Praise for *The Misadventures of a Cross-America Kayaker*

"In 2008, a man of sixty-five years, with a crippled shoulder, two replaced hips, a bad heart, and poor eyesight, launched his kayak into the treacherous Columbia River, near its mouth on the Pacific Ocean. Nine summers later, he completed a journey of 4,700 miles and reached the Atlantic Ocean. He traced Lewis and Clark's route as far as St. Louis, headed south through the Tennessee Valley, east along the Gulf Coast, and then crossed Florida on the Suwannee and Saint Marys Rivers, finally reaching the Atlantic north of Jacksonville.

"Along the way, the intrepid paddler (some would call him foolhardy) defied constant dangers of drowning, crippling injury, snakes, fire ants, alligators, exhaustion, thirst, and bewilderment.

"Landau's story is much more than a travel adventure. Hank is a keen observer who reflects on the American Northwest occupation, Indian cultures along the way, the hydrology and geology of vast river systems, local flora and fauna, colorful personalities he encountered, and the role of his supportive family.

"There is something for everyone in this amazing tale by an extraordinary man."

—**William Ellis**, Retired Minister in Foreign Service

"Anyone who loves rivers, sea kayaking, adventure, or just a great yarn about an ambitious and eventful journey will enjoy this book. Hank Landau set off on what would be an audacious challenge for anyone, but especially for someone beyond the typical age for such quests. Setting out to retrace the upriver journey of Lewis and Clark by sea kayak on the Columbia River, he ends up going much farther than planned, eventually traversing the entire nation and multiple great rivers. As he battles weather, currents, waves, ships, fatigue, wet campsites, and unexpected calamities along the way, he also encounters beauty, history, kindness, and inner discoveries about life, challenge, and change. This is both an entertaining and an inspiring tale, reminding each of us that with grit, determination, and a spirit of adventure, there may still be limits imposed by age and circumstances, but those limits are far beyond what we might have imagined."

—**Brian Baird**, PhD, Psychologist, College Professor, Former Member of Congress, Recreational Sea and Whitewater Kayaker

"*Misadventures of a Cross-America Kayaker: An Old Man's Quixotic Journey* describes Hank Landau's almost decade-long, 4,700 mile adventure following the Lewis and Clark expedition from the Northwest of the United States to the Missouri River and then extending his journey from Missouri to the Atlantic Ocean near Jacksonville, Florida. Dr. Landau intersperses his tale with historical references, geographical and geological explications, reflections on train travel in America, and descriptions of the natural beauty and daunting challenges of his adventures. While this is a solitary tale of courage and perseverance, the narrative is effectively punctuated by the many encounters with other tenacious naturalists and numerous hospitable citizens along the way. Hank Landau's amazingly supportive family provided company during several segments of the trip, timely information about impending weather events, unending supplies, and logistical support. The story is Hank Landau's, but perhaps his wife, Joyce, is the heroine."

—**R. Barbara Gitenstein**, President Emerita, The College of New Jersey; Senior Vice President, Association of Governing Boards (AGB) Consulting; Author of *Experience Is the Angled Road: Memoir of an Academic*

"Hank Landau had great adventures that he captured in his book with warmth and humility. His determination, keen observation of the rivers and the surrounding environment, and care for the people he met shine through."

—**James C. Card**, Retired Vice Admiral and Vice Commandant, US Coast Guard

"An inspirational tale of grit and determination in the face of adventures both alarming and amusing."

"Who doesn't love being a time traveler? Landau paddles across a nation and brings you into his time portal, where the river takes us to the days of old, yet the experiences are new and fresh. We all need to experience the pace of the river, to bring us to the best days of our lives.
"The book is great and needs to be in the hands of everyone."

"*The Misadventures of a Cross-America Kayaker* is a tale of action, adventure, endurance, and grit, spiced with danger and discovery. I greatly appreciated Hank Landau's observations regarding the history of America, the evolution of our disparate cultures, his reflections on preserving our natural heritage, and his graphic descriptions of flora and fauna. . . .
". . . Encounters with rapids and dams, alligators and snakes, and animals of the two-legged variety are described with humor and warmth. Hank Landau's use of simile and metaphor and his precise details bring his story to life in a way that most holds readers' attention."

"Hank Landau tackles rivers the way he tackles life: through tenacity, determination, perseverance and grit. Kayaking challenging rivers despite physical, mental, and emotional obstacles along the way, Landau describes the historical significances of his travels and the people he meets in a way that lets the reader experience the Columbia, the Snake, the Suwannee, and more."

"Do you want to read the true story of a remarkable man performing an extraordinary feat? Then read Hank Landau's *The Misadventures Of A Cross-America Kayaker: An Old Man's Quixotic Journey*. In this book, Landau chronicles his 4,700-mile trek from the Pacific Ocean to the Atlantic. Landau, at seventy years old and with severe health and physical disabilities (heart arrhythmia, both hips replaced), paddled and portaged his kayak the whole journey, refusing any powered support. This is impossible, of course. But he did it! Read this book and be amazed at the hardships he overcame, the friends he made, and the history he accomplished. On top of all this, the educational value of his story is immeasurable."

—**Samuel G. Tooma**, Physical Oceanographer and Author of
The SOOF and *Assassin's Revenge*

"A captivating memoir of adventure and exploration, reminding us what it means to truly live. Encountering dangerous conditions and uncertainty, Hank Landau set off to retrace . . . Lewis and Clark's route, much of it in a kayak and with minimal gear, and experienced a truly remarkable journey. Landau's book is a breath of fresh air, and it was a privilege to live vicariously through him! This is a must-read!"

—**Ryan Lindner**, Author of *The Half-Known Life: What
Matters Most When You're Running Out of Time*

"Having grown up on the Fort Peck Reservation, just fifteen miles north of the Missouri, I was captivated by how vividly Landau captures the essence of this last best place. It brought me home after decades of East Coast life. I could smell the sage. Hard to put it down."

—**Jim Murray**, Nationally Acclaimed Trial Lawyer and
Occasional Storyteller

"Hank Landau's goal to follow the route of Lewis and Clark; his combination of experience and lack thereof; his willingness to risk and be wrong but somehow survive; and his brutal honesty in his mistakes and in his confession that he received unexplained good luck, plus his ability to develop friends along the way, kept me engaged until the end of the journey. . . . What surprised and delighted me was his clear awareness of and appreciation for the beauties of nature that he saw . . . and his honest description of the damage being done to our amazing planet . . . Luckily, the overarching theme is one of determination, goodwill, and appreciation for both the Lewis and Clark Expedition and the spectacular nature they uncovered and which still remains."

—**Gayla L. Shoemake**, PhD, Vice President for Instruction, South Seattle College, retired; Founder and Chair, Interfaith Climate Action; Chair,

"*The Misadventures of a Cross-America Kayaker* is a richly textured and vivid account of how one man, Landau, alone in a kayak named Whisper, backtracked the journey made by the Lewis and Clark Expedition in the 1800s and continued on to the Atlantic Ocean. Landau's story is an exciting and harrowing odyssey, sometimes made worse by a myriad of health issues, self-doubt, age, weather, snakes, and insects. But beyond this, the history lessons interwoven and documented throughout educate and remind us of our storied past and often unforgivable treatment of the native population. I highly recommend this book to anyone who has dared to dream the impossible and found a way to make it happen."

—**Joe C. Rice**, Former President and CEO (Headmaster) of Mid-Pacific Institute, Contributing Author of *One Way Out: The Greater Good*

The Misadventures of a Cross-America Kayaker:
An Old Man's Quixotic Journey

by Hank Landau

© Copyright 2022 Hank Landau

ISBN 978-1-64663-780-5

Picture Credits:

Page 226
Olmsted Locks and Dam, by Jacqueline Tate, Defense Visual Information Distribution Service, Public Domain
The appearance of U.S. Department of Defense (DoD) visual information does not imply or constitute DoD endorsement.

Page 227
U.S. Army Corp of Engineers Digital Library, Nashville District, Public Domain

Map services and data available from U.S. Geological Survey, National Geospatial Program.

The author will donate all royalties to Native American not-for-profit organizations.

Published by

◤ köehlerbooks™

3705 Shore Drive
Virginia Beach, VA 23455
800-435-4811
www.koehlerbooks.com

Hank Landau

The Misadventures *of a* Cross-America Kayaker

An Old Man's Quixotic Journey

VIRGINIA BEACH
CAPE CHARLES

To my family, without whom there would have been no voyage

Table of Contents

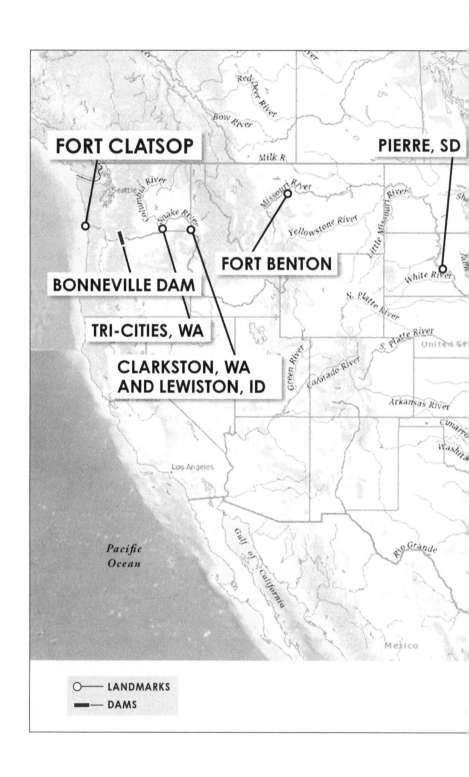

FORT CLATSOP

PIERRE, SD

BONNEVILLE DAM

FORT BENTON

TRI-CITIES, WA

CLARKSTON, WA
AND LEWISTON, ID

Pacific
Ocean

○── LANDMARKS
■── DAMS

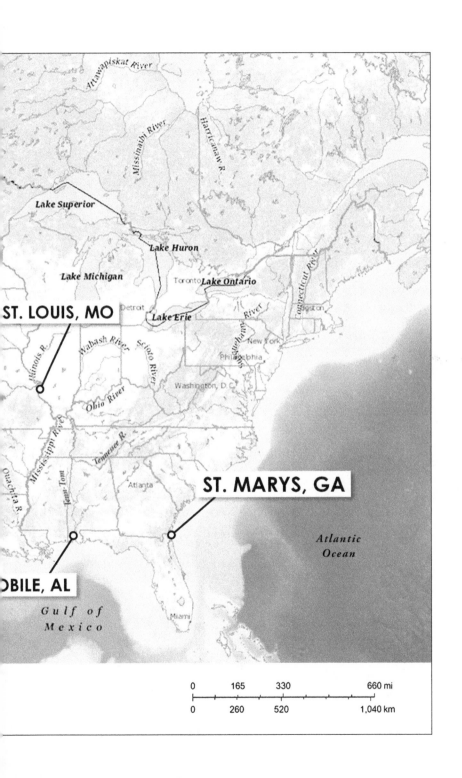

ST. LOUIS, MO

ST. MARYS, GA

ОBILE, AL

Lake Superior

Lake Huron

Lake Michigan

Toronto Lake Ontario

Detroit

Lake Erie

Atawapiskat River

Missinaibi River

Harricanaw R.

Connecticut River

Wabash River

Scioto River

Illinois R.

Ohio River

Mississippi River

Tennessee R.

Ouachita R.

Tenn Tom

Atlanta

Susquehanna River

New York

Philadelphia

Washington, D.C.

Boston

Atlantic Ocean

Gulf of Mexico

Miami

0	165	330	660 mi
0	260	520	1,040 km

Prologue

My pulse raced. My battered but dependable kayak was locked in the current of the flood stage Mississippi River. I was rapidly losing control, and in moments I would hurtle a big wave over the Chain of Rocks diversion dam with construction debris, whirlpools and class three rapids lying below. I was flush with both exhilaration and fear that I would become the dam's latest victim. The Gateway Arch in St. Louis, Missouri was within reach. My year-end destination for 2013 lay just minutes away.

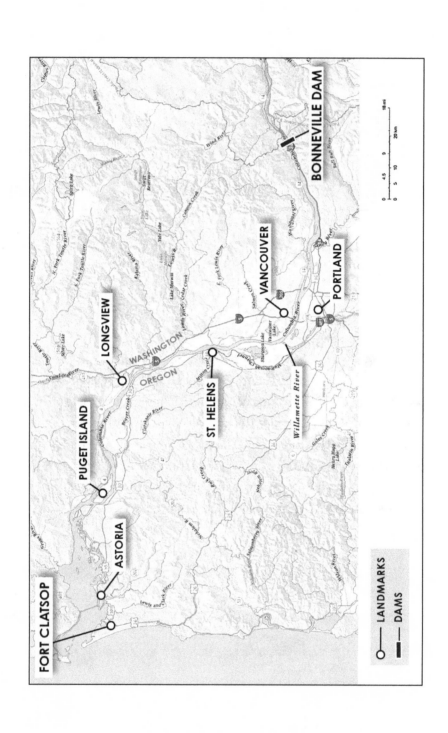

FORT CLATSOP

ASTORIA

PUGET ISLAND

LONGVIEW

ST. HELENS

VANCOUVER

PORTLAND

BONNEVILLE DAM

WASHINGTON

OREGON

Willamette River

○——— LANDMARKS

■——— DAMS

I

The Lower Columbia River

2008

The author departing Netul Landing on Lewis & Clark River

The Call of the River

The day dawned cloudy at our campsite in Warrenton, Oregon, across Youngs Bay from Astoria, where my wife, Joyce, and I had spent the night. When we opened the tent flap that sodden August morning in 2008, the damp mist put me in a dreary mood. I dwelled on the embarrassment and loss of self-esteem I would experience if I was unable to reach my announced goal of paddling upstream to Bonneville Dam.

When we checked in at Fort Clatsop where the Lewis and Clark Expedition spent the winter of 1805-1806, we met a ranger in the busy visitor center. With a look of concern, he warned me not to kayak across nearby Youngs Bay because of heavy ship traffic and changing sea conditions. Later, a woman, who appeared even older than my sixty-eight years, cautioned me. "You had better be wary of big ships," she said as we crossed paths along the riverbank. Other than extensive mud flats, I hadn't expected any difficulty in Youngs Bay. Had I missed something in planning this trip?

I kissed Joyce goodbye, guessing she was looking forward to a break from my running monologue on Lewis and Clark and kayaking, and what might happen during the ten-to-twenty days I thought it might take to reach Bonneville Dam.

As I pushed off, I interrupted the cries of the gulls to call out, "See you in two to three weeks"

"Don't drown," were Joyce's last words to me.

The Corps of Discovery left Fort Clatsop in heavy dugout canoes. I left Fort Clatsop in my fourteen-year-old, two-person fiberglass Eddyline Whisper kayak. I borrowed the manufacturer's name, *Whisper*, for my boat because it reminds me of the music a kayak makes when it slices through still water. Whisper is eighteen feet long, weighs seventy-three pounds, and has a twenty-eight- inch beam (width). Even if Whisper were not my only kayak, I preferred a tandem kayak because it carries more gear below deck and because it would allow one of my adult children to help me paddle if I ran into trouble. I was also willing to sacrifice slower speed—and most things short of world peace—for the greater stability offered by a wider kayak. The tide was slowly rising when I paddled Whisper past the tourists mingling on the pier at Fort Clatsop and turned my sights to Youngs Bay. On this windless morning, the small tidal river flowed between its winding banks as gracefully as the birds flew through the calm air. I turned out a rhythm with my paddle as a kingfisher, cormorant, and great blue heron took turns leapfrogging me and greeting me, the cormorant in silence, the kingfisher sounding like a prolonged rattle, and the great blue heron with its raucous *"graak."*

Soon after gliding under the last bridge crossing the Lewis and Clark River and entering Youngs Bay, Whisper ran aground on a sloping mud bank, hidden out of sight in the silty water. The mud beneath Whisper wouldn't support my weight and was too soft to push off using my paddle as a pole. With the mud gripping my kayak like a vice, I feared being stuck in the middle of the bay for many hours.

With time to think, I admitted to myself that I was no longer in top physical shape. Running had worn out my hips, and a near-death bicycle collision made it difficult to continue riding. To make things worse, my heart had started beating irregularly, which resulted in the need for a pacemaker. I couldn't keep up with Joyce and our friends, and my three children Greg, Amy, and Mike, had long since passed me by. It was depressing. The only thing I still had going for me was my ability to propel a rowboat or kayak over long distances, at least until the pain in my deformed left shoulder, broken when I was much younger, forced me to stop.

I peeled open a candy bar and leaned back to enjoy the view. By the time the rising tide gently lifted Whisper, I was eager to get back to the rhythm of paddling. I hadn't been paddling long when I was jolted from my reverie by the signal of five short blasts from a ship's whistle, the nautical danger signal to move out of the way. With nervous sweat gathering on my forehead, I spun around expecting to see a ship bearing down on me, but the only ship was far in the distance. I doubted the signal was meant for me. Sound travels far on the water.

I sometimes claim that my trip began at the Pacific Ocean, but Fort Clatsop is on the tranquil Lewis and Clark River. Three miles west of Fort Clatsop, the formidable Columbia River discharges over the Columbia River bar, known in maritime circles as the "Graveyard of the Pacific." I chose to avoid graveyards. The challenge of paddling upstream on a river I barely knew would sufficiently test my body and my determination.

Rounding Smith Point at the western end of Astoria, Oregon, I felt reassuring puffs of wind at my back. Wind blowing in the same direction as the incoming tidal current meant lower waves. That's what I was hoping for. I smiled. Whisper felt like a bobsled beneath me as I dug into each stroke and rode the flow.

A few minutes later, I glided under the 4.5-mile-long pale green Astoria-Megler Bridge linking Oregon and Washington. I recalled the coastal bike trip with my son Greg in 1998 that took us over this bridge, freezing in the April morning rain. When the Astoria Bridge opened in 1966, it completed US 101, an unbroken link between the Canadian and Mexican borders. With its circular ramp on the Oregon side, the bridge reminded me of an enormous green snake.

Beyond Astoria

The Columbia River Water Trail by Keith G. Hay (Hay's Guide) is the only aid to navigation other than road maps, topographic maps, and tide tables that I brought for this trip. It cautions about rough conditions when the wind is blowing against the current at Tongue Point, just east of Astoria. Nearing the Coast Guard station at Tongue Point, I remembered that on their downstream journey, the wind and waves forced Lewis and Clark to camp there for ten days, from November 27 to December 7, 1805. While previously camped on the Washington side near Point Ellice about a mile west of today's Astoria-Megler Bridge, they allowed all adult members of the expedition to vote for their choice of winter encampment. According to Stephen

Ambrose in his classic saga, *Undaunted Courage*, this marked the first time in American history that a woman and a slave (Clark's slave, York), were allowed to vote. York's vote was counted in the tally. Sacajawea's was not. How free was America if fifty years would pass before African American males could vote in America, and more than a hundred years before women and Native Americans got to vote.

I took note of Lewis and Clark's rare combination of democracy and military leadership. I hoped to join other paddlers or have a friend or one of my children join me in Whisper if I needed help. A democratic form of leadership would be preferable to my behaving like a dictator. Of course, I'd have to cede some control.

Approaching Tongue Point, I was battered by eddies and white caps. My habitual optimism led me to believe that if I were to capsize, I could swim Whisper to shore close to the Coast Guard station, a quarter mile away. Sea conditions never approached those endured by the Expedition, and to my palpable relief I made it to the lee of the Point with only a little sea spray on my face.

Lewis and Clark's Routes over and West of the Rocky Mountains

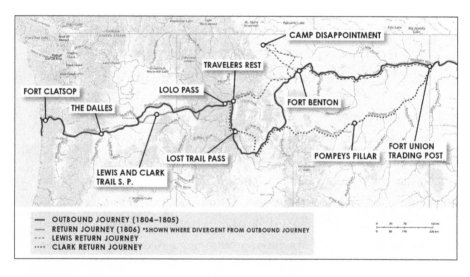

In favorable conditions, I could sustain a paddling pace of about 3.5 mph. I would make no headway if the combined river current and adverse tidal current exceeded this speed. On this first day, the tidal current was in my favor with a tailwind. The three-to-seven-mile width of the estuary dissipated the river current to one knot (1.15 mph) or less. Great for the first day, but my radio was predicting a marked change in the weather.

After about four hours of paddling, cramps locked my arms, threatening to end my day. I took a break to chug some water and then resumed at a more relaxed cadence. Twenty minutes later the pain subsided, however, the increasing wind and choppy sea made it difficult for my exhausted arms to propel Whisper in the direction I intended.

I sought more protected waters along the south shore of Cathlamet Bay. While the wind was less of a trial, I soon became disoriented in the many blind sloughs. I made several wrong turns trying to find a passage. Time and again, I ended up stymied in the reeds at the bottleneck end of yet another slough. I was beginning to feel like Humphrey Bogart and Katherine Hepburn, lost in a leach-infested swamp in the movie *African Queen*. Served me right for not carrying nautical charts as suggested in Hay's Guide.

Stabilizing Whisper in the stiff brown reeds, I dug a topographic map from a drybag, and finally found what might (or might not) be my location and continued along what I hoped to be the Lewis and Clark route. It would have been great to find a fellow boater to wave down and confer about my predicament, but I seemed to be the only one on the river.

When the Corps of Discovery traveled the Lower Columbia, they were rarely out of sight of a Native American village, despite the death toll taken by old world diseases since the arrival of Europeans. Gone now are the numerous Native Americans encountered by Lewis and Clark, the trappers and traders who soon followed, and most of the fishers and loggers following them. I passed a few old and apparently vacant cabins and houseboats, but other than two large container ships traveling upriver far in the distance, I saw no signs of human activity. Sometimes the most important features are those we never see. I would observe many examples of lost land, liberties, and opportunities in the miles ahead.

While struggling along the reed- and brush-covered wetlands that dominated the shoreline from Astoria to this point, I had not seen any suitable campsite. My worries shifted from making good mileage to finding a place to spend the night. By late afternoon, the shoreline vegetation had transitioned to brush and trees—a sign of stable ground—but I still worried that I wouldn't find a campsite before dark.

When the light blue of the eastern sky turned dark gray, I saw a sliver of a dock peeking out of a clearing along the south shore. With my arms leaden from paddling in chop and current for more than six hours, I gladly pulled over at the remote boat ramp and old floating dock in a small calm eddy at Aldrich Point. It was hardly the white sandy beach I'd hoped for earlier in the day, but I was ready to settle for any river egress.

Whether camping was allowed I honestly could not say, but I was too tired to care. There were no facilities at the ramp, but two friendly fishermen arrived soon after me in an outboard powered aluminum boat. I generally don't drink much beer or other alcohol, but the cold bottle of Corona they gave me sure tasted good. I had covered twenty-five miles in six hours and thirty minutes. For a first day, it was better than I'd hoped for. Soon, I'd look back on it as a benchmark I wouldn't often achieve again.

I began to establish my evening routine. First things first, protect my vessel. I pulled Whisper high enough to avoid losing it to rising water and secured it with a painter, a line connecting Whisper's bow to a metal stake. After opening Whisper's waterproof hatches and unpacking, I set my tent under a slight but steady drizzle and shivered while washing the sweat from my body in the cold river. I stretched my legs with a short walk before preparing a simple meal of peanut butter, cheese, and crackers. I slathered ointment on the blisters on my hands, stretched my joints and muscles, and decided my plans for the next day should start with checking maps for a target campsite about twenty miles upriver. After jotting some notes in my journal and reading for a few minutes, I tried to sleep. I was already worried that my goal of reaching Bonneville Dam was beyond my abilities.

A Change in the Weather

Early the next day, I woke to cloudy, cool weather with thunder roiling in the distance, a prelude to the miserable conditions predicted on my weather radio. Rest had renewed my energy and my spirits. I reminded myself that my family and friends probably thought that it would take more than bad weather to stop me. Resolved to move on, I was dismayed to find that the adverse current stayed strong during an otherwise pleasant morning. A river otter stared at Whisper and me while we traveled along the Oregon shore with the old Spokane, Portland, and Seattle railway grade marching along the shoreline beyond. I imagined the ghosts of the passenger and freight trains that once ran on this scenic segment of the line. I had hoped to one day take that ride, but the last train to Astoria, an excursion train, was terminated in 2006.

Puget Island, a low flat lump of land populated by Norwegian dairy farmers and fishers, divides the Columbia into two navigable channels. Through the thickening fog and heavy overcast, my nose detected the sweet smell of the Georgia Pacific pulp mill at Wauna, Oregon. I bounced and bobbed nervously in the wake of large ships as they passed less than two hundred feet from me in the narrow channel between Puget Island and the Oregon shore. The ships heading to and from Portland and other Columbia River ports were not unwelcome sights, although I had to remind myself to look behind frequently. With their stern-mounted engines, these vessels could sneak up like stealth warriors.

Near Wauna, I concentrated on safely negotiating the high current at the end of a wing dam, a line of wooden piling extending from shore. The thickening fog limited visibility to about three kayak lengths. Moving away from shore to get around the barely visible dam, I feared Whisper would be invisible to the crew on a ship's bridge high above me and I knew that a fiberglass kayak is not readily visible on radar.

Straining to hear a foghorn, I heard nothing above the low whine of the pulp mill. Suddenly, the calm was broken. My heart launched into race mode when I looked over my right shoulder to see a freighter larger than the City of Portland emerge from the fog so close that individual rust spots, looking like red pimples, were visible on the white hull. I turned to prevent getting sucked in any closer to the enormous propeller, which looked to me like an executioner's blade each time it broke the water's surface. Fortunately, the big ship was moving slowly. I avoided capsizing in its wake by steering Whisper's bow into the oncoming wave, while the ship disappeared in the fog.

The predicted change in the weather brought an unappreciated change in wind direction. Fair weather in the Pacific Northwest is generally accompanied by wind from the north or northwest. On a typical August day, the Columbia River valley tends to channel the wind such that it blows upriver. Inclement weather is often associated with an in-your-face wind from the south or southeast, the direction I was heading. This sort of weather might be expected in the shoulder seasons; in August, it was just plain irritating.

After leaving Puget Island behind, I found myself exposed between Wahkiakum County's Cape Horn to the north and Oregon's Wallace Island to the south. I could have, and should have, avoided this area by paddling the longer more protected southern route through Wallace Slough. The wind picked up to the point where I felt threatened, so I looked for a place to pull ashore. Neither the steep bluffs on the Washington side nor the marshy islands on the Oregon side offered an attractive landing. Although the wind coming from dead ahead slowed me to a crawl, a crosswind or tailwind would have added the unwelcome danger of broaching or capsizing. I have capsized many times in kayaks and small sailboats, but never in cold, rough water. I was much relieved when the wind died down.

By midafternoon, I rounded Oak Point and arrived at the primitive Lewis and Clark Columbia River Water Trail campsite on Gull Island. The island is roughly a mile-long sandbar, probably formed from dredged material. I bathed in the river, walked the island, ate a cold meal of beef jerky and American cheese slices, wrote in my journal, planned for the next day, and read until nightfall. While awake in my sleeping bag I began to wonder if I had forgotten anything. Suddenly remembering *Rule one,* I crawled out of my comfortable sleeping bag and tent and rushed down to the water's edge to find that the river had risen, and the wakes of larger ships threatened to set Whisper afloat. Embarrassed and relieved that no one saw my gaffe, I set some logs under Whisper and pulled her further up the sandy beach. As with the previous night, I was the only one at the campsite and already felt lonely. It had taken me more than eight hours to paddle 21.5 miles. I was paddling longer and harder and in more difficult conditions than I had expected, but I did not yet regret that I had begun.

A Lesson in Combined Currents

The next morning, I shoved off under cloudy skies, calm wind, and an opposing current. Two hours later I reached a side channel inside Walker-Lord-Dibblee Islands, conjoined at low water but now undergoing a trial separation with the river at high water. A wind blowing directly in my face all but stopped me. I pulled ashore in a small, wooded cove on the south shore of Lord Island, tied Whisper to a willow branch and sat there eating a snack and giving my tired arms a rest.

When the wind didn't abate after twenty minutes, I shoved off. I had little choice. I knew of no place nearby to get off the river. A few minutes later I saw an inflatable boat speeding toward me. Just before colliding with Whisper, the lone operator, dressed in a seemingly official dull-brown uniform with shoulder braids and colorful patches, put the engine in reverse and aggressively pulled to a stop as his bow wave pushed Whisper aside. The bold letters on the side of the boat spelled *Marine Security Patrol.* The officer, a middle-aged man seemingly impressed with himself, told me that I was heading too close to an old rusting abandoned ship. He didn't offer a reason why my proximity to the old ship mattered. His tone and aggressive behavior annoyed me, but I resisted contesting his authority even though I'm not a big fan of extreme security at the expense of freedom. With the added energy that comes from being agitated, I steered away from the rusting ship.

After returning to the strong adverse current on the main channel, I followed the shoreline along the small community of Rainier, Oregon. On the other side of the river, I saw the moored ships and white concrete grain silos at the Port of Longview and heard grinding and heavy metal sounds emanating from the industrial city of Longview, Washington. I was careful to avoid large freighters maneuvering to moor at the piers and buoys.

Within an hour of first sighting industrial Longview, I looked up to see the high-arching Lewis and Clark Bridge far above me. Also known as the Longview Bridge, it appeals to engineers like me who see it as an almost symmetrical spindly-legged sister of the Astoria-Megler Bridge. The Longview Bridge is the only structure spanning the Columbia River between Astoria and the almost twin cities of Portland, Oregon and Vancouver, Washington. Having pedaled my bike over this bridge more than a dozen times, I knew to watch out for debris falling from logging trucks. While preparing to take evasive maneuvers, I pressed on.

A few minutes after passing the bridge, the increasing wind and strong current both set against me. It took me more than ten minutes to pass a hundred-foot-long tugboat—tied to a dock. The crew offered me a tow. The tug captain didn't agree although he seemed to take pity. He warned me that the current in Longview changes three hours after Astoria and rarely moderates for more than ninety minutes.

Adding to my discouragement, I slipped backward every time I put down my paddle to look at a map, pee, or take a drink of water. I later figured that if I peed enough to feel comfortable, looked at a map enough to know my location, and drank enough to avoid dehydration, I would have ended my voyage where I began.

I stopped at a well-maintained public boat ramp in Rainier, Oregon to call my family. The ramp was busy with fishers pulling their boats out and bragging about the few fish they caught. I tied up to the dock, trying to keep out of the way, and looked for a pay phone. I didn't bring a cell phone, despite the pressure from my family to do so. I am averse to technology and a fan of logic. I couldn't convince myself to push the button on the cell phone labeled *end* in order to begin a call. I found one of the few remaining pay phones in the region, but I didn't have the correct change. A friendly fisherman offered to let me use his cell phone and wouldn't accept my money. Not able to reach anyone at home I left a short but upbeat message that I was tired but safe.

In recent years, my body had undergone some significant alterations and repairs, most notably two new hips, fifteen broken bones, and a titanium plate in my skull from a near-death SUV-bicycle collision (as you might guess, I was on the bike). My most recent addition was a pacemaker, a device that will apparently keep my heart ticking after death, much like Edgar Allan Poe's "The Telltale Heart." My oldest injury, and the one that torments me when kayaking, is a broken clavicle from a long-ago bike accident that deformed my left shoulder. While preparing to leave for the Columbia River, my wife Joyce reminded me of all my artificial body parts. At first, I thought she was concerned about my health until she added that if I died, she planned to take me to a recycling facility. I wanted to show Joyce, and myself, that I was not quite ready to be recycled.

The truth was that much of my body was crying out for attention. The important news, pain wise, was that my after-market hips and my original equipment spine and back were doing fine.

Back on the river again I fought wind, waves, and newly arrived driving rain. I felt like I was pulling a sinking log raft. To give my left elbow and shoulder some relief I applied a little right rudder. My right arm was now doing most of the work, although with the rudder no longer aligned with the kayak there was more work to be done. There was little solace to be gained in knowing that the expedition encountered even worse conditions when they passed this place on March 26, 1806. In addition to a strong headwind and rain, they battled flood currents and cold temperatures.

Why am I doing this? I began to wonder if I should have undertaken this trip and whether I would make it to Bonneville Dam, or even Portland. *Could I have prepared better? Should I have enlisted a paddling partner?* Listening to my family or friends who suggested that I was too old might have been a good idea. I was glad I didn't tell too many people about my plans. That way there would be few to whom I would have to admit defeat.

I had admitted defeat too often when I was young. I gave up baseball after going a complete Little League season without ever hitting the ball. My eye-hand coordination was so bad that trying out for football or basketball would have been hopeless. Failing my tryout for the 100-yard dash was a harbinger of my future. Slower runners were assigned to distance runs; this is where my stamina proved an asset. I had moderate success in cross-country runs, climbing, bicycling and, later in life, rowing, and kayaking. Friends said I was indefatigable. My wife called me mule headed.

My other distinguishing characteristic is a high level of skepticism. Prior to being sent to Vietnam in 1969, my Army unit marched along in training, chanting, *"Delta Company, we are the best"* over and over. The drill sergeant fell back and approached me, leaning in to listen. He stopped the march and asked what I was saying. I replied, "Delta Company, we're pretty good." He demanded to know why I wasn't saying that we were the best. I told him that I had no basis for comparison. I knew that the Corps of Discovery completed a monumental task. They were the best. I just couldn't fully appreciate how monumental it was until I experienced some of it myself.

My wife Joyce doesn't appreciate this anecdote. She seems to think that it reflects poorly on her ability to choose a mate. I'm still not sure what the drill sergeant thought. A few days after the march he handed me a form and suggested filling it out if I wanted to become an officer.

I did. I suppose that much of my life involved taking chances, often with some success. I hoped this kayak voyage would be seen as such.

The stronger the wind and rain, the more my physical world shrank. Rain hitting my glasses rendered them useless. I could barely see the Oregon shoreline less than a hundred feet away, and through the driving rain I had only a glimpse of the now-closed Trojan Nuclear Power Plant, its concrete cooling towers reaching into the clouds. I knew there was a campsite on the Washington side of the river but couldn't see that far and feared that boaters and ship's crews would not be able to see me if I tried crossing the river. If I didn't power through against the wind and current, I might not arrive at my next campsite until long after dark or, worse, might have to turn back to Rainier or scramble off the river on a rocky shoreline with breaking waves that could destroy Whisper. But if I paddled too hard, I might injure my elbow or shoulder, rendering me unable to continue. I decided to move on at a slower pace.

Paddling slower didn't last long. Fear overcame pain and I again pushed hard, my paddle spinning like a windmill. After each bend in the river, I expected to find my intended campsite. I began to worry that I had passed it because it was hidden in the rain. As the sun set and when I was about to give up hope, my intended destination, a quaint marina linked to an RV park and general store appeared through the raindrops. Scipio's Landing, in Goble, Oregon, is very close to where Lewis and Clark spent their fifth night. For five dollars, Mr. Scipio, the son of the owner, provided me with a campsite and a tie-up at his floating dock, just like *real* boats. For a few more dollars he offered a microwave pizza, a local newspaper, and a hot shower, which warmed me and soothed my aching muscles. Mr. Scipio wasn't interested in learning about my kayak trip, so I read the newspaper. The weather report—100 percent chance of heavy rain and a headwind for the next day. I had paddled nine hours and covered only seventeen miles. I could have walked faster.

My battle with the tidal current convinced me that I had to plan better, or my increasingly sore left shoulder and elbow might give out. I placed my tide tables, tidal corrections, and charts on the tent floor and began calculating. As best I could tell, low water and low current would be at about 1:30 p.m. While trying to fall asleep to the sound of pouring rain, I debated whether I should paddle at all the next day.

I twisted and turned all night long, favoring my aching shoulder. If the pain in my shoulder hadn't kept me awake, shivering in my soggy sleeping bag and shaking every time I heard thunder or saw a flash of lightning would have. Thunder and lightning storms scare me. They are not common west of the Cascade Mountains, especially in the summer, so I hadn't prepared for a storm of this type or intensity. I did know that wet ground would conduct electricity from a nearby strike to my body if I didn't have some form of insulation. The National Outdoor Leadership School reports that "there is a large change in the electrostatic field out to 30 m from the ground strike point." The potential for serious injury or death was said to be dependent on several factors in addition to distance and ground moisture, such as the proximity to trees, elevation, and assumption of the "lightning position" (squat or sit, ball up, put feet together, wrap arms around legs). I found it impossible to sleep in such a position.

Wing Dam Danger

The next morning, I lay in my soggy sleeping bag and listened to the wind gust through the swaying branches of the fir trees. Falling rain found its way through the tent roof creating rivulets on the tent floor. Finally, after 9 a.m., I dragged myself out of bed. While eating a microwave egg and sausage sandwich at the marina store, I listened to Mr. Scipio senior, the eighty-five-year-old proprietor, lecture on the river and the weather. He told me that yesterday's rain exceeded the August record in Portland.

By noon, the rain was little more than the drizzle we Northwesterners experience on most winter days, but the wind still formed threatening whitecaps on the river. I waited until after lunch before my impatience and the coin I flipped in my mind told me to pack my wet and heavy gear and move on.

It was early afternoon when I launched Whisper into a strong headwind and a light drizzle. Mr. Scipio Sr. had advised me to paddle on the west, backwater, side of Sandy Island, a two-mile-long sandbar covered with brush and low trees that forms a narrow channel along the Oregon shore. Less than an hour after shoving off, I left Sandy Island behind and entered the half-mile wide main channel below Kalama, Washington, just when the drizzle turned to a steady rain.

A violent wind blew up the main channel. My vision in the rain suffered, and an adverse current almost as bad as yesterday continued to make upstream progress difficult. Digging deeper with my paddle while still trying to time my strokes with the crest of the waves, my paddle sometimes "caught a crab" in a trough, causing my pulling arm to lurch backward. During one such mishap, I uttered a silent scream; my middle fingernail on my right hand broke off when it jammed on an amateurish gel-coat patch I had applied to Whisper's hull before starting this trip. My broken fingernail, along with the unrelenting rain and strong current, led me to second-guess my decision to leave the security of Scipio's Landing.

I looked across the river to see two powerful Burlington Northern-Santa Fe freight trains and the sleek and speedy Amtrak Cascade train traveling with ease from Seattle to Portland. I was envious of the speed and power of the trains and even more envious of the passengers, some of whom were probably watching a battered kayaker struggle on the river below while they reclined in warmth and comfort.

I began to encounter more wing dams, perhaps one every few hundred yards. These dams, also called groins and dikes, extend into the river, sometimes as far as the navigation channel. Their purpose is to increase water velocity to keep the channel free of sediment, but they greatly complicate travel by human-propelled craft like Whisper. Having learned that wing dams create an upstream eddy current near the shore, I took advantage of this favorable situation by paddling close to shore until it was time to punch out into the main stream to get around the dams.

A long wing dam that jutted far out into the river took me by surprise. Whisper's bow was suddenly spun downstream by the water coursing around the end of the dam. The current hitting Whisper broadside tilted us precariously. Bracing with my paddle was all that kept us from capsizing. I fought the current and managed to turn Whisper's bow upstream only to find that a hill of water, much like a speed bump, had formed near the end of the dam. My first attempt to get around the dam was such a dismal failure I considered portaging. During my second attempt, I tired quickly getting over and past the bump. Anticipating a break from the strong current, I exited the main channel by turning toward shore.

I turned too soon. The water bunching upstream of the dam swept me downstream. If we hit the dam, Whisper would capsize. Once trapped against the dam, bracing wouldn't help. Accounts of people drowning when they lodged against dams or moored boats are all too common. I had often lain awake thinking of two Boy Scouts who drowned when they became entangled in the branches of a downed tree on the Wildcat River near Lafayette, Indiana. I didn't want my life to end that way.

Whisper was still pointed upstream and was several boat lengths from the dam when I dug in stroke by stroke. My adrenaline surged, but I only managed to hold ground. My energy flagged and I felt the tug of Whisper drifting back toward the dam. More by accident than experience, I turned Whisper to head diagonally upstream towards the shore, like swimmers are taught to do when encountering rip currents. I began to make progress and finally found a measure of safety in the calmer water downstream from the next dam.

Needing a break, I decided to risk paddling in the narrow, reed-filled passage inside of Goat Island, even though my maps didn't show the route to be passable. While entering the tranquil channel whose banks were so close, I could almost touch them, the sky turned dark, and an ominous black cloud bore down on me.

A few minutes later the wind changed direction, making it hard to steer. The rain soon became a frog strangler. Water flowed down my jacket and somehow found its way past my spray skirt and into the cockpit where it pooled on my seat and soaked my bottom. *How much more of this terrible weather can I take?* My question was made moot thirty minutes later when, to my profound relief, the sky cleared, and the sun brought welcome warmth.

All was good and I began to relax until I attempted to re-enter the main channel at the upstream end of the island. Here I confronted another wing dam, this one stretching across the channel. Reviewing my limited options, I berated myself for believing this route would save me time and effort. I could turn back and retrace my path to the main channel or unload the heavier gear from Whisper and attempt a portage through the mud. I was in the process of turning around when I noticed that one of the worm-infested pilings had rotted away, allowing Whisper barely enough room to squeeze through.

Once through, I wondered if this was the same river, I had left an hour before. In place of black clouds, the sun shone, and a double rainbow glowed directly in my path. Conditions had so improved that I even imagined the current to be in my favor. I began to sing "America the Beautiful."

In the early evening, I arrived at St. Helens' Sand Island Marine Park, a clean and free campground on a small well-cared-for island. Across the narrow slough separating the island from the mainland sat the imposing stone-and-white, wood-trimmed Columbia County Courthouse, highlighted in the setting sun and conveying the image of governmental power, the likelihood of a crime-free stay and the confidence that my kayak would probably still be at my campsite the next morning.

A Long Day's Paddle

I awoke before sunrise, no longer hearing the wind in the trees or the rain falling on the tent roof. Still tired, I almost decided to roll over and go back to sleep in my still damp sleeping bag, laying on a deflated air mattress. What most prompted me to get out of bed was a tree root poking me in my back.

I shoved off still unsure which route to take. If I stuck to the main river channel to the east of 16.5 mile long Sauvie Island. I would have to paddle 22.3 actual miles with shortcuts before reaching my next campsite, or I could take the Multnomah Channel, actually a branch of the Willamette River on the west side of the island. That route would add eight miles to the trip but has a campsite along the way.

I tossed aside my calculations when I remembered that one purpose of this trip was to see the river the same way Lewis and Clark saw it. That led me to prefer the main channel, which would skirt the Shillapoo Wildlife Management Area and the Ridgefield National Wildlife Refuge, once the site of the Chinookan village of Cathlapotle. After observing osprey nesting on pilings among the lush wetlands, riparian forests and oak groves engulfing the riverbanks on the main channel, and the heavy industry and ship traffic on the Multnomah Channel, my decision was easy.

At the point where the Columbia River and Multnomah River channels divide, I passed Warrior Point Lighthouse on the Oregon side of the river and the basalt lava outcrop of Warrior Rock on the Washington side. To my left, the landscape was much like that observed by Lewis and Clark, while to my right signs of the big city of Portland began to emerge.

Warrior Point was named by Lt. William Broughton of the Vancouver Expedition. On October 28, 1792, thirteen years before the Corps of Discovery, Broughton led an exploration party that rowed upriver all the way to Cape Vancouver, about 115 miles from the mouth of the Columbia River. When the expedition briefly anchored off Warrior Point, they found themselves surrounded by twenty-three canoes, each carrying three to twelve Natives attired in war garments and prepared for combat. Broughton ordered his launch's swivel gun primed for discharge and fired a ball from his musket into the water. After this brief show of force by both sides, the parties disarmed and traded bows and arrows for buttons and beads.

That conflict reminded me of a story told to Joyce and me the first time we lived in South America about one of Brazil's many revolutions.

With the two opposing forces confronting each other, the generals in charge met, each bringing a list of the number of troops and number and type of armaments. A comparison of the two lists determined the victor.

An approach like that of the Brazilian generals or Lt. Broughton's encounter with Native Americans may seem fair, but, at another level, illustrates the concept that *might makes right.* I would be reminded of its power to corrupt as I paddled past the remnants of many indigenous nations along my route.

It was just about noon when I arrived at Kelley Point Park where the Willamette River curls to the north and joins the Columbia to form the alluring shape of a woman's breast. As I had hoped, many ospreys, herons, ducks, and gulls greeted me when passing the wildlife areas during the morning hours. Based on the rate at which I left fixed objects behind, I moved slower and slower while the morning progressed. I realized that releases from Bonneville Dam, forty-five miles upstream, combined with an outgoing tide, had probably increased the adverse current. Although I didn't know when releases were planned for the remainder of the day, I decided to wait at Kelley Point, hoping the current would subside. I thought about camping at Kelley Point Park, but camping wasn't permitted. I walked around the park with my primary and spare paddles in hand but never lost sight of Whisper. Should someone be bold enough to take Whisper, I would be up the creek, but they would be the one without a paddle.

By midafternoon I was becoming impatient. Since branches floating downstream didn't seem to be moving as fast as they had been when I pulled ashore, I concluded that it was time to get back on the river. To avoid the heavy Portland and Vancouver Washington ship traffic I took the side channel between Hayden Island and the mainland. Had I taken the main channel I would have passed historic Fort Vancouver, a location where the Expedition stopped on March 30, 1806. Lewis and Clark found this area, near the confluence of the Columbia and Willamette Rivers, to be the most heavily populated land along their route. Native Americans in the numerous villages dotting the riverbanks subsisted on the abundant game, fish, and wild plants. Today, the greater Portland-Vancouver area remains the most heavily populated area along the Lewis and Clark Trail.

It was sunny and warm when Amtrak's Coast Starlight left Portland and ambled across the river on a rusty bridge not far above my head. Beyond the railroad bridge and downstream from the I-5 bridge, I paddled through Portland's large houseboat community with many expensive homes and fancy yachts.

A pudgy middle-aged man launched his red plastic kayak from the shore and paddled up to me. We talked about kayaking and for a few minutes he discussed his current misfortunes. Although I couldn't hear everything he said because of the railroad and motorboat noise, I gathered that he was killing time on the river because he was out of work and couldn't find a job because he didn't have a car. After paddling together for about a mile, my accidental companion peeled off and headed back to shore.

I welcomed a late-day surge in energy and finally saw my intended campsite in the distance 12.5 hours after leaving St. Helens. It was a beautiful golden evening, the sun's rays shimmering on the water, when I approached Lemon Island. The primitive campsite at the downstream end of the low-slung island was home to many birds and was surprisingly tranquil, given that it was bounded by Portland International Airport to the south, I-205 to the east and the Burlington Northern Railway to the north. The many recreational boaters tied up along the sandy beach seemed to evacuate the island when sunset and I approached.

I would have preferred a shorter paddle than the 22.3 miles covered that day, but I was pleased to make it all the way to Lemon Island, and the sandy campsite I found negated the need to blow up my leaky air mattress. It was not far from my campsite where Lewis and Clark spent the eighth night of their return trip. In place of airplane noise, the Expedition complained about too much attention and theft by the Chinook Tribe. I didn't have to worry about being robbed unless some thief arrived by boat during the night.

The Landscape Changes

A fawn stared at me the next morning while I shoved off into the side channel to the south of Lemon and the Government Island Wildlife Refuge. The sun came out from behind low clouds when Whisper passed under the I-205 Bridge spanning Government Island. Suddenly, the symmetrical cone of 11,235-foot-high snow-covered Mount Hood loomed in the distance. This noble peak served as a beacon for Native Americans and the westbound Expedition after they left the Snake River Valley. I had hoped to climb it before my failing hips made that impossible. Some describe the trip to the summit as a long walk. Many who thought that way did not adequately prepare and died. A similar worry stayed with me for much of my trip, whether I had adequately prepared for the uncertainties that lay ahead. I didn't know what I didn't know.

A little more than two hours after leaving Lemon Island, I stopped at the Chinook Landing Marine Park to make another phone call, this time to Greg. I was relieved when he told me he would be available to paddle with me over the weekend if the river current below Bonneville Dam proved overwhelming. He also invited me to spend the night before with him and his family.

I was also glad I had remembered to obtain change for the payphone while at Scipio's Landing. I felt somewhat superior to cell phone users because I didn't have to worry about losing, dunking, or charging what my grandchildren, in their attempt to rewrite the English language, refer to as a *device*. The prisoners doing cleanup duty at the park stared at me, seemingly finding my chosen method of recreation, and my kayak attire amusing. I could have said something about their orange jumpsuits but wisely resisted the impulse.

The Corps of Discovery stopped on the Washington side of the river near Chinook Landing between March 31, and April 6, 1806, in a successful search for game. They had been told that the absence of game above the Gorge was causing starvation among the Indians. Clark took that opportunity to explore the lower reach of the Willamette River, a stream that had remained hidden from the Expedition on their downstream voyage. They had learned about the Willamette from Native Americans and had planned to explore it to satisfy their curiosity, and to meet President Jefferson's mandate to explore the main rivers and their tributaries. Through broken translation, and from a rough sketch, they learned that not far upstream there was a majestic waterfall, and above that a vast tract of country between "the western range of mountains" (the Cascades) and "those on the seacoast" (the Coast Range) and as far south as the "waters of California." This was an amazingly accurate description of the Willamette River valley, a land that proved so attractive to early explorers, especially farmers. I vowed to explore the Willamette someday and have since paddled most of its length in the company of friends and family.

I felt the wind picking up while paddling a back channel near Point Vancouver. It was here that William Broughton of Captain George Vancouver's 1792 expedition turned back to the mother ship, having fulfilled his mission. I began to question if I, too, should stop here but hubris prevailed, and I decided to move on.

Rooster Rock lies farther up and across the river from where the back channel enters the main river. The Columbia River didn't seem to pose a threat, but like the swimmer who encounters warm water near the surface only to be chilled when diving deep, the calmer water near the shore became more threatening when I pushed onward. Brackish spray from the whitecaps stung my eyes. Fighting both the current and wind on my diagonal path across the mile-wide river, I needed every other stroke to correct my direction, so Whisper wasn't swept downstream.

The threat of capsizing was real. I never learned how to roll a two-person fully loaded kayak, so a water exit would be the preferred option. I had recollections of people drowning because they couldn't release their spray skirts while they were upside down. I would have practiced reaching forward to find the pull tab on my spray skirt, but both arms were needed to paddle. Except for being trapped upside down, I didn't fear drowning. All I had to do was hold onto Whisper until we washed up on some distant shore. I remember remaining remarkably calm, or is my memory selective? Perhaps I gained a measure of comfort from the presence of motorists on an overlook along U.S. Highway 30. The likelihood that most of them were carrying cell phones gave me the confidence to continue. (Okay, so maybe I am a hypocrite when it comes to technology.)

I was hurting and running on empty when I arrived at the serene side channel leading to Rooster Rock Park. The basalt tower glistened in the afternoon sun and welcomed this lone paddler to the Columbia River Gorge National Scenic Area.

I performed needed maintenance on Whisper and my gear while waiting for Greg to shuttle me to his home. I left Whisper tied to a floating dock and hoped she would still be there when I returned after my day of rest. It was convenient that Greg and his family live close to the river. I later suggested to Joyce that we have more children so they could be positioned at strategic locations along all the rivers I might eventually paddle. I don't believe Joyce was thinking geographically when she told me where I could go.

Dam in Sight

Over the years Joyce and I have come to realize that we have three wonderfully caring children. When Greg agreed to paddle with me, on what was likely to be the last day of this year's trip, I wasn't surprised. Greg is a strong paddler and a wonderful companion. Our experiences together have become safer and more pleasant now that he is no longer reluctant to tell me when I am wrong.

Greg developed his small-boat skills while rowing crew for the University of Puget Sound and Washington University in St. Louis. He even made it to a pre-Olympic training camp. But rowers tend to be very tall, and because Greg, at six-one, was on the short side, he was assigned to the lightweight boat. The weight loss expected of him became too difficult to sustain.

I spent the afternoon playing with my grandchildren Kyla and Landon and then enjoyed a relaxing evening with Greg, his wife Tara, and the children. The next morning, Greg and I drove back to Rooster Rock and were relieved to find Whisper where we had left her. We reloaded and paddled Whisper down the slough to the main channel. Sunny weather, a modest adverse current, and a tailwind gave us a fair start to our day, my only regret being that we somehow missed the nearby clothing-optional beach. When Greg asked, "Why are you interested in nude women?" it reminded me that children don't like to be informed that their parents are interested in sex.

All around us towered the dramatically beautiful Columbia River Gorge; the sheer basaltic cliffs of Cape Horn (the second Cape Horn of this trip), Bridal Veil Falls cascading from a basalt bluff, and the imposing Multnomah Falls, a string of whitewater dropping 620 feet, and the most popular tourist site in Oregon. Our view from the river accentuated the majesty of the gorge and high peaks, as the multiple shades of green receded in the distance, but I had to admit that I remembered even more fondly feeling the mist blown from the falling water of the falls when Joyce and I last visited.

After twelve miles of hard paddling, we arrived at a boat ramp at Fisheries Marina in Dodson, Oregon. We bought candy bars and soft drinks in the rustic camp store and read several signs cautioning boaters about water depths exceeding one hundred feet, severe currents between five and eight knots below Bonneville Dam, and about twelve boats that had recently capsized, resulting in two deaths by drowning. Demonstrating that the warnings were not idle, soon after returning to the river we had to churn our paddles at full force to make any progress. At times we even found ourselves slipping backward. Somehow, I found it reassuring when Greg asked, "How are you doing, Dad?"

We tried to hug the shore, where the slower current overshadowed the increased bottom drag but travel near shore proved impossible because of the many fishers casting their lines and the few reeling in to allow us to pass. At one slight bulge in the shoreline the current bunched much like it had above the wing dams. The hill at the outer end of the bulge stopped us cold. Sprinting together we should have been able to paddle at 5 knots or more, but even this wasn't enough. Greg didn't want to debate the fishers on water rights, so we angled over to the Washington side of the river in hopes of finding a slower current. Fortunately, we made some headway there. Expecting slower current on the inside of Ives Island, we entered the pass between Ives and Pierce Islands. The current in the side channel was still powerful enough to stop us, but this time there were no fishers to dodge, and the water was shallow enough for us to push, pull and drag Whisper until we could get around Ives Island and return to the main channel.

Lewis and Clark spent the night of April 9, 1806, on the Oregon side of the river near the present location of the Bonneville Fish Hatchery just downstream from the dam. Greg and I had also intended to pull out on the Oregon side of the river at Tanner Creek Fishing Area, just below the fish hatchery. However, the posted warnings at Dodson remained on our minds. "What do you want to do?" Greg asked. I answered that challenging the rough water below the dam wasn't worth the risk.

Midafternoon on August 24, 2008, we completed our journey at the Hamilton Island Boat Ramp on the Washington side of the river. The boat ramp is adjacent to Fort Cascades National Historic site and marks the eastern terminus of the 146-mile Columbia River Water Trail from the dam to Fort Clatsop. Soon after we arrived, the shouts from Kyla and Landon, "Hi Dad, hi Papa," put a smile on our weary faces.

Postscript I

Despite headwinds, heavy dugout canoes, and the need to hunt or trade for food, it took the Expedition only ten paddling days to reach this location from Fort Clatsop. My goal of following in their wake took seven paddling days. My adventure for this year had come to an end. I was more relieved at not having failed than I was at having finished.

The Expedition still had thousands of miles and many adventures to go before they returned to St. Louis. It wasn't long before I began to consider following farther in their wake. Maybe I wasn't as old as my years and rebuilt body suggested.

Warrior Point Lighthouse

Wing dam at confluence of Columbia and Willamette Rivers

Rooster Rock

Author's son Greg and granddaughter Kyla in
Whisper below Bonneville Dam

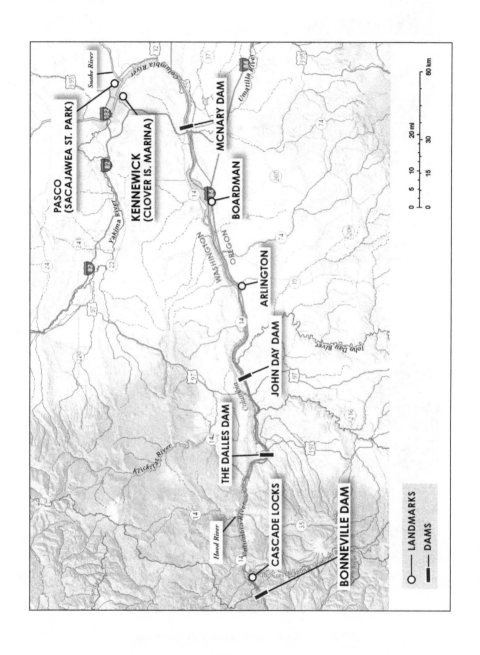

PASCO
(SACAJAWEA ST. PARK)

KENNEWICK
(CLOVER IS. MARINA)

MCNARY DAM

BOARDMAN

ARLINGTON

JOHN DAY DAM

THE DALLES DAM

CASCADE LOCKS

BONNEVILLE DAM

Snake River

Columbia River

Umatilla River

Yakima River

Klickitat River

Hood River

John Day River

Columbia River

WASHINGTON

OREGON

○── LANDMARKS

▬── DAMS

| 0 | 5 | 10 | 15 | 20 ml |

| 0 | | 30 | | 60 km |

II

The Mid-Columbia River

2009

Bridge of the Gods

Ominous Introduction

When I thought of last summers' journey on the lower Columbia River downstream of Bonneville Dam, I remembered fighting the rain, wind, and the high river and tidal currents. In a brighter mood, I recalled snow covered Mount Hood emerging from behind a tree, and Rooster Rock glowing the color of marmalade in the afternoon sun. Eastern Washington has a different type of beauty. Rolling hills juxtapose with sharp cliffs and sudden drops across the golden-brown shrub-steppe landscape. It's a dramatic scene that recalls the ice age Missoula flood that carved its way to the Pacific, a vista that is not always easy to appreciate when the summer temperature hovers around that found in a boiler room.

I had even less confidence in completing this year's trip than last year's, in large part because of my lingering arm and shoulder problems. I had hopes that my arms would become stronger as this year's trip progressed, but my deformed left shoulder was not likely to improve.

The river would challenge me. In addition to debilitating temperatures, every kayaking reference warns about the strong winds and high waves, especially during the summer in the Columbia River Gorge (famous for kite boarding and wind surfing), as well as the long barren reaches of the river near Arlington, Oregon and the wind torn Wallula Gap downstream from Pasco, Washington.

Paddling with Mike

I welcomed my son Michael's offer to accompany me for up to five days. There was a time not long ago when, like most young adults, Mike didn't want to do much with his parents. But recently, like bacteria and antibiotics, he seems to have built up an amazing tolerance to Joyce and me.

Mike and I left our home in Washington before sunrise on August 2, 2009, and drove my 1996 Volvo to the Cascade Locks Marina, upstream of Bonneville Dam and Bridge of the Gods, arriving just before 9 a.m. The marina managers allowed me to leave my vehicle there while Mike and I were on the river. Learning from last year's navigational missteps, I now had charts from the *2006 Evergreen Pacific River Cruising Atlas for the Columbia,* Willamette & Snake River ("The Atlas"). Resentfully succumbing to the technology craze, or maybe it was family pressures, I even brought a cell phone. Now, all I had to do was overcome the absurdity of having to press the end button in order to begin a conversation.

Sweat was already dribbling from my forehead late that morning when Mike and I launched Whisper. The mild west wind beat against the current to create small waves and occasional whitecaps. Mike sat in the bow and set the pace while I navigated and steered. After knocking our paddles together a few times like prizefighters testing each other, we were soon able to synchronize our strokes.

This reach of the Columbia River— the Gorge—transitions between the lush green western Pacific Northwest and the dry brown, unforested expanse of the eastern Pacific Northwest. From Wind River to Hood River—a distance of only fifteen miles—the average annual rainfall drops from a hundred inches to twenty-nine inches, further plunges to fourteen inches at The Dalles, and drops even below that in the desert near Arlington, Oregon. Between Portland and Pasco, the average daytime summer temperature increases in step with the elevation gain.

The strong adverse current just above the marina quickly moderated where the river recast itself as Bonneville Lake. As we stroked past Swell City, aptly named for its rough water, three-foot waves combined with a crosswind woke me from my daydreams and brought me back to the river's challenges. The waves sprayed clean cool fresh water on my face, much preferable to last years' eye stinging salty brine.

"How are you doing Mike?" I yelled in order to be heard over the wind and waves.

"Just fine," he answered.

We paddled hard and braced often to keep from broaching.

In early afternoon, approaching Hood River, Oregon, we found ourselves weaving amid hundreds of wind surfers and kite boarders. They zigged and zagged like a convention of angry rainbow-colored hornets. Being so much faster than us, they whipped across the water, contributing to the froth as much, it seemed, as the crosswind and current. Plodding forward, we could do little to avoid them and the noise from the wind and their flapping sails prevented them from hearing us when we called out in warning. They frequently headed right towards us only to veer off at the last possible moment. I closed my eyes just before each anticipated impact. Whisper would survive a collision, very likely, but I really didn't want to practice rolling or exiting the boat in the cold current.

We were relieved to pass Hood River on a calm day. The wind didn't exceed 20 knots and the waves were no more than three feet, a far cry from the six-to-eight-foot waves we were told to beware of. Aided by a following wind in the afternoon, we paddled twenty-eight miles at an average speed of 4 mph, almost doubling my average speed of last year.

At the end of the day, we found a small cobble covered cove near Oregon's Memaloose State Park situated on a low hill south of the Union Pacific Railroad, and north of I-84. The footpath crossing the railroad tracks was near a blind curve. Because my hearing is not that good, Mike assumed the role of train listener. When he gave the "all clear," we hustled Whisper across. We climbed a rough trail winding through sagebrush and found a campsite somewhat isolated from groups of noisy campers. After pitching our tent, we made separate meals, our prime area of incompatibility being food preferences. I don't know where Joyce and I went wrong. Mike will only eat healthy food. He prepared oatmeal, peanut butter, and a couple of apples. I had beef jerky, trail mix, and peaches in sugary syrup. Before preparing to sleep, we agreed that we were off to a good start. Other than blisters, I felt fine. Mike reported a strange tingling that coursed down his right arm. Neither of us knew the cause, or where it would lead.

The next day, after a three-hour paddle, we reached the Dalles Dam. The city of The Dalles is on a reach of river that Lewis and Clark named the Long Narrows. Native Americans had occupied the Long Narrows for ten thousand years and, at the time of the Expedition, it remained a Native trading center. On their downstream voyage, the Expedition astonished the Natives by running the treacherous rapids in their dugout canoes. They camped just below the rapids at a site they called Fort Rock Camp, now known as The Dalles.

Detour at the Dalles

Reaching the Tri-Cities (Kennewick, Pasco, and Richland), where I planned to end this year's voyage, required traversing three dams, one of which (the John Day Dam) was once the highest single lock dam in the free world. Alas, the world is not so free that it allows human powered boats through the Columbia River locks. I was bothered by this apparent discrimination considering that powered recreational boats are permitted to pass through. There is a cost to operate the locks, of course. If what I read is correct, that a tax on marine fuel pays for lock operations, the exception made for travelers like me didn't seem quite so unfair.

The US Army Corps of Engineers had told me that it would be preferable to portage the Dalles Dam on the Washington side because the Oregon side involved pulling our kayak several miles through the city of The Dalles. While in mid-river, we questioned this advice. Climbing the steep boulder-covered slope on the Washington side seemed hazardous, at best. We paddled to The Dalles Marina on the Oregon side for a second opinion. While there, a gruff and impatient fisherman commented, "Kayakers should stay in Washington," underlining our belief that it would be unpleasant, and perhaps risky, to pull Whisper through the town.

We crossed back over to the Washington side where we landed near a rickety Native American fishing platform less than a mile downstream from the dam. The platform was reminiscent of the lattice work Native

Americans balanced on while netting and spearing thousands of salmon that struggled to pass Celilo Falls. It seems unlikely that many salmon now pass the fishing platform.

We made several trips carrying our gear up the steep twelve-story high, boulder-covered slope with Mike shouldering most of the burden. We then gingerly moved Whisper from one rock to another while working our way over and around the sharp basalt boulders. At the top of the slope, we found an almost level gravel road leading to the dam. We made good progress, pulling Whisper on her wheeled cart until our path was blocked by a ten-foot-high chain-link fence topped with barbed wire. We took stock of our limited options.

"Let's go back the way we came and pull the kayak through The Dalles," Mike suggested.

"We might damage Whisper, or me, going back down that devil of a slope," I countered.

"Okay Dad, it's your trip.," Mike said without a hint of resentment.

I convinced Mike we should dig a hole under the fence. A friendly contractor working nearby lent us a large breaker bar to move the boulders but was not otherwise complicit in our effort. Coincidentally, this was the same contractor Mike had worked for right after college, and perhaps the one who had erected the fence. I scooped sand out with my bare hands and used the breaker bar to roll boulders out of the way, one heavier than the engine in my vintage '66 VW.

Mike, my reluctant accomplice, intent on establishing a case of plausible deniability should someone object to what we were doing, nevertheless helped me move big rocks as rapidly as if we were breaking out of prison. Mike half-jokingly said he would scan the sky for Homeland Security helicopters. He was much less likely to be spotted than me. While we both thought that stylish dress for men should, at a minimum, be a low-level felony, I vented my frustration with the clothes culture by wearing colors so bright and antagonistic they looked like they might go to war with each other. Whether it is because he is color blind or because he doesn't want to stand out, Mike avoids all primary colors. To an eye in the sky looking down from above, Mike, in his greige colored clothes, would resemble a large rock.

Mike also reminded me that he was starting his career while mine was dwindling and that a criminal record would not be of much benefit in finding a job. It is ironic that the career Mike chose involves regulating power generation from Columbia River dams and other energy sources.

I might have been disappointed with Mike letting me do most of the digging if he hadn't paddled so hard. I would soon learn that he had a very good reason for slacking off. We made it past the dam without further complications and ended our four-hour-long portage at Railroad Island Park where we devoured a long-delayed lunch of overly healthy food. Later, when back home, I contacted the Corps of Engineers and advised them of our problem with, and solution to, the portage. I had been afraid they might issue me a citation. Instead, they graciously promised to take corrective action to restore the portage route.

Continuing upstream after lunch, I noticed that Mike wasn't paddling very hard, which was unlike him. As the afternoon progressed, I was doing most of the work. Mike never complained, but when I finally asked if anything was wrong, he showed me his swollen lower right arm. It looked like his bicep had migrated from north of his elbow to the south and parked itself on his forearm, like Popeye's arm in the old comic strip. Mike told me that the pain had begun the day before and was now intense. After discussing the options, and the likelihood that his arm would worsen with forced use, we agreed that this should be his last day on the Columbia River.

Coincidentally, it was near here that the Expedition abandoned their canoes and proceeded on horseback and on foot along the Washington side of the Columbia, to the confluence with the Walla Walla River. While camped near here on October 22 and 23, in 1805 and again April 19 and 20, 1806, just when the salmon arrived, the Expedition noted that this vicinity was the dividing line between the Chinookan people on the lower Columbia and the Sahaptian speakers above. Unlike most European settlers, and probably because of Jefferson's tutelage, Lewis and Clark recognized that the Indians who populated this area represented many distinct nations. Clark noted that the Sahaptins were well outfitted with deer, elk, ibex, goat, and wolf-skin robes. Clark's unusually comprehensive study of Native Americans resulted in him being a strong advocate for them when he later became Superintendent of Indian Affairs for the Louisiana Territory.

Mike and I stopped briefly at Avery County Park, a launch ramp with limited camping adjacent to what were once the famous Celilo Falls and Tribal fishing grounds before the river was dammed. Mike called Joyce to ask if she could meet us at the Celilo Campground to drive him home. I mused that if I had called Joyce with a similar problem, she might have put me on hold while considering her options. When children call their mother for help, the response is visceral and instantaneous.

What puzzled us both was why Mike would have been the one to develop tendonitis. I knew that he was working harder than me, but there may have been another factor. My training built tolerance for repetitions while his built strength. What was clear is that we pushed too much on our first day. I had overlooked the importance of pacing.

That evening, I found one of the few green campsites at the otherwise brown but quiet and free Corps of Engineers' Celilo Campground. Experienced arid land campers would not make my mistake. Mike and I were lying in our tent talking when Joyce arrived after a 250-mile drive. After bidding Mike and Joyce goodbye, I was tucking into my tent for the night when the campground sprinklers kicked in, spraying my exposed gear and me inside my open tent. Not yet to the car, Mike jumped into action and found some empty garbage containers to put over the active sprinklers while I rushed to move gear before it became soaked. Getting irrigated served me right for not questioning why our campsite was so much greener than the surrounding terrain.

I had hoped Mike would remain with me for up to five days, encompassing the difficult portages and the dangerous reach of the river downstream from Arlington, Oregon. After that, his schedule would have made it necessary for him to return home to continue his job search. Now, without his comforting presence, my self-confidence was on the verge of collapsing.

During a restless night I dwelled on missing Mike for the rest of the voyage. The following day would involve another portage, this one at the 113-foot-deep lock of the John Day Dam.

Alone Again

While Michael was with me, I put aside some of the fears I had about the widening river ahead. Now alone, I began to think more about the stories of others who had traveled this route. In 1995, William Least Heat-Moon, his faithful first mate Pilotis, and a support crew traveled from New York City to the Pacific Ocean in a cabin cruiser named *Nikawa* (River Horse) powered by two big outboard motors. Heat-Moon noted in his book *River Horse* that every few days he and his crew encountered conditions that could easily cause the death or destruction of a lone paddler in a kayak. If high wind and waves on the Columbia River could threaten to sink the twenty-two-foot-long high powered *Nikawa*, what would these conditions do to me? Perhaps Heat-Moon took liberties in telling his story, but I feared that he did not.

The next morning, after fastening my spray skirt, and while sitting snug by the shore, I realized how lonely I would be in Whisper. To dispel that haunting feeling, I busied myself considering upcoming moves. My first decision would be whether to paddle the shorter and narrower channel to the north of two-mile-long Miller Island or the longer route to the south. I decided to avoid the shorter route with the ominous name of Hell's Gate.

A mild tailwind, and the company of many fishers at the mouth of the Deschutes River, lifted my spirits. Added to this was the comforting feeling of Whisper wrapped snuggly around me as I paddled the next four hours to John Day Dam. It would have been thrilling to pass through the deep lock at this dam, but the rules precluded me from doing so. To portage around the dam, I searched the shoreline for the designated take-out location at Cliffs, not knowing whether "Cliffs" referred to a community or a geographic feature. Eventually, admitting that I had probably missed Cliffs, and not wanting to advance too close to the turbulent water below the dam, I pulled ashore. The current was running fast enough even along the shore for me to fear losing Whisper when I exited. After searching without success for an eddy, I tied a line from Whisper to my life jacket. The connection might prevent me from losing my kayak but just as surely could cause me to be dragged downstream. With all the agility of a flying hippopotamus, I tumbled out of Whisper, struggled to gain my footing, and stumbled up the steeply sloping gravel bank suffering nothing more than an embarrassing dunking.

The portage proved consistent with the Corps of Engineers' guidance. I learned that unless you have vehicular support or can carry much more weight than I can, wheels for a solo paddler with a kayak are necessary. With wheels, the portage length is less important than the grade and composition of the path. On this occasion, the two-mile-long, flat-to-moderately sloped packed gravel road was a cakewalk compared to the portage at The Dalles.

Just upstream of John Day Dam I waved to many of those fishing in a dozen or so recreational fishing boats near the mouth of the John Day River. These were the last private recreational boats I would encounter on the river for the next sixty miles. What waited ahead was a lonely and dangerous reach of river.

I finished the day at Le Page Park, a secluded Corps of Engineers campground with a protected bathing beach on the John Day River, just upstream of the Union Pacific Railroad and I-84. It was blow-dryer hot, so a bath in the rejuvenating river was first on my list of activities. The ice-cold Sprite, a gift from Ken Cardwell, the soft-spoken campsite host, tasted as refreshing as anything I had ever drunk. Responding to my concern about rattlesnakes, Ken offered little comfort. "At least," he said, "there are not so many as last year." As I prepared to sleep, the weather changed dramatically. Ken had warned that it would. Gusts of wind almost collapsed my tent while thunder roiled in the distance.

Struggling against the wind, I secured additional restraining lines and tent pegs and draped a flapping rain cover over the tent, all the while taking care not to step on a rattlesnake.

The view upstream on the Columbia River the next morning was dominated by the sharp gray basalt riprap rock placed to protect the riverbank and the railroad embankments from erosion. An otter walked the rocky shore near the mouth of the John Day River, but after that I saw no animals other than gulls, and certainly no fellow kayakers. The *Boating Guide to the Middle Columbia River (The Guide)* was correct when it said to expect little company between The Dalles and Umatilla. It was hard to imagine a more desolate stretch of river.

Three things held my interest during this lonely stretch—the wind, the waves, and the railroads. The railroads were constant companions, riding high above me behind rocky slopes, the Union Pacific on the Oregon side, and Burlington Northern on the Washington side. Long, heavily laden freight trains passed me many times each day and night. Amtrak's Empire Builder passed twice a day, once in each direction, a reminder of home where trains on the Seattle-bound spur of the Empire Builder toot their horns twice each day.

Rail lines and rivers are frequent companions. The gradient of most rivers rarely exceeds the relatively flat grade negotiable by trains. The Columbia River is no exception. The Burlington Northern line incorporates the once thriving Spokane, Portland, and Seattle Railway (SP&S). An early example of false advertising, the SP&S railroad never made it to Seattle, but did extend to Astoria, Oregon, as I had observed during my journey last year. The mournful whistles I heard while paddling combined with the mystery of not knowing where the trains were headed triggered fond memories of family rail trips to Spokane, Boise, and Salt Lake City. I've read that overnight passenger trains may soon go the way of the passenger pigeon. I felt sorry for those who would never experience the romance of the rails and vowed to take my grandchildren on an overnight train trip before it was too late.

Between Le Page Park and Arlington Oregon, a distance of

twenty-four miles, there are only two places to pull off the river on the Washington side, and no pullouts on the Oregon side. The straight, basalt-lined river corridor with walls that appeared to converge in the distance, looked like a pathway to oblivion. I was duly concerned about this area after having read Karl Adams account of entering this reach during a period of flat calm in 1987, only to have the weather quickly change. He was driven upon the rocky shore by fifty knot winds and "waves that broke with five-foot white caps." Adams almost drowned. The hull of his kayak split open, but he somehow managed to pull his damaged kayak and himself up the embankment.

The wind was still mild when I shoved off. With the threat of high winds always on my mind, I didn't want to cross the mile and a half wide river unless necessary, so I hugged the Oregon shore with its procession of angular basalt boulders.

Guessing that it would take me at least eight hours of hard paddling to reach Arlington, I realized I had a long watch ahead for dangerous wind and waves. My eyes constantly scanned the shore for places where a landing might be attempted, but I found none. I also looked for other boaters but saw only a single tour boat moving out of my sight in the early morning hours, bound for Portland. In light wind I might be able to pull out over the riprap shore, but the wind usually increased as the day progressed and hauling Whisper out of the river with even moderate waves would certainly damage her hull, possibly putting a hole in it as it did to Adam's kayak.

The first few hours went well. The initial sign of trouble was a deceptively refreshing breeze on my face. Then the wind increased. The waves grew higher. The swells were above my head and the following sea pushed the waves over Whisper's stern. Every so often, a wave sprayed me with cool water when it crashed against Whisper's side. I braced to remain upright. I began to develop an escape plan in the event the waves got much higher. I could attempt a risky 180 degree turn and paddle into the wind, but I had never attempted such a turn with high wind and waves. If I failed, I would almost surely capsize. How long I would remain coherent before hypothermia took its toll, I couldn't guess.

I didn't broach, but whether this was skill or luck I don't know. Churning my paddle as fast as I could, and not willing to stop to eat, I began to feel hunger's effects. I was afraid my arms would cramp, or the wind would change direction and drive me onto the rocks. Just when I thought I couldn't paddle another stroke, my dimming hope of making it safely to shore got a boost when I saw a grain elevator in the town of Roosevelt on the Washington shore. This was a sign that Arlington, Oregon, and my escape from this dangerous river corridor was approaching.

Even had I been able to put my paddle down long enough to eat, I'd have found it difficult. In very hot weather I have no appetite, and though I didn't carry a thermometer my estimate was temps upward of 95 degrees Fahrenheit. About the only food I can stomach in such heat is a snack of jellied fruit drops, but the drops had melted and congealed into an unappetizing mass that resembled a giant dead amoeba.

The Guide reported that conditions were generally better on the Washington side along this reach, but it was now too risky in this wind for me to cross the river. Through steep chop and with the whistle of wind swirling around my head, I finally reached Arlington's small boat basin and breathed a long sigh of relief. Even at the floating dock, Whisper was pounded by small whitecaps. Aided by a tailwind, I had averaged 4 mph that day. At least there was that triumph.

A Long Walk from Arlington

After tying Whisper to the lee side of the dock I crossed under I-84 and walked to town. Not finding a place to camp, I checked into a motel. After a short nap, I ordered a steak and salad in Arlington's Village Inn Restaurant. The server's welcoming smile reminded me how pleasant a small town can be. "It's so nice to find a good restaurant, a clean and comfortable place to stay, and a grocery, all within easy walking distance," I said. I could have added my appreciation for the town's tranquil and lush green park, which contrasted so pleasantly with the brown of the surrounding Alkali Canyon. The waitress, when I shared this pleasantry, smiled, and said, "Did you know that it hit 116 degrees last Saturday?"

Waking the next morning to a blaring alarm clock in place of chirping birds, I noticed there was barely a breeze at the motel, which was nestled in the canyon. My hopes for calm conditions were soon dashed. On the river, high waves crashed against the breakwater. My pulse quickened when I observed that leaving the marina would put me broadside to the waves pushing from the west. I also remembered the warning in *The Guide* that the wind can make entry and exit from the Port of Arlington difficult. There was no one nearby on the churning river to assist should help be needed.

I waited at a picnic table at the Port of Arlington, hoping that sooner rather than later conditions would improve. Instead, the wind turbines on the surrounding hills spun faster and faster. As the morning progressed with the wind showing no sign of abating, I jury-rigged two fenders to protect Whisper from damage as it chafed against the dock. John Kennedy, a boater who came down to the river to check on his cabin cruiser, told me, "Don't expect improved conditions until you get to Quesnel Park about fifteen miles upstream." On this not so optimistic note I went back to the motel and took a nap. Returning to the marina shortly before noon, I took temporary refuge from a downpour in the office of the CDL Grain Elevator. CDL's manager had been monitoring weather and river conditions through the morning. "Even higher winds and six-foot-high waves are predicted for the next day. You might find a more hospitable place to launch up there," he said, while pointing to a distant bend in the river.

Impatient to get on with my journey, I checked out of the motel and set off pulling Whisper over a rough gravel road that paralleled the railroad tracks heading for a place known as "up there." Where the gravel was loose, I strained to make progress. Every so often, where the road crossed the tracks on irregularly spaced timbers, I envisioned the wheels getting stuck between the timbers at the same time vibrating tracks warned that a train was about to destroy my kayak.

My company included passing Union Pacific freight trains and one lonely coyote with eyes as sad as Mike's Brittany spaniel, Paco, when he begs for food I'm not supposed to give him. With its long legs and fur coat, the coyote reminded me of an undernourished fashion model. Unlike any fashion model I ever met (one), it followed me at a distance, apparently hoping I might drop some food along the way. Not wanting the coyote to rely on humans, I resisted the strong urge to give it my lunch.

Ultimately, I dragged Whisper ten-and-a-half miles with the wind-wracked river to my left and brown desiccated land to my right. I found a possible place to camp at the Heppner Junction Union Pacific work yard just west of the railroad bridge over Willow Creek. I had hoped to make it farther, but when I stood at the edge of the creek peering across the 700-foot-long bridge a chill went down my spine. I recalled a scene in the movie *Stand by Me* where several boys just barely made it across a similar trestle as a train bore down on them—and they weren't pulling a loaded kayak. Rejecting the trestle alternative and the equally uninviting choice of detouring to I-84 and following it eastward, I went back down the grade to the work yard. I saw No Trespassing signs but convinced myself they weren't meant for me. It was getting late. The wind was howling. I struggled to pitch my tent. Before crawling in and collapsing in my sleeping bag, I choked down a meager cold supper of beef jerky and dried fruit.

Pulling Whisper had not been as bad as I anticipated. Surprisingly, it gave my sore shoulder a break. I made a mental note to study my maps for similar escape routes—low traffic roads that ran roughly parallel to the river.

"The Rescue"

I returned to the river early the next morning to avoid the high wind predicted for the afternoon. The wind at this location was no better than yesterday in Arlington, but accessing the water was much easier. I was also relieved that yesterday's riprap-blanketed shoreline was now broken by occasional green coves, which afforded places to pull ashore.

It was an easy morning's paddle. Late morning, I observed Crow Butte, a large island connected to the Washington mainland by a causeway. It's a familiar marker I look for when flying between Seattle and Boise to visit my daughter Amy, her husband, Sean, and my grandchildren Owen, Katy, and Jack. While passing Crow Butte I had my first sighting of a pleasure boat since leaving LePage Park. A forty-foot power yacht passed me heading downstream, seemingly unaware of my presence.

I reached Boardman, Oregon, before noon. I had wanted to paddle farther but the next camping area was more than twenty miles upstream, too far to paddle before the wind was predicted to increase. I pulled ashore at the well cared for Boardman Marina and park, isolated from the nearby railroad and highway by groves of irrigated trees. After tying Whisper to the guest dock, I walked up to the park office where two delightful young women told me where I could find refuge for my little tent among the assortment of huge recreational vehicles. As predicted, the wind picked up soon after noon, just when I was setting up camp. After securing Whisper and adding more tent pegs, my growling stomach reminded me that I needed food. I gorged myself at the nearby C&D Drive Inn on a sloppy bozo burger with grilled onions hanging off the side and a super-delicious icy cold milkshake with real strawberries. I then went for a long walk.

Upriver from Arlington, the shoreline had been transitioning from relative wilderness to low intensity development. The rolling hills on the Washington side were now patch worked in shades of green by vineyards and tall poplar trees planted to protect the grapes from the wind and frost. The Oregon side featured food processing plants in Boardman and motorized irrigation machines, creators of the big green crop circles. Between Boardman and Irrigon, I paddled past what appeared to be hundreds of small islands near the center of the mile-wide river. The islands, combined with an irregular shoreline consisting of small bays and coves, offers excellent habitat for wildlife. Deer scampered across the hills in the distance and numerous herons, ducks, and the occasional gigantic white pelican with a wingspan considerably wider than that of a bald eagle, crossed Whisper's bow. I saw my first magpie, a sure sign that desert was nearby despite the green resulting from artificial irrigation. The squawk of the great blue heron was a welcome reminder that I was passing the Umatilla National Wildlife Refuge. I was in a land that belonged to deer, shore birds and magpies—not to me.

I took advantage of the many islands to seek protection from the wind and waves. In unprotected areas, I was bothered by two-to-three-foot waves, but after five days of steady paddling in similar or worse conditions, this seemed easily manageable. I almost lost that confidence near Long Walk Island when I noticed a rogue wave that topped out above my head approaching from my left. It threw Whisper into a broach. Just before the moment when capsize was inevitable, I instinctively braced against the river bottom with my paddle and pushed upright. Had the water been a little deeper I would have capsized, and had it been only a few inches shallower I would probably have been swamped by breaking waves.

Catching my breath from the near miss, I pulled out my chart with the resolve to be more careful. It wasn't possible to avoid all exposed water. The Oregon side of Long Walk Island appeared more protected than the Washington side, but my chart indicated that a sandbar at the upstream end might block my path. Not wanting to get trapped in a dead-end channel, I reluctantly paddled in the less protected main channel. The wind soon died down. I could almost relax.

Arriving at McNary Dam in Umatilla, Oregon just past noon, I began a portage of three miles around the dam. I stopped at the underground observation window for the fish ladder, but the murky view into the green migration channel showed only random bits of dancing and swirling vegetation and flotsam. Given another month in a normal year, the fish ladder should be gushing with salmon returning to their breeding grounds. Would this be a normal year? After returning home I checked on the Corps of Engineers website and found that it was.

Prior to the arrival of European settlers, anecdotal evidence suggests that more than a million salmon passed this point each year, far more than fish ladders could accommodate. Even before the dams, overfishing by settlers had depleted the fish runs to the point where Native Americans were starving. Louie Dick Jr., a member of the Confederated Tribes of the Umatilla Reservation, said it well. "The salmon made a commitment to return and give life. He's following his law by coming. We are violating our own law by not doing everything we can to get him back."

Though traveling solo, I was enjoying this day as much as Lewis and Clark enjoyed the few days, they had spent with Chief Yellept, and the Walla Walla people in 1806. The Chief graciously presented Clark "a very elegant white horse," a gesture emblematic of the treatment afforded the Expedition. On May 1, 1806, Clark wrote in his journal, "I think we can justly affirm to the honor of these people that they are the most hospitable, honest, and sincere people that we have met with in our voyage."

After I pitched my tent on the black sand at the Sand Station Recreation Area nine miles above McNary Dam—another free Corps of Engineers campground—a fellow camper asked me to help a lone kite boarder becalmed in the middle of the mile-wide reservoir. I paddled out to see what I could do. The kite boarder named Josh seemed reluctant, and maybe a little embarrassed, to accept help. He told me that the light early evening wind was insufficient to propel his board. He was already tired from the day's boarding, and it was a long dogpaddle back to shore. With the sun setting, hypothermia was a possibility. After staying nearby for twenty minutes while he waited for the wind to increase, Josh reluctantly straddled Whisper near the front cockpit, and towed his kit alongside while I paddled him back to shore.

My effort did not go unrewarded. Upon returning to my campsite, the Parks, a friendly Korean couple from Yakima, shared their steak dinner with me as we spoke about their dry-cleaning business in Pasco and some of the hardships they had faced as new immigrants. This had been my most relaxed day of paddling, but relaxation led to the realization that my body was hurting, especially my shoulders, and, despite wearing new paddling shoes, my heels had developed large blisters.

I had finally resigned myself to press the *end* button on my cell phone to make a call. Now that I was a communications expert, I called Joyce to report my progress and health. Joyce told me that Mike's arm was still swollen.

Meeting Sacajawea

My final full day of paddling this year required passage through the Wallula Gap, a narrow slot in the Horse Heaven Hills where the river makes a wide bend to the north. I started early in hopes of making it through the gap before the wind picked up and had positioned more of my gear in the bow compartment than usual to keep Whisper from behaving like a weathervane. While the sun rose, the wind began to build. Whitecaps crashed against Whisper. I switched to paddling in the lee of the east bank. The cliffs blocked some of the wind and most of the bright, rising sun.

There were no other boats on the river and almost no people visible from my vantage. At one gap in the cliffs, visibility hindered by the sun in my eyes, I was startled by the sharp tug of a thin line across my windpipe. The garrotes used by professional assassins came to mind. This was no crazed killer. An amiable young woman with the distinctive high cheek bones of a Native American sitting on a rock high above me expressed her chagrin that her fishing line happened to cross my path.

The waves continued to build through the Wallula Gap where the steep cliffs on both sides funneled the wind and the narrow river accentuated the opposing current. *The Guide* cautions, "the river and wind combine forces regularly to rip loose 'slow no wake' buoys even though they are anchored with five-gallon buckets filled with concrete." My adrenaline was pumping while I powered full speed ahead to make it through the gap before the wind forced me to seek shelter on the rocky shoreline. Getting off the river without damaging Whisper or myself would have been even more difficult than it had been on the reach below Arlington.

My worry about swells that barely reached my shoulders seemed rather silly when compared to the story geologists tell of an event that happened about 15,000 years ago at the end of the last ice age. A wall of water several hundred feet high, known as the Missoula Flood, roared through this canyon and carved the route of the Columbia River. The flood occurred during the age of the glaciers when a gigantic ice dam on the Clark Fork River suddenly broke. In a fit of fantasy, I imagined myself surfing down that wave.

As the song, "Only the Strong Survive" suggests, only the most steadfast rocks still stand along the shores of the Columbia. Being a geotechnical /environmental engineer, I am also an amateur geologist, but even with my amateur status I knew that the black cliffs I was passing, and the top-hat-shaped column known to Lewis and Clark as Hat Rock, which I passed yesterday, are the most resilient remnants of the Columbia River basalt geologic formation.

Off to the left, briefly visible from the river, an even more impressive geologic feature emerged—Mt. Hood's white capped symmetrical cone, which looks the same as it appeared to the Expedition when they passed here in 1805 and 1806. According to Bernard De Voto's review of Clark's journal, Clark described the mountain, which he didn't identify by name, as "bearing S.W. conical form Covered with Snow." It seems amazing that Lewis and Clark, probably with the aid of Native Americans, recognized Mt. Hood, 170 miles distant, based on descriptive notes made during Vancouver's 1792 expedition.

In late morning, I passed through the narrowest part of the river, the official Wallula Gap. The river spread out before me. The waves became less threatening as the river transitioned to Lake Wallula. While the risks diminished, annoyance increased. My kayak and paddle became tangled in milfoil and pondweed.

I soon reached the mouth of the wallowing Walla Walla River to my right. This marked the end of Lewis and Clark's upstream voyage along the Columbia River Valley. Here they crossed the river and camped from April 27 to April 29, 1806. From this camp, the Expedition proceeded by land to Travelers Rest near Missoula, Montana. They walked and rode horses they obtained from Chief Yellept and the Walla Wallas. I elected to travel a little farther on the Columbia River, to its confluence with the Snake River, before closing out this segment of my journey.

At long last I observed the railroad bridge just downstream from the confluence of the Snake and Columbia Rivers. The mile-long steel truss bridge appeared in surprisingly good condition for a structure that recently passed its hundredth birthday. I hope I look as good if I reach that age. Low humidity meant little rust. I looked forward to crossing it by Amtrak on my planned return to the beginning of this year's trip.

In my eagerness to complete my journey, the last ten miles seemed to take forever. I arrived at Sacajawea State Park, the official end of this trip, in midafternoon. It had taken me nine days to travel 165 miles. The elation of finishing was diminished by the absence of anyone with whom to celebrate. To compensate, sensing I needed a boost, the friendly park ranger directed me to a campsite reserved for river paddlers and told me he would open the shower whenever I was ready. While I was making camp, a pudgy fisherman named Red Dot introduced himself. With a tuft of bright red hair emerging from his otherwise bald head, he resembled a giant fishing lure. Whether his hair was a lure or not, fish sought him out. It didn't take Red Dot long to catch two nice-sized bass.

The next morning, after circling clockwise around Sacajawea State Park, I paddled another four miles upstream on the Columbia River to the Clover Island Marina at the Port of Kennewick. The marina staff graciously allowed me to store Whisper in a fenced enclosure for the time it would take me to travel to Cascade Locks to retrieve my vehicle. The Clover Island Inn offered me a riverside room for only ten dollars more than a room facing land. Having seen enough of the river for a while, I opted for the land view.

Postscript II

I spent the afternoon arranging travel on Amtrak back to Vancouver, Washington, and borrowed one of the marina's loaner bicycles to ride to and from the Yakima River, a side excursion something like the one Clark and a small group of soldiers made in a small canoe in October 1805. I also pedaled through all three of the Tri-Cities—Pasco, Richland, and Kennewick—all sleepy bergs before the Manhattan Project of WWII made the nearby Hanford Atomic Energy Reservation famous.

The next morning, I trundled out of Pasco aboard Amtrak's Empire Builder. Embraced in the cocoon of a comfortable padded seat, the rumble of the train speeding westward on the Washington side of the river lulling me into a veritable trance. I realized, looking out over the very early morning becalmed river, how unthreatening it would look to anyone who had not traveled it. Easy, it was, to remember the envy I felt for the passengers on the Amtrak trains that passed me when I was on the river struggling and hurting and worrying about survival, but now that I had this comfort in hand, I envied that paddler on the river.

Greg picked me up in Vancouver and took me back upriver to my Volvo at Cascades Locks. I then drove back to Kennewick to retrieve Whisper from Clover Island Marina before heading home. Driving eastward along the Columbia River on I-84, I saw that the afternoon wind had kicked up some big waves, reminding me how dangerous the passage had sometimes been. Driving past Boardman, I remembered to stop at the C & D Drive-In for another strawberry milkshake. The long drive gave me time to reflect on my accomplishments and my failures, and to consider accompanying Lewis and Clark even farther on their eastward voyage.

Hank at the start of the Gorge

Author's son Mike portaging at the Dalles

Arlington, Oregon in Alkali Canyon

Entering Wallula Gap

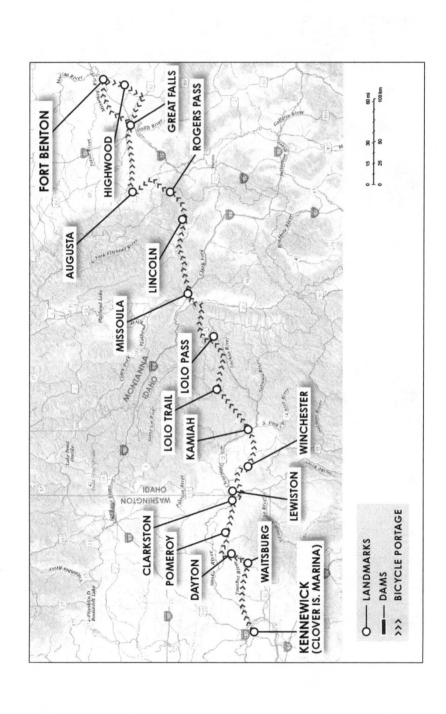

FORT BENTON
GREAT FALLS
ROGERS PASS
HIGHWOOD
AUGUSTA
LINCOLN
MISSOULA
LOLO PASS
LOLO TRAIL
KAMIAH
WINCHESTER
LEWISTON
CLARKSTON
POMEROY
DAYTON
WAITSBURG
KENNEWICK
(CLOVER IS. MARINA)

MONTANA
IDAHO
IDAHO
WASHINGTON

Marias River
Missouri River
Teton River
Smith River
Sun River
Gallatin River
Jefferson R.
Big Hole River
S. Fork Flathead River
Clark Fork
Flathead River
Bitterroot River
Clark Fork
Flathead Lake
Saint Joe River
Lochsa River
Selway River
Salmon River
S. Fork Cle... Cle... River
Snake River
Clearwater River
Palouse River
Snake River
Spokane River
Lake Pend Oreille
Columbia River
Franklin D. Roosevelt Lake
Tucannon River
Touchet River
Snake River

60 mi
100 km
30
50
15
25
0
0

O —— LANDMARKS
—— DAMS
>>> BICYCLE PORTAGE

III

Rocky Mountain Portage

2010

Author's son Mike on Weippe Prairie

Crossing Washington

Mike and I shared the driving on the trip to Kennewick from our home in western Washington. It was in Kennewick, near the confluence of the Columbia and Snake Rivers, that I would switch from river to road in order to bicycle portage the Rocky Mountains and the Bitterroot Range, a part of the Rocky Mountains that runs along the Montana and Idaho border. What a relief when Mike offered to join me on this trip, the off-road portion of which, I feared, was beyond my ability to do alone.

If you are a betting person, it would be safe to wager that nights in a desert climate like the Tri-Cities, even in mid-summer, are cool or even cold due to the absence of heat retaining moisture in the air. So it was that even though Mike and I started our bike ride after breakfast on August 1, the air that would soon exceed 100 degrees F was still relatively cool.

A soft breeze buffeted us while we crossed the landmark cable stayed bridge over the Columbia River into Pasco WA, the most industrial of the Tri-Cities. When completed in 1978, the Inter City Bridge was the first major cable-stayed bridge in the US. The diagonal cables create an efficient angular appearance, well suited for a city of industry.

A short ride past rail yards and the Port of Pasco took us to Highway 12 and the dual truss bridges over the Snake River, graceful only to an engineer like me. Bridges often intimidate me while cycling, but wide shoulders and few vehicles made for a smooth beginning for our trip.

Soon after crossing the Snake River, we turned east on WA 124, a rural two-lane highway. With the temperature already climbing, we welcomed the infrequent passing cars for the burst of turbulence that stirred the air around us. Rivulets of sweat dripped from my forehead and stung my eyes. We pedaled in silence, passing through lush green irrigated Snake River vineyards, orchards, and fields of row crops. As we gained elevation, we came upon an ocean of wheat fields, which undulated in the heat, sprouting rusty brown in contrast to the gray native vegetation and rock outcrops. There was a hint of new mown hay in the air, likely from an early wheat harvest somewhere beyond the rolling hills.

When the expedition left the Columbia River valley in late spring of 1806 they continued on foot and on horses provided to them by Chief Yellept and the Walla Wallas. The friendliness and support they received from the Walla Walla tribe, relatives of the Nez Perce, allowed Lewis to forget the hatred he had developed for the Chinooks, whom he accused of being thieves—despite that the Expedition stole a canoe from them.

It's no longer possible to follow the exact portage route taken by the Corps of Discovery when they headed east without trespassing on large tracts of private property. Lewis and Clark followed a route used by the Nez Perce, Palouse, and other Native Americans in their endless quest for game on both sides of the Rocky Mountains. The route Mike and I cobbled together crossed the Expedition's path at numerous places and was about as close as you could get to walking in their footsteps while remaining on public roads. Sometimes referred to as the "Forgotten Trail," this segment is often ignored by historians, probably because other parts of the Expedition's journey were more eventful.

Between Eureka, WA and Prescott, WA, we followed the verdant swath of the Touchet River. By the time we stopped for a snack and cold drinks in Prescott, my polyester jersey was drenched in sweat, a condition that would persist for the rest of the day. Soon after a stop at Sandy's Market, an unadorned square gray building with a friendly attendant, we left US 124 and reconnected with US 12 in the small town of Waitsburg, WA, with its unusually broad Main Street and brightly painted refurbished buildings. East of Waitsburg we rested at the Lewis and Clark Trail State Park along the Touchet. We took relief by resting in the shade of the many ponderosa pine and cottonwood trees in this microclimate oasis. The Expedition passed this area on May 2, 1806. Even in May, they shivered from the rain, hail, snow, and high winds. We, on the other hand, were hot and tired from pushing through endless walls of stagnant, blazing heat.

Back on the road, a slight crosswind did little to cool us but also did little to slow us down. We hadn't yet encountered any steep hills but the added weight of camping gear in my panniers slowed me on all hills, no matter how steep. I was grateful that Mike carried our tent and more than half our food, and often broke the wind by riding ahead of me. Hills, heat, and wind, hardly noticeable to motorists, can make or break a bicycle ride.

Drawn to shade, our next stop was at the town gazebo in Dayton, WA. More thirsty than hungry, we guzzled water and electrolyte drink and had a light lunch of apples, trail mix, and fresh locally baked bread beneath the gazebo. Reluctantly leaving the shade behind, we moved on past Dayton's railroad depot. The care lavished by the town on the oldest surviving passenger train depot in Washington State, tastefully and meticulously painted pale orange with brown trim, was impressive. We might have considered throwing our bikes on a train, but the last train left the modest station in 1974.

My fascination for rail travel stems from the times my grandfather took me to see the steam trains arriving at the small station at the end of the line in Ocean City, NJ. The engine's drive wheels towering above me, combined with the cacophonous noises and pungent odors, fired up the imagination of a young boy. Soon before my father died in 1997, he lamented the passing of rail passenger travel. With the resurgence of rail travel around the world, I wondered if the Dayton terminal would ever again host waiting passengers.

We had a moderate climb and then a steep descent after leaving Dayton. I used my brakes when the speedometer hit 27 mph. Riding with loaded panniers in the building crosswind had eroded my confidence. I feared that a gust of wind would blow me off the road or my bike's frame would crack as happened on my cross-country bike ride in 1999.

Just before Delaney, while on a long downgrade, we saw our first rattlesnake, dead on the side of the road. We stopped to speak with five hot and tired bicyclists, four students and a professor, who were resting not far from the rattler. They said they were enjoying their ride from

St. Louis to Seaside, Oregon despite the heat. My bicycle computer read 102 degrees, perhaps a little higher than the actual temperature, but not by much.

Mike and I both experienced the minor pains typically felt at the beginning of long rides. Mike's only discomfort so far was a dull pain in his lower back, but it was potential damage to his ego that he feared most. He felt bad that tendonitis in his arm forced him to drop out of last year's kayak trip, telling his mother, "It's rather embarrassing not being able to keep up with someone twice your age."

I had trained hard for this trip but riding my bike outside had been limited because of intermittent episodes of sciatica and recent complications following hip-replacement surgery in the spring of 2008. I was concerned that these conditions would force me to stop.

My right foot felt like I was stepping on a bed of burning coals, as we approached the junction with WA 127, a condition that may have been the result of nerve damage I had experienced during my cross-country ride. I dismounted and walked for about ten minutes, which restored circulation in my foot and relieved the pain. The break gave Mike a chance to stretch his lower back.

We followed Pataha Creek from Delaney to Pomeroy, WA. Exhausted, we arrived in midafternoon and checked into the clean, simple, and appropriately named Pioneer Motel. We had covered almost a hundred miles, considerably more than our target of eighty miles per day. Mike settled into the room while I walked to the lone grocery store where I guzzled an admittedly weird combination of chocolate milk and orange juice. A cold drink dispenser at the store sold 12 oz. cans of pop for forty cents. This was a town locked in time.

On the way to the grocery store, I purchased Dr. Scholl's footpads at a well-stocked drugstore, hoping they would alleviate my hotfoot. I passed a bar on the main street with two substantially inebriated middle-aged men sitting outside in the shade of a sign noting that a designated driver was available at any time of the day. I wondered how these men spent their days when they weren't drinking. Then I wondered what they thought about an old guy like me walking around town in funny looking bicycle clothes. Other than a few motorists rumbling down Main Street, the three of us were the only ones outside in the oppressive heat.

The next morning, after breakfasting in our room on bananas and instant oatmeal made with tap water, we left Pomeroy on a short upgrade followed by an exhilarating five-mile descent. The surrounding terrain, while hilly, is much softer than the mountainous terrain we knew we would encounter later. Infrequent patches of green irrigated crops appeared to have sprouted among the otherwise arid land. We soon began a more gradual relaxing descent for about eight to ten miles, after which we rejoined the gently winding Snake River at Chief Timothy State Park and followed the river into Clarkston. We arrived at the Hellsgate Marina in Clarkston at 8:45 a.m., about the time a civilized person should be eating breakfast.

The logistics of the Discovery Expedition were complicated. On their return trip, the Expedition passed close to Clarkston on foot on their way to retrieve the horses they'd left over the winter with the Nez Perce. They planned to use horses until Lewis arrived at the Missouri River and Clark arrived at a tributary to the Yellowstone River. Three small groups would break off from the two main groups for independent exploration. It was an ambitious and risky endeavor. One small group led by Sergeant Pryor had their horses stolen by a band of Crow Indians, and Lewis's group was forced to flee a Blackfeet war party.

I had considered portaging by horse, but my two artificial hips and my limited skills would have endangered the horse, and me. About ten years ago, while visiting the Boise Historical Museum with my daughter Amy, I complied with a sign on a full-sized stuffed horse that said, *Try Me*. I succeeded in mounting but couldn't bend my leg enough to dismount. Amy had left the room, so I had to endure several children asking their parents why the old man was sitting on the horse. My embarrassment ended when Amy returned and helped me down.

Land of the Nez Perce

The sun was high when we left Clarkston, Washington and crossed the Blue Bridge to Lewiston, Idaho. We followed the lush valley of the Snake River on a paved trail before climbing a gradual grade to the rolling Weippe Prairie of Nez Perce County, the endless wild camas still displaying remnants of a scene Merewether Lewis described as resembling "lakes of fine clear water."

It was here that Native Americans and knowledgeable pioneers harvested the edible blue camas bulbs. Those with less knowledge ate the poisonous white death camas, often with disastrous results. When the starving westbound members of the Expedition emerged from the Bitterroot Mountains in October 1805, the Nez Perce provided them with fish, berries, and dried plants, probably including baked camas bulbs. Many members of the Expedition became ill, but it was almost definitely due to eating food with which they were not accustomed, not poisoning.

Each spring, my family and I delight in walking the trails among the blue-and-white camas beds at the south end of Lopez Island, Washington. Crossing the Weippe Prairie, imagining the virtual sea of camas lilies the Expedition would have seen, connecting that image to the camas lilies on Lopez Island, I felt closer to the Expedition and wondered, had I been among them, would I have trusted that licorice-tasting mash that nourished the Nez Perce through the long, cold winters?

My right foot again felt like it was on fire when we reached the start of Web Cut Off Road. After walking a few hundred feet to restore circulation, we peddled uphill for about a mile and then began a breath-taking descent on a winding road that followed a small stream in a narrow tree lined and shaded valley to US 95. While on US 95, I got some rest drafting in Mike's tailwind until we arrived at Cul de Sac, a town not much larger than its name implies. With the sun now directly overhead, we found no shade outside the small convenience store. My bike computer thermometer read 104 degrees. We drank as much water and electrolyte drink as we could hold while eating a light lunch of fruit and peanut butter.

We were now on the Nez Perce Reservation, or what is left of it. Lewis and Clark had learned to trust the Nez Perce more than other tribes. That trust was well deserved, but the trust the Nez Perce had in the US government was not. Before the federal government twice reneged on the tribe's treaty rights, the limits of Nez Perce treaty land would have extended well beyond my view, covering a vast territory in present day Washington, Oregon, and Idaho.

Leaving the store, we turned off Highway 95 and began a switchback climb on the Old Winchester Grade Road from about elevation 2,000 to 4,200. The long, steep climb offered little shade. But the lack of traffic and the expansive views of golden-brown Nez Perce prairie country rewarded me with beauty and with musings on what life would have been like during the nineteenth century. I could almost see Chief Joseph and his tribe, who, along with their dogs, horses, and few possessions, prepared to flee their home as the US Cavalry bore down on them.

Short of breath much of the way, I stopped a couple times to restore circulation in my right foot and took my glasses off when sweat cascading from my bald head and forehead made it impossible to keep both eyes open.

The sun was past its zenith when we arrived in Winchester, Idaho at the foot of the Craig Mountains. Debilitating leg cramps began just before reaching our destination. We had climbed 4,900 feet over seventy-five miles but had averaged only 10.8 mph. I had an energy drink, a pop, and an ice cream bar at the local convenience store, and took three electrolyte pills, which helped relieve my leg cramps. Mike drank water. We checked into Winchester Lake State Park and pitched our tent among the Ponderosa pine and Douglas fir near the placid lake. A printed guide for the park informed us that we need not worry about the local wolf pack.

We left Winchester Lake about an hour after sunrise the next morning and rode fast to the town of Green Creek. The nine-mile downhill before Kamiah was perfect riding. I felt comfortable, only hitting the brakes once to keep below 30 mph, my new speed limit. We arrived in Kamiah shortly before noon. Mike took control of purchasing Clif Bars, taco shells, individually wrapped American cheese slices, trail mix, peanut butter, honey, and dried apricots. He doesn't have much confidence in my knowledge of nutrition, while I consider him to be a food radical. He even takes the extreme position that Good & Plenty licorice is not one of the basic food groups.

While eating our lunch outside the grocery store, a "friendly" Middle Ages (the spelling is deliberate) truck driver approached us. Somewhere between Mike's age and mine, his appearance was more like an early pioneer than a gainfully employed truck driver. He began the conversation by telling us that he rides a bike. Next, he issued a mandate that bike riders keep within one foot of the edge of pavement. He admitted wanting to hit riders who failed to abide by his rule. I don't usually let comments like this pass without a response, and I had an unspoken wish that Mike would toss him into the Clearwater River, but there didn't seem much point in debating the matter. Were we to encounter him on the road, we would be at his mercy. We got a good look at his big rig and resolved to stay well clear of him.

The Lolo Trail

We tackled a steep grade, surrounded by the remnants of old-growth cedar, spruce, and fir forests, on the paved start of the Lolo Trail after lunch. As with most long climbs, every curve seemed like it should be the last until we passed it. I was hot, cramped, and very relieved when the road leveled off after an exhausting two-hour climb of 1,800 feet.

We filled our water bottles at a cool spring near Pheasant Camp at the end of a paved road late in the afternoon. The gravel road from Pheasant Camp to Canyon Junction, our next waypoint, was rutted or wash boarded, and the loose gravel slowed me appreciably, sometimes grabbing my tires and forcing me to release my shoe clips from my peddles to prevent a fall.

At Mike's suggestion, I had purchased a cyclocross bike for this trip. The cyclocross is a hybrid intended for both on- and off-road conditions, but perfect for neither. I bought a Specialized Cycle Cross with 700 x 32 tires, not quite wide enough for loose gravel. Also, because I was inattentive, I was sold the previous year's model, which lacked dual brake levers, an important feature on steep off-road downhills because it allows a cyclist to avoid hand cramps by switching hand positions. Mike rode a true mountain bike, which, combined with his greater off-road skills, allowed him to negotiate the trail with relative ease.

We saw one truck, one SUV, and one motorcycle in the few miles after leaving the pavement. We saw no hikers or other bicyclists on this section of the trail, or at any other time on the Lolo Trail. We looked west to the Weippe Prairie while crossing a high ridge. Near the same location, the starving members of the westbound Expedition encountered the Nez Perce and were given food, which included the camas-bulb mash they had no idea what to make of and were reluctant to trust.

As the sun was beginning to set, we pitched camp at Canyon Junction. We were alone. Our elevation gain for the day was 4,900 feet over a distance of eighty-three miles. I was too tired to eat, but the friendly ground squirrels gathered around our camp were not so finicky. I apologized to Mike for slowing him down. He allayed my concerns when he said he was impressed with my off-road riding. He added that the only time he saw me having difficulty was when I tried to choke down a Clif bar.

While we sat at a broken-down picnic table on this warm, wind free August night, I reflected on some of my lapses as a parent. I told Mike I wanted to apologize for criticizing the work he and Greg did spreading broken basalt rock along a steep slippery trail on our Lopez Island, Washington property. The boys did a good job spreading the rock, but it wasn't exactly what I envisioned. Instead of thanking them, I criticized their work. Mike groaned. "Dad, you have been apologizing at least once a year for almost twenty years. You can stop." I didn't want to stop. I said that apologizing was a good reminder to me never to repeat what I had done. What I didn't say was that my apology was also intended to be a lesson for Mike, his brother, and sister. "I know there is a parental lesson hidden in there somewhere." Mike responded with a roll of his eyes.

When darkness fell, Mike turned in. I worked on my journal and read while waiting for my foot and leg cramps to subside.

We left Canyon Junction after breakfast and headed for Twelve Mile Saddle, a seemingly short thirty-nine miles away. The US Forest Service recommended this double-track path only for high clearance vehicles. Compared to the conditions they encountered, Lewis and Clark would have found the trail to be an excellent portage despite the fact that it was very steep and consisted of loose gravel, loose sand, rocks and ruts. I rode slowly along the worst parts of the trail to avoid falling and injuring my artificial hips. Even so, I fell four times. Luckily, no dislocated hips.

I walked some of both the uphill and downhill portions of the route including much of the 1,000-foot climb after Pete's Fork Junction and much of the 1,200-foot climb after Horse Sweat Pass. Horses aren't the only ones to sweat. Rolling downhill I unclipped my right foot and let it dangle. This helped me brace in the event I started to fall, and restored circulation to my foot. Cramps in my hands made it difficult to squeeze the brake levers. I risked running off the trail and slamming into a tree during high-speed turns on downhill runs. At just the right time, when I really needed words of encouragement, Mike told me that I was doing great. Somewhere on this trip the roles of parent and offspring had been reversed.

We pulled into Twelve Mile Saddle Campground after riding or pushing our bikes for twelve hours. Despite averaging little more than a walking pace, I was so hot and tired when we arrived that I had trouble speaking, or even thinking. We encountered a crowd, the Valley Cats Off-Road Club from Kamiah, ID. About twenty or so people were just finishing a scrumptious-looking steak dinner spread out before us on a long table. The aroma of broiled beef made my mouth water and my empty stomach growl.

The Valley Cats ranged from Mike's age to a decade younger than me. Even though they arrived in motorized vehicles, they appeared trim and healthy. They had gained access to the campground from one of several US Forest Service Roads that connect with US 12, and which could provide an escape route for us if needed. I was introduced to Jim, Sonny, and Nancy, none of whom seemed to take notice that exhaustion had caused my speech to be slurred.

They made us feel like we were fellow Valley Cats. Our concern with encountering what we thought might be a rowdy crowd declined as rapidly as the end of the day temperature when these gracious people offered us what remained of their dinner—steak, salad, onions, potatoes, a soft drink, and dessert. Even Mike, my minimalist son, was willing to forgo our normal fare of peanut butter, individually wrapped cheese slices and dried fruit. Mike later accused me of pleading for an invitation by acting half dead. I told him I wasn't acting.

Sonny took us to their portable toilet, a real luxury in such a remote area. Nancy provided me with warm water for a sponge bath. It felt great to remove some of the dirt and wash my sweaty feet so my toes wouldn't stick together. It sure beat bathing in the ice-cold stream that flowed by the camp, as Mike did.

We were invited to their evening campfire, but the event was called off when thunder, lightning, and rain suddenly arrived. Without a rain fly for our tent, Mike and I covered the mesh openings with our emergency blankets. The fix was largely successful. Through the night, only about a half-inch of water gathered at the low end of the tent by our feet. Except for the bottom ends of our sleeping bags, we didn't get wet. Before going to sleep Mike advised that I take a pain reliever to prevent cramps. Pills scare me, but I found an Advil, took it, and quickly fell asleep.

Early next morning, we tried not to wake our neighbors while we broke camp, but several people were already attempting to rebuild the mess tent that had blown down during the storm. We thanked the Valley Cats for their hospitality and were off. We were surprised and refreshed when the morning broke cool and cloudy. We even encountered a few drops of rain.

Given our slow progress the previous day, we were apprehensive about this day's ride and our chance of reaching Powell and the Lochsa Lodge on US 12. By late morning, we were running low on water purification tablets and decided to chance drinking cool, clear water directly from some natural springs, emerging on the high side of the trail in a mossy bed of ferns and shrubs.

The morning ride was very difficult for me. Mike took a photo of me at the marker for Indian Post Office, a Native American resting place at elevation 6,966 feet. I'm wearing my long sleeve bike jacket, a sign that it was cool at this high elevation. I have a faint smile but look rather forlorn while I lean on my bike for support.

I soon fell again. I had trouble getting my foot unclipped from the pedal. While toppling, I had time enough to decide if I should, at least, attempt to avoid falling on a big rock. I missed the rock but hit the ground hard enough to warrant checking all my body parts. No broken bones. I was lucky, as I would learn a few years later when I broke one of my artificial hips in a similar fall during a rock scramble.

I looked back and couldn't see Mike. At first, I thought he had stopped to pee. It seemed unlikely we could have taken different trails, but the thought plagued me until he emerged from around a bend. One of the two bolts holding his seat to the seat post had sheared. He was somehow able to borrow the bolt from his seat clamp to reattach his seat. That meant that his seat moved up and down, although a tight fit slowed the process.

My butt hurt, but I didn't have much time to think about it because my shoulders hurt even more, and my wrists and hands had lost feeling from applying the brakes on the downgrades. My theory that a person could not feel pain from more than one source at the same time was disproven. When we stopped for a lunch of American cheese slices, dried apricots, and trail mix at Cayuse Junction, we were not at all optimistic that we would complete this off-road ride before nightfall, but we were set on trying.

The trail we rode after lunch followed the forested ridge tops of the Clearwater National Forrest. It was this segment of the trail that Clark called "a most intolerable road on the sides of steep mountains." Unlike the Expedition, we didn't have to contend with many downed trees, and most of the large rocks had been cleared from our path. The mercury never reached the heat of the previous day. I was able to ride almost all the way up the dreaded 1,600-foot climb after Cayuse Junction, where we exceeded 7,000 feet elevation, the highest point on our trip.

I stayed riding for almost all the way downhill. For the first time on the off-road trail, I felt almost comfortable. Early evening, we reached US 12 and the historic Lochsa Lodge, rebuilt in 2002 from a 1929 commercial hunting lodge deep within the then isolated Lochsa River Valley.

It was near this place on September 14, 1805, that the Expedition became lost despite being guided by "Old Toby," a Shoshone. They were shivering, almost out of food, and were forced to kill a colt for sustenance. Our problems were minor by comparison. Although we were too late to get a room at the lodge, we found a campsite at the nearby US Forest Service Campground. After I showered, we both enjoyed a delicious dinner at the Lodge. Mike had yellow tuna and Asian salad. Craving protein and fat, I opted for steak and French fries. On this day we gained 5,400 feet in 40.5 miles, averaging only 4.5 miles per hour. My high cholesterol dinner caused me no guilt given our rough days on the Lolo Trail.

Back on the Road Again

Early the next morning Mike and I decided to ride US 12 rather than continuing on another segment of the Lolo Trail after a ranger told us the trail was blocked by many downed trees. A bonus of this decision was that we would not have to rush to arrive in Missoula before the bike shops closed for the weekend. Tourist traffic on two lane US 12 was lighter than we expected. In its place we had to contend with the many large trucks that buffeted us as they travelled between Missoula, Montana and Clarkston or Boise, Idaho.

The "friendly" truck driver we met in Kamiah had told us that US 12 in Idaho had adequate shoulders, but we did not find this to be true. He had also told us that US 12 in Montana had wide shoulders, but we found them to be generally less than two-feet wide. Worried that the truck driver or one of his disciples could be approaching from behind, we rode fast and looked back often.

While riding briskly in the valley of the turbulent crystal clear and freely flowing Lochsa River, I was reminded of Lonesome George, the last Chinook salmon to reach Idaho. Since George was a male and not a female with eggs, his death meant the extinction of his species in Idaho. This didn't seem to bother one Idaho congresswoman who commented that she preferred her salmon in cans, not rivers.

A friend, Peter Hallson, had told me that the climb over Lolo Pass (elev. 5,233) in the Bitterroot Range of the Rocky Mountains at the Idaho / Montana border would be difficult. Since Peter is an excellent rider, I was worried we'd be forced to walk, especially given the added weight of loaded panniers. I was stronger than I thought, though, and that felt like a victory.

After crossing the pass and gliding down the east slope, we observed a group of about twelve heavily laden young bicyclists struggling up the mountain, probably envying the ease with which we traveled. I would have been more sympathetic to their plight had we not experienced the grueling climbs on the off-road trail.

We stopped for lunch at a convenient convenience store, conveniently located at the junction of US 12 and US 93 in Lolo, Montana. While stopped, I adjusted my bike seat in an attempt to relieve my butt discomfort. While traveling both west and east, the Expedition rested nearby at a location they called "Travelers Rest." This place, on Lolo Creek, was used by the Salish people for hundreds of years as a hub for an intricate network of trails. The nearby areas supported, and still supports, good hunting, fishing, and the gathering of camas and other plants. It was also at Travelers Rest that the eastbound expedition temporarily split in two with Lewis taking a small detachment to explore the territory near the Blackfoot, Sun, and Marias Rivers, while Clark, guided by Sacajawea in the land she knew, headed southeast through Crow and Shoshone territory to the Yellowstone River.

Travelers Rest is the only campsite on the Lewis and Clark Trail with physical evidence of the Corps of Discoveries visit, albeit in the form of toxic metals mixed with native soil. Mercury was used for medicinal purposes and lead used in the repair and manufacture of firearms.

Big Sky Country

We rode a tailwind on busy US 93 from Lolo to Missoula where we stopped at a bike shop for Mike to buy a bolt to fix his seat. We crossed the Clark Fork River on a day when hundreds of scantily clad college-aged students were enjoying the sunshine walking and bike riding on paths close to the river, rafting in the river and just relaxing. Near the confluence of three scenic rivers, the Clark Fork, Bitterroot, and Blackfoot, and at the convergence of five mountain ranges, Missoula is nicknamed "Hub of five valleys." Established just prior to the Civil War and several decades before settlers arrived in Seattle, it is an attractive mix of classic and new buildings.

We checked into a Quality Inn in downtown Missoula that, at $100 per night, was more than we were used to spending. We would have looked further, but a few phone calls revealed that most lodgings were full or nearly so, and we, or at least I, was too tired to search further.

We had to settle for a smoking room and its musty odor. Mike went shopping for fresh fruit while I took a very long shower and washed my clothes. After Mike returned and showered, we had a delicious dinner at an elegant restaurant satirically named The Shack. My healthy dinner of grilled chicken, salad and ice cream for dessert went down very easily. After dinner, Mike suggested I put Nu-Skin on my butt wounds. His butt was also beginning to hurt, probably because of his broken seat.

The next morning, I almost jumped out of my skin in pain when I applied the Nu-Skin to my chafed skin. I had trouble getting a Band-Aid in the correct location without placing the adhesive on my scabs. I reluctantly asked Mike to do the honors. He objected until I reminded him that I changed his diapers when he was an infant. He finished applying the Band-Aid before he remembered that it was almost always his mom who changed diapers. I also switched from my heavily padded Sugoi shorts to an old pair of Pearl Izumi shorts with natural leather chamois to which I applied chamois cream. The combination of remedies relieved much of my discomfort.

Leaving Missoula on MT 200 in the rugged Blackfoot River Valley, we traveled past the depressingly deserted and soon to be ghost towns of Milltown and Bonner, near the confluence of the Clark Fork and Blackfoot Rivers. The lumber mill had recently closed leaving behind boarded up stores and run-down houses, well beyond the point of repair. Adding to the gloom, mining operations a hundred and twenty miles southeast of Missoula in Butte, and the Anaconda copper smelter close to Butte, had deposited toxic sludge in the Clark Fork River above Bonner Dam, rendering the river unfishable.

It turns out that my conclusion that Milltown and Bonner would soon become ghost towns was as premature as the exaggerated 1897 report of Samuel Clemens' (Mark Twain's) death. The dam was removed in 2008 and the toxic sludge was soon hauled away. Stimson, the owner of the mill cleaned up the 170-acre property and sold it to two enterprising developers. According to multiple news reports, the Stimson property is now the home of multiple businesses, and new luxury homes are being built on the surrounding land. Fishers are now pulling prized trout from the rivers.

About an hour later, thunder echoed in the distance as the sky darkened. Mike suggested we put on our rain gear but, with my infinite wisdom, I told him we could seek shelter in the town of Potomac that was just ahead. It turned out that there was no shelter because there was no town, only a few buildings with their bright paint long since faded and now rapidly reaching the end of their lives. The heavy rain blasted us, and the temperature dropped by the time we donned our rain gear. Heavy rain lingered for about thirty minutes. We shivered even though we were riding hard. Thankfully, we were soon able to get hot chocolate and breakfast sandwiches at a convenience store at the intersection with MT 83 that heads north to Glacier National Park.

Approaching Lincoln, Montana, I observed many reddish-brown dead and dying pine trees on the hillsides, apparently infected with pine bark beetles, which have now extended their range due to warmer winters. I asked Mike if this could be related to climate change. Mike said that he couldn't distinguish the dying trees from the healthy. I had never realized his color blindness was so severe.

Pushed by a modest tailwind we arrived at the appropriately signed Three Bears Motel (Welcome Adventure Cyclists!) in Lincoln, Montana while the sun was still high in the sky. I had hoped to stay at the same motel where Mike stayed when he reached Lincoln on his Continental Divide ride from Canada to Mexico, but he couldn't remember which motel it was. On that ride he had endured several hours of heavy rain north of Lincoln and so much mud on the trail that he had to carry his mud caked bike several miles into town. While Mike shopped for dinner and I waited for the proprietor of the motel to return, I met Stewart Iden, who appeared slightly younger than me, and who was riding cross-country from NYC to Portland. He invited me to join him for dinner. I later decided to do so when Mike told me he was tired of eating in restaurants.

Most interesting to me, Stewart grew up in Syosset, NY, an up-scale version of neighboring Hicksville, my boyhood home nestled on the banks of the Long Island Expressway. He also worked in the Plainview Shopping Center where I worked in Mickey's luncheonette while a teenager. I was paid only seventy-five cents per hour, but I got to eat as much as I wanted, just like I was doing while we spoke. Stewart was divorced. He told me he retired from the computer industry, but not by choice. He blamed his current unemployment on low-cost international labor. I got the distinct impression that this ride, and a previous one he had completed across the southern US, were his attempts to find new meaning to his life. Looked like he and I had more than a little in common.

Crossing the Continental Divide

The next day offered enjoyable riding despite being forced to cover our longest distance yet. The morning was cool with little wind. This made the climb to the Continental Divide at Rogers Pass, Montana (elev. 5,610) easier than it would have been in the heat of the day. The moderate upgrade allowed for a speed that rarely dropped below 6 mph. On the downgrade I reluctantly transposed useful potential energy to waste heat by using the brakes, but not so much as to cause hand cramps.

Lewis and his party had a more difficult journey in the vicinity of the Continental Divide than did Mike and me. On their eastward journey they crossed what is now known as Lewis and Clark Pass, a few miles north of Rogers Pass and, at 6,424 feet in elevation, more than eight hundred feet higher. It has more gradual approaches than Rogers Pass, which made it possible for Native Americans to pull loaded travois with horses and dogs. Some tracks still remain. It is the only pass traversed by the Expedition not now occupied by a road and the only pass that received more traffic in 1806 than it does today.

After crossing, the Expedition headed north to explore the upper Marias River Valley. This is the land of the Blackfeet, a tribe once feared by other Northwest Native American tribes. Lewis experienced one of the lessons taught him by Jefferson; each Native American tribe has its own culture and traditions and should be dealt with as an independent nation. Lewis found the contrast between the peaceful Nez Perce and the warlike Blackfeet to be extreme. During a violent skirmish with a band of Blackfeet, the men of the Expedition killed two Blackfeet warriors. While pursued by a Blackfeet war party bent on extracting justice, Lewis and his detachment made a hasty, successful retreat to the Missouri River near what is now Fort Benton. The end of Lewis's landward journey at Fort Benton also marked the end of Mike's and my portage.

The ten miles on MT 200 before the intersection with MT 287 were the toughest stretch of the day for me. Our maps didn't adequately prepare me for a climb, which seemed steeper and almost as long as that before Rogers Pass. At the intersection with MT 287 there was supposed to be an inn at which we hoped to eat and rest. I later read that it was closed on Mondays, the day we arrived, although the absence of any observable activity suggested that it might have closed permanently. I called Adventure Cycling, the publisher of the maps we were using, to learn why they recommended turning left onto MT 287 rather than going straight. Turning meant the equivalent of covering two legs of an isosceles triangle rather than staying on MT 200 and riding only one leg. Reception was too poor for me to understand their answer. After observing light traffic on MT 287 and noting that it approximated the route taken by Lewis and his men, we selected the road less traveled and had a fast tailwind-assisted ride to Augusta. The almost treeless landscape with snowcapped mountains in the distance afforded a magnificent entry to Big Sky Country.

We stopped for lunch at the rustic grocery store in Augusta, where the road turned east to follow the Sun River. It was the land of cowboys and big pickups. We looked and felt out of place in bicycle garb, but we were treated well while we recharged our bodies. I remember thinking that Mike's muscular build may have warded off smart-alecky comments.

We had a crosswind and slight headwind for the twenty miles after Augusta. As we approached Simms, the sky darkened behind us and on both sides, but bright blue sky lay ahead, and a tailwind pushed us along. Mike's butt bothered him, and he later told me that this was his most uncomfortable day. I now had bandages on both sides of my backside, which gave some relief from the pain.

Nearing Great Falls, a growing tailwind combined with a slight downgrade. We raced the building storm at an exhilarating 20-plus mph, reminiscent of the way Lewis and his contingent raced the Blackfeet war party.

Great Falls, Fort Benton, and Home

We crossed the Missouri River on Central Avenue and entered downtown Great Falls, one of the few planned communities in the west. Rain obscured the river and the falls, which dropped five hundred feet in the eighteen-miles portaged by the Expedition. The imposing restored tower of the Chicago, Milwaukee, and Saint Paul railroad station was there to welcome us but, like Dayton, Washington, the last passenger train left Great Falls many years ago. We checked in at the downtown Econo Lodge, where we would remain for two nights. It was early evening when we went to eat. We walked for several blocks during which time we encountered few people and several boarded-up buildings. We ate at a small and almost empty pizza place. The talkative, and apparently lonely proprietor told us that in 1950 Great Falls was the largest city in Montana. The loss of several resource extraction industries and accompanying railroad traffic, and little tourism, has seen Great Falls fall to third place. The recent Great Recession hadn't helped. Mike later referred to downtown Great Falls as "dead," but I saw considerable potential and preferred to think of it as "sleepy." In the years after Mike and I finished our ride it appears that Great Falls has woken up to its strong potential by focusing on its abundant natural resources, including the scenic river, the largest fresh-water spring in the world and the exploits of the Lewis and Clark Expedition.

The next morning Mike told me that he had changed his mind and now wanted to ride with me to Fort Benton, near where Lewis and his party rejoined the Missouri River after fleeing the Blackfeet warriors, and the planned end of our portage. Mike and I would then return to Great Falls where we would catch a westbound bus. We left Great Falls on the historic concrete arch 10th St. Bridge, built in 1920, and headed northeast on US 87. This road has almost no shoulder for the first twenty miles, and although traffic was moderate the speeding vehicles kept us (literally) on edge. We were able to relax a little when the shoulder increased to about three feet for the final twenty miles. There were almost no trees until just before Fort Benton where we stopped to drink in the expansive view from a bluff overlooking historic Fort Benton and the green valley of the Missouri River. Our view encompassed the fast-flowing river surrounded by natural habitat for deer, antelope, bison, and predators as large as grizzly bear, as it tumbled and rumbled through a narrow canyon with steep black cliffs on the far bank.

In Fort Benton I visited the Interpretive Center and police station to obtain information needed for kayaking the Missouri River, should I feel capable of continuing eastward. Mike took a nap on a park bench. The police told me they would look after my vehicle while I was on the river. After his nap, Mike and I had lunch in a small cafe where the friendly and talkative owner served us the largest Reuben sandwich I had ever been served.

During our southerly return to Great Falls via Highwood and MT 228, the morning tailwind from the south became an almost overpowering afternoon headwind, unblocked by trees. A curious antelope stared in sympathy at our slow-moving procession from the other side of a fence before bolting away. I would have had much difficulty keeping up with Mike had he not slowed when he saw me tiring. I wondered if I had been as considerate of Mike, Amy, and Greg when they were young. As we re-entered Great Falls, we made our final crossing of the portage route taken by the Expedition on their westward journey.

Postscript III

Mike and I put 676 miles behind us in the ten days it had taken us to travel from the Tri- Cities to Fort Benton. It took the Expedition most of May and June 1806 to travel overland from the confluence of the Columbia and Walla Walla Rivers in Washington to Travelers Rest near Missoula. The heavy snow and other hardships they faced were immeasurably greater than the obstacles we encountered. After the Expedition split at Travelers Rest it took Lewis and his group about a week to reach the Missouri River, followed by the disastrous week-and-a-half detour into Blackfeet Territory.

Our last morning in Great Falls, we boxed our bikes and took them to the nearby bus station. From Great Falls to Butte, we traveled in an overcrowded van. The transit company had substituted the van for our bus, which had broken down on the way to Great Falls. In Butte we transferred to a larger Greyhound bus, which took us to Spokane. From there, we took Amtrak to Pasco. I walked about four miles to Kennewick to get our vehicle while Mike watched our gear. Mike drove the whole way to Edmonds where Joyce greeted us with congratulatory signs on the home windows. Upon arriving home, exhausted and butt sore, I was filled with mixed emotions. The return to my familiar world, time playing Scrabble with Joyce and trying her patience with tales of daring do, held a strong appeal. But already I regretted that my journey with Mike had ended.

The trip was all I had wanted it to be and inspired me to travel farther. I had been afraid that I wouldn't be able to follow in the footsteps of the Expedition across the Bitterroot Mountains on the grueling Lolo Trail, but with Mike as my guide I did better than I could have hoped. Mike was very considerate and never let frustration with my lesser riding abilities or eccentric eating habits show. He is a private person, but on this trip Mike and I got to know each other as two adults, while on an adventure we both enjoyed.

When we reached Fort Benton, he spoke words that, I hope, will forever remain in my memory. "Dad, I'm so proud of you."

Author on the Lolo Trail

Author at "Indian Post Office"

Rogers Pass / Continental Divide

Big Sky Country

Approaching Fort Benton

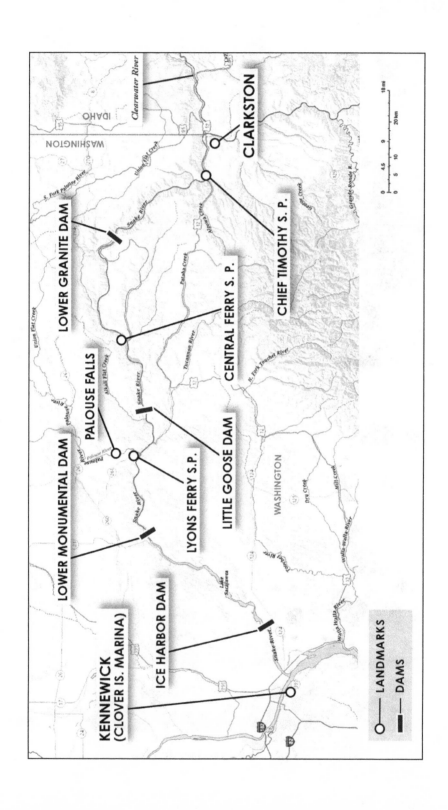

IV

Snake River

2010

The author's friend Bob on the approach to Lyons Ferry Bridge

Kayaking with a Friend

I n a strict sense there was no reason for me to kayak the Snake River. My growing intent was to travel the path Lewis and his party traveled on their return to St. Louis. On their eastward passage, the entire expedition left the Columbia River valley at the confluence with the Walla Walla River downstream from the Snake River. They then travelled overland on a route almost identical to that taken by Mike and me until Travelers Rest, near what is now Missoula, where the Expedition split apart. Kayaking the Snake from the Tri Cities to Lewiston/Clarkston would be, for me, a bonus. I had the impression that this would be an enjoyable part of the trip. With the company of my good friend Bob, I would experience some of what the Expedition encountered when they headed west on the Snake River.

After picking Bob up at SeaTac Airport, we crossed the Cascade Mountains in my 1996 Volvo Station Wagon for an overnight stay in Kennewick, with most of the day spent catching up on friends and family.

Bob and I both grew up in Hicksville, NY about thirty miles from Manhattan and about as far from salt water as you can get on Long Island. Neither of our families was well off, and since Bob had more siblings than me, I suspected his family had little financial reserve. We became friends on the track and cross-country teams. He was considerably faster than me, but I had a bit more endurance.

We spent many evenings at Bob's home, playing ping pong with friends Carl and Jack. Bob almost always won, even when he, a right hander, held the paddle in his left hand. We were more closely matched in the debates we had after ping pong. Even when we agreed with each other, we picked different sides of the argument. Many years later, I learned to appreciate how well this prepared us for the real world. Late one night we predicted our future careers. Jack would become a lawyer, Carl a computer expert, Bob an industry leader, and me a forest ranger. I didn't become a forest ranger, but three out of four correct predictions were not bad.

After high school I attended the US Coast Guard Academy while Bob worked his way through the State University of NY at Oswego with support from the Marine Platoon Leaders Program. After college we both went to Vietnam, Bob with the Marines, and me with the Army. Bob married Barbara, who ranked far above Bob and me in our high school class. He also introduced me to Joyce who he had been dating and who was one year ahead of us in high school. Upon returning from 'Nam, Bob took a job with a major steel corporation. It wasn't long before he was the company's president. For a while we drifted apart. As with our competition in shorter distances runs, I couldn't keep pace with Bob professionally, and Joyce's and my casual Pacific Northwest plaid-shirt lifestyle was far from that of Bob and Barbara's.

My greatest concern with the Snake River trip was that Bob had never kayaked any extended distance. Surely, he would be in good shape for the trip, given his competitive nature, but experience taught me that just being in great shape wasn't enough. Last year my weight-lifting son Mike suffered severe tendonitis on his second day of kayaking. I tried to plan a trip that would break us in gradually and limit us to about twenty miles of upstream kayaking per day. Knowing that adverse current and high wind could severely impact our schedule, and that keeping on schedule was very important because of Bob's post-trip commitments, I identified alternatives to paddling that included long portages around dams and on roads following the river.

Ice Harbor Dam

We launched Whisper at the Clover Island Inn on the Columbia River where I had finished paddling last year. Leaving the Tri-Cities Blue Bridge behind us on a sunny morning in late August 2010, we headed for another blue bridge connecting the twin cities of Lewiston, ID/ Clarkston, WA. After a downstream run of three miles on the Columbia River, we arrived at the confluence with the Snake where we turned east, heading upstream. Along the north bank of the river, we saw grain barges and Tidewater petroleum barges with their smiley face logos.

Tidewater transports petroleum products from Vancouver to Pasco in Washington. A few years ago, several oil companies proposed building a pipeline across the Cascade Mountains, including a run through an abandoned railroad tunnel at the top of Snoqualmie Pass. I consulted for a group that believed the pipeline failed to address environmental and safety concerns. When a pipeline explosion in Bellingham, Washington killed three boys, it put an end to the Cross Cascade Pipeline proposal. Hence the petroleum barges still ply the Columbia and lower Snake Rivers.

As the day warmed, jet skis displaced heron, egret, pelicans, and osprey. In a competition for most offensive sound, the whine of jet skis far outdid even the grating squawk of the blue heron. We were moving slowly upstream, and the sun was near its zenith when we arrived at Ice Harbor Dam, the first of four concrete gravity hydroelectric dams we would have to portage to reach Lewiston/Clarkston. The four dams are between ninety-eight and a hundred feet high (difference in upstream and downstream water levels), and all have navigation locks that we, in our kayak, could not enter unless chaperoned by a power vessel. All four dams on the lower Snake River are what is known as "run of the river" dams. In contrast to the dams on the Columbia River, they impound very little water and are not meant for flood control. They generate power, provide irrigation water, and open the river to navigation while impeding fish passage. Many environmentalists want the dams removed to save the salmon runs.

By early afternoon I began to experience pain in my lower right arm leading to concerns that, despite my preparation, tendonitis might end this trip for me as it had ended Mike's paddling last year. As with the first day of the previous two years, I also experienced arm cramps. After taking some electrolyte tablets, the cramps faded. Bob paddled strongly for most of the day, only slowing and taking more frequent breaks during the last couple hours. The level of effort needed to hit mileage goals isn't always easy to predict. So far, we were doing okay.

Portaging Ice Harbor Dam took a little more than an hour—quick compared to the four dams portaged on the Columbia River in 2009. We unloaded Whisper, carried it up a rocky twenty-foot-high slope, and then pulled it on its two-wheel carrier about three quarters of a mile on an unpaved road to a ramp upstream of the dam. We ate ham-and-cheese sandwiches prepared for us by the Clover Island Inn and shoved off soon after noon, paddling past fields of green crops and golden-brown native vegetation.

It isn't easy debating sensitive subjects while kayaking, especially when both paddlers have less than perfect hearing. Whisper silently sliced through the calm water but splashing from our paddles and the difficulty of turning to face each other caused us to repeatedly mishear what was said. Even so, the temptation to debate was irresistible. I interrupted my off-key singing of "America the Beautiful" to revisit a topic that Bob and I began arguing over fifty years ago. I accused Bob of being patriotic, although at first, he heard unpatriotic.

"I'm proud to be patriotic," he grumbled. "What's with you this time?"

I said that his brand of patriotism, "my country right or wrong," will never correct the wrongs we, as a country, have inflicted on Native Americans and others. I added that I would gladly become a patriot if we only lived up to the ideals espoused in our Constitution.

I expected him to blow up, like he has done before, and tell me to leave the US if I wasn't happy here. Instead, he responded in a voice that was all too reasonable. "You are too idealistic and live too much in the past. It's time you placed more emphasis on our future."

I replied, "As a history major you should know the importance of learning from the past. Idealists like me change the world for a better future."

"Don't keep me waiting too long for your changes," he said.

Two hours later we arrived at Fishhook Park located near what was once, and would be again if the dams are removed, Fishhook Rapids. Fishhook Park is a large Corps of Engineers campground where my

Golden Age Pass earned us a 50 percent discount. A park ranger told us to take our pick of one of the eleven primitive campsites. She added that Fishhook Park sits next to the largest fruit orchard in the world, one for which the owner built a small town for the workers.

First Fruit Orchards, owned by the Broetje family, may not be the largest orchard in the world but, with 2,500 seasonal employees and 6,000 acres, it is the largest employer in Walla Walla County. Broetje Orchards lives up to its mission of, "Bearing fruit that will last." The Broetje's provide affordable housing, childcare, early learning, and medical care for their employees, and the Vista Hermosa Foundation they established invests in sustainable communities throughout the world. This all came about because, at the age of fifteen, Ralph Broetje decided to make it his life's mission to help the less fortunate. Broetje Orchards was fined $2.25 million in 2015 because they employed undocumented workers.

"The Broetje's should have been rewarded, not fined," I said.

"A fine for illegally helping immigrants is okay with me," Bob responded.

This precipitated a long discussion on whether we should both be shipped back to Europe because of the illegal or unjust ways our ancestors treated Native Americans.

In late 2018, Broetje Orchards was sold to the Ontario Teachers' Pension Plan that said it would continue many employee-support programs.

I wanted Bob to enjoy this trip—but not too much. Knowing he would place more importance on creature comforts, I was concerned about the weight and volume stored in Whisper. I resisted when he wanted to add a more voluminous air matrass and a beverage cooler. However, his suggestion we bring a compact camp stove and freeze-dried dinners proved to be welcome advice. After we set up our tent and showered, Bob cooked freeze-dried mandarin chicken on our new Jetboil stove. With mixed nuts, mandarin oranges, peaches, and candy for dessert, it was definitely high style compared to the Clif Bars and packaged cheese slices Mike and I had eaten on our escapades.

Dinner with Bob at our campsite on the bank of the Snake River reminded me of the time Joyce and I joined Bob and Barbara in New Orleans. We had made tentative plans for a bus tour. Instead, Bob announced that he had arranged for a private car and driver. Joyce and I have never traveled that way and are unlikely to ever do so again. We went along out of curiosity. At the end of an admittedly relaxing tour, our driver took us to Commanders Palace in the Garden District, a highly rated restaurant Barbara wanted to try. The dinner was the best I had ever eaten, and the most expensive. Yet, except for female company, our meager dinner of mandarin chicken eaten while sitting on a log on the bank of the Snake River was almost as satisfying.

While on their westward journey along the Snake River, the Expedition had far fewer choices of food than Bob and me. There was little game and even less firewood. They subsisted on fish and dogs bought from the Indians. Clark wouldn't eat dog. Lewis would, even though his dog Seaman accompanied the Expedition.

The Expedition would have been glad to eat horsemeat, but the Nez Perce prized their horses. They were the only tribe known to Lewis and Clark who bred their horses for specific traits. Nez Perce would only eat horsemeat when desperately close to starvation. Clark, fed up with eating fish, shot blue wing teal on October 15, 1805. He dined on them on the shrub-steppe landscape with nary a tree in sight, very close to where Bob and I ate our chicken dinner.

The lake above Ice Harbor Dam that Bob and I paddled had replaced the once turbulent river, and irrigated land and transplanted trees had replaced much of the original desert landscape. Not being familiar with camping in Eastern Washington, neither Bob nor I knew what wild animals we might encounter at the camp. Vicky, the young, blond, blue-eyed camp host, told me it was not necessary to protect our food at night from animals. She said there were no raccoons, squirrels, rats, or skunks in the camp because there are no nut-bearing trees. Later, she added that six rattlesnakes were sighted this year, and that even more were sighted last year when the river was higher. I began to wonder if the absence of small mammals might be linked to the abundance of snakes. Maybe the snakes also limit the number of park rangers. According to Vicky, a park ranger had recently been bitten and spent a week in the hospital. This news did nothing to quell my fear of snakes.

Lower Monumental Dam

After midnight, it became quite cold. Although I slept fine, the 45 F. sleeping bag was barely adequate for Bob. We woke while the sun and the rated temperature were rising. Bob made coffee to warm up and chomped on a breakfast bar while I scurried around breaking camp. As in prior years, I put off eating breakfast until we were underway. Sunshine, a mild temperature, a slight tailwind, and pleasant company made for an enjoyable day of paddling between dams.

The Lewis and Clark Expedition faced more than eighty sets of rapids on the Lower Snake where we now see placid water and dams. Even more difficult than "seeing" lost rapids in our mind's eye, is imagining the many other things that were lost, like migratory fish, traditional ways of living, and buried or forgotten history. Somewhere ahead in the flooded valley was the ancient Marmes Rockshelter site, used by early people for a fishing camp from over 11,000 years ago to relatively recent times.

We began a three-mile portage at Windust Recreation area and ended it immediately above the dam at the Devils Bench undeveloped campground. Although we could have paddled closer to the dam before beginning our take-out, we would have encountered more rock riprap, a higher bank and stronger current. Since we were able to balance the load in Whisper over the kayak cart wheels we had packed, and because we shared the work, the portage was easy.

After setting up camp, I took a bath in the river at the end of a very slick concrete boat ramp. I intended to warn Bob to be careful, but on the way back to our tent an older couple stopped me, asking questions about paddling upstream. Bob walked by while I was talking to them. I tried to break off the conversation, but the couple persisted. I saw Bob slip, utter a string of profanities, and go down hard on his back. He didn't complain, but I knew he was hurt.

That night we slept to the hum of the dam's generators. Bob, who was bothered by the noise and probably pain from his fall, would have spelled the word "dam" differently. I found the hum soothing, though not sufficient to cure the headache I had had for the past two days, likely the result of long exposure to mid-ninety-degree temps and the sun beating down like a sledgehammer. After reluctantly taking an Advil, the headache dissipated, and I slept.

A Pleasant Diversion

The next morning, Bob applied bandages to the broken blisters on his hands. Living in Florida, he apparently hadn't chopped enough firewood. My hands were calloused, so I applied duct tape in a failed attempt to impress him. As is his nature, Bob said nothing about injuries caused by his fall at the ramp. Like my children, he is not a complainer. The wind had blown during the night and there were small whitecaps on the river. Bob expressed some concern but was not opposed to continuing. As I had hoped, we seemed to have a similar risk tolerance. If mine was a little greater it was only because of my experience.

Soon after we shoved off it became unbearably hot, and by early afternoon sweat dripping from my bald head and forehead caused my eyes to sting. After arriving at Lyon's Ferry and tying Whisper to a dock, I guzzled thirty-two ounces of Coca Cola and and another thirty-two ounces of Sprite. Bob also chugged two big containers of soda. Kate, the charming young attendant at the Lyons Ferry Marina, referred us to Jesse, the dock attendant, who agreed to take us to Palouse Falls after he got off work. This diversion was intended to show off the stark beauty of Eastern Washington, so different from the white sand beaches Bob was used to in Florida.

Shortly after 4 p.m., we crowded into Jesse's small pickup, drove over the bridge spanning the Snake River, past the inundated Marmes Rockshelter Site and another eight miles northbound on Hwy 261 to Palouse Falls State Park. For the final two miles, we travelled on a gravel road that zig and zagged past low basalt outcrops on a broad plateau overlooking the falls. The parking lot for the 105-acre camping park was half full of tourists and campers. We walked through dry scrub vegetation on the upper path to the edge of the 200-foot-high drop off, careful not to step on hidden rattlesnakes. The shimmering water cascading over the falls in the bright afternoon sunlight was an incredible sight. "Really beautiful," I said. When Bob only nodded, I asked him why engineers, at least this one, were more appreciative of beauty than liberal arts majors like him. He ignored me. I would have to wait for another time to provoke a debate.

After dropping us at our campsite, Jesse told us that his boss had checked the weather forecast. Dangerous winds up to 35 knots were predicted for the next day. Before we could narrow down the time, the marina lost power, a precursor of the coming storm. If conditions were even reasonably calm when we woke, we'd high-tail it out of the marina early and hope to beat the wind.

I had taken a shower before we left for the falls. Bob had hoped to shower upon returning, but the loss of power prevented him from doing so. It also prevented us from using the internet to check the weather, and from getting a hamburger or steak for dinner, something we had looked forward to all day. In place of our planned feast, we settled for an unmemorable freeze-dried dinner.

Bob worried about falling behind schedule. He had to be in New York in time for a meeting involving the conversion of an aluminum smelter to a steel rolling mill. He and his wife, Barbara, also wanted to attend the US Open ("Open what?" I asked). Waiting for the wind to pass, would certainly set us back. We decided to get up at 4:30 a.m. and launch if the river was calm enough. If not, we'd pull Whisper on wheels along Hwy 261, which ran parallel to the river.

Little Goose Dam and the Predicted Wind

The river was calm when we woke so we pushed off toward Central Ferry State Park. We'd identified on the map several emergency pullouts along the river in the event the wind became too strong.

The sun had not yet risen when we shoved off. An almost full moon cast a brilliant beam of light on the water. While the moon set and the sun rose, the temperature became more comfortable. Bob started our day of paddling wearing a long-sleeved shirt. I stayed with my normal practice of paddling in short sleeves, a life vest, and spray skirt. I should have followed Bob's lead. Even after applying copious amounts of sunscreen, as was my daily custom, I developed brown spots on my arms. Upon my return home, they were diagnosed as pre-cancerous lesions and had to be removed by a dermatologist.

We saw more mammals on this day than on any other—a beaver or muskrat, an otter, and a coyote. The coyote, spotlighted by a moonbeam, was so large Bob mistook it for a deer. We saw kingfisher, swallows, gulls, blue heron, and cormorants. Fish were abundant, especially in shallow water. Jesse, our guide yesterday, had told us that they were probably carp or suckers.

Upstream of Lyons Ferry, the river narrowed and the current increased. I wanted to move faster to beat the windstorm, but I didn't want to be too bossy. A more democratic management style worked for Lewis and Clark, so why not for Bob and me?

In preparation for this trip, I looked up some jokes about Marines, basing this on my theory that provoking him with jokes would be a better way to encourage cooperation than preaching. "What do you call a Marine with an IQ of 160?" I asked when we'd hit a lull. When I got no answer, I told him "A platoon." Still no verbal response other than a grunt, but I noticed his strokes got longer, deeper, and stronger. We were moving faster. If I could have remembered a joke that was even less fair, we might have been able to tow a water skier.

The closest pullout below Little Goose Dam shown on our map was at Riparia, almost seven miles below the dam. That was more than we wanted to pull Whisper. Proceeding upstream, we passed Texas Rapids on a narrow reach of the river, the rapids having been inundated when Lower Monumental Dam was built. We scanned the shore for a possible exit while worrying that the current would stop us if we got too close to the dam. We eventually moved to within a quarter mile of the dam, where the current was still manageable, and pulled ashore at a steeply sloped gravel beach on the north side of the river. After balancing Whisper on the wheel carriage and tightening the straps that held her in place, we pulled the kayak along a paved road over the dam to a small dock. We now used a yoke, made by inserting a paddle through the bow loop, to pull Whisper in tandem. While portaging, we called the operations people at the dam. We were told that high wind was expected after 11 a.m. but should die down by 11 p.m. After a quick snack of peanut butter, crackers, and dried fruit, we launched at about 10 a.m. and left the dam behind us.

For the first five miles above the dam, we paddled in a wide placid lake with very little wind. A tug with two barges passed us going in the opposite direction, the first commercial vessel we'd encountered above Ice Harbor Dam. When we passed a railroad trestle at Brown's Gulch, about five miles above the dam, the wind arrived. A tailwind, approaching gale force, pushed us along like an impatient NYC pedestrian. None of our emergency exits were nearby. When the river curved, we were faced with a dangerous crosswind. Adrenaline pumping, we paddled hard to keep from broaching and capsizing.

Glancing at the map, searching for obstructions, I took my eyes off our intended heading and the wind blew us toward shore. In a blink of an eye, the sharp basalt rocks near the railroad embankment on the north shore were only a few feet away.

"Watch out Hank," Bob yelled. I turned away from the rocks just in time to avoid ramming them. "You scared the living **** out of me," Bob added. Bob reminded me that he only refers to me as Hank during periods of stress. I responded that we were never that close to shore, and that even if we experienced a glancing blow with the rocks, we would probably not have had much of a problem.

"We would not have had much of a problem because we would be dead," Bob snapped. This from a man who would stand on a rickety platform ten feet from a heat of red-hot molten steel and act as if it were nothing more than tea poured from a kettle.

With the wind pushing us we made the seven miles from Brown's Gulch to Central Ferry State Park in less than an hour and a half, an average speed of almost 5 mph against the current. We couldn't find the park office or instructions on where to camp. Another camper advised us to pick a site, and someone would come by later to take our money. The park attendant finally arrived and told us we were in an area scheduled for watering. Using her golf cart, the attendant kindly helped us move our gear to a nicer spot, but one more distant from the boat launch. Bob finally got his warm shower, although he thought that the seventy-five-cent charge should have been included in the campsite fee. Like many events during the trip, this precipitated another debate. After I showered (and paid with no objection), I went to the camp store for pop, candy, and ice cream. Bob prepared soup to make sure we had a balanced diet.

Late in the afternoon, the wind picked up, again with gale force gusts. One or both of us held position at our tent to keep it from taking to the sky like a kite. Joyce later told me that gusts of 35 knots were reported. The sky became hazy with dust. The sun seemed to set far earlier than usual. The following week, Washington State issued a health advisory because of high wind and dust caused by the wind blowing over plowed fields. The river looked very dangerous, but more because of the wind than the waves which were probably not much higher than two feet. I attributed the low waves to the short fetch over which the wind blew, and to the short duration of the storm.

The strong wind kept us hunkered down in camp. Perfect time for another debate. I accused Bob of becoming wealthy at the expense of the environment.

"You are an environmental extremist," he argued. "I've seen you straightening old bent nails for reuse. I bet you even recycle paper clips, and you want to get rid of the automobile and the Snake River dams."

He was mostly correct. I chose to respond by going on the attack. "You make steel for the fracking industry, even now when we have a glut of petroleum on the market and when petroleum products and the methane vented to the atmosphere during their extraction are major sources of greenhouse gas."

"You drive a gasoline powered automobile, don't you?" he countered. "And besides, what my company does is completely legal. The market for petroleum products justifies fracking."

"The lobbyists for the petroleum, auto, and steel-making industries are the ones who justify fracking. The economics would turn upside down if the legacy costs passed down to future generations were included," I noted.

"It isn't my fault that legacy costs aren't included," Bob said.

I ended the debate with a low blow. "But it is your fault that you expect other park users to pay the cost of your shower."

Bob called Barbara to wish her happy anniversary. I felt bad forgetting the day, since I was best man at their wedding. He grimaced when his cell phone call dropped. I tried to call Joyce to ask her to relay Bob's message to Barbara but was unsuccessful. The camp host told me that the wind interferes with cell phone calls. Bob blamed the dust.

After a hot dinner of chicken soup and freeze-dried chicken, we both dozed off quickly in the cool breeze and slept well—me for the first time this trip without taking a pill.

Lower Granite Dam

We woke at first light to a glowing red sun, thanks to the remaining dust in the sky. Once on the water we averaged over 4 mph with a gentle breeze coaxing us along.

As a test, we drifted with the wind and against the current. Bob estimated we moved upstream at about .5 mph. And that was with our load greatly reduced by not having been able to replenish the food we'd consumed due to the power outage at Lyons Ferry. It now looked like we'd go hungry before reaching Clarkston, WA, the end of our journey, still two to three days off.

In contrast to the dammed reach of the Columbia River, the Snake River is so narrow I felt I could almost reach out and touch the shore on both sides. I had expected the Snake River to be featureless, as described by at least one member of the Expedition, but there were frequent patches of green and wildlife management areas nestled below the gray cliffs, and the birds and other wildlife they attracted raised my spirits. On this day we were joined by Canada geese along the shore, osprey and gulls circling above us, heron and egret wading in the shallows, and one lone robin, which seemed to be lost and calling to its mate.

Bob was paddling stronger every day, especially during one of our political discussions. However, the pain in his back and ribs from the fall on the boat ramp caused him to make frequent adjustments. Being in the bow, he set the stroke, with only his adjustments breaking our rhythm. I navigated and steered, having survived his call for my demotion after that close call with the rocks during the windstorm. We had become accustomed to and comfortable with our tasks.

We tied up to a crowded floating dock at the Boyer Park Marina with the sun just passed its zenith. We got one of the few remaining tent sites. It was a long haul to our campsite from the shoreline location where the camp host instructed us to leave Whisper. We bought cold drinks at the marina office and cooked our last package of chicken soup before calling ahead to Lower Granite Dam on the marina's house phone, using my calling card. Good thing. The Corps of Engineers had previously told me we could portage on either side of the river, but they didn't warn me about a fence that encased a construction project blocking the road just above the dam on the north side. Since Bob and I didn't want to repeat the Dalles Dam misadventure Mike and I survived last year, we decided to cross the river at or below the dam in the morning.

We were later told that motor vehicles were allowed to cross the dam, but pedestrians (even those pulling kayaks) and bicyclists were not. Apparently, this is for some obscure security reason and not because the dam operators don't like spandex. The only available option was to cross the river below the dam and portage on the south side.

An attendant at the marina told me that the weather the next day was supposed to be much cooler with a west wind of about six knots. For the following day, there was a 20 percent chance of rain and thundershowers. Bob called Barbara and gave her the good news that, barring a weather delay, we remained on schedule. I called Joyce and Mike with the bad news that the trip would soon end.

We had not seen any trains moving along the Camas Prairie railroad (the Union Pacific and Northern Pacific Railroads, according to our chart) until about 5 p.m. when two locomotives pulling about sixty cars rumbled past our tent site. Another train passed during the night so loudly that I wouldn't have been surprised had we been run over in our sleeping bags. It seems likely that freight transport by rail would increase appreciably if the dams were removed, a compromise I would be happy to make. Bob went to sleep quickly. The unintelligible yelling of a man and the shrieks of a woman, camping in a nearby tent, kept me awake until almost midnight.

Approaching Lewiston/Clarkston

The first leg for the day was little more than crossing the river to a portage take-out. We found a gradual beach with scattered driftwood about one hundred yards downstream from the posted official portage site. An older couple (old like us) was at the site, him fishing and her sitting on a rock and reading.

I said, "Good morning."

He replied in a very unfriendly voice, "What do you want?"

"We want to portage the dam."

"Go use the official portage site," he grumbled. "Why do you think we paid to build it?"

As far as I could tell nothing was "built," and the current would have made a take-out at the official site risky. Without further conversation, and with the risk of him throwing a rock at us, Bob and I loaded Whisper on its carrier and began our portage.

In contrast to our meeting with this couple, the Expedition experienced nothing but friendliness from the numerous Native Americans whose villages lined the Snake River. Led by Chiefs Twisted Hair and Tetoharsky, the Nez Perce had moved along the riverbanks afoot or on horseback, serving as guides and provisioners. Clark attributed the friendliness to the presence of Sacajawea who "we find reconciles (sic) all Indians as to our friendly intentions, a woman with a party of men is a token of peace."

We arrived at the Lower Granite Visitor Center as it opened. Six miles beyond the dam, and beyond our view, was the granite mound, isolated among the dominant dark basalt plain, for which the dam is named. We watched a short film about the dam, observed a few fish navigating the fish ladder through a viewing window and were greeted by a friendly, knowledgeable, gray-haired volunteer docent. The few fish that now pass this dam are a fraction of the pre-dam annual passage estimated to have exceeded four million fish in a good year.

By mid-morning, only twenty-seven miles from Clarkston, our destination, we checked the weather report before shoving off from the upstream boat ramp at Offield Landing. The predicted intermittent tailwind, that soon became a sustained breeze, gave us a welcome boost. While the morning wore on, the sky darkened, leading us to worry that rain and thundershowers would soon arrive with lightening. We pulled up on a sandy beach at Chief Timothy State Park early in the afternoon. For the first time, we were ahead of schedule. We considered trying to beat the storm to Clarkston. When the camp staff assured us that the storm would pass, we decided to stay.

After we setup our tent, Bob went off looking for better cell phone reception. He rescheduled his flight out of Seattle to allow time for him

to help me with the complicated logistics of getting Whisper back to
my home in Woodway.

The Meeting of the Clearwater
and Snake Rivers

The paddle to the confluence with the Clearwater River, the official
end of this year's trip, went faster than I thought it should have given
the very slight tailwind. It had taken us seven days to travel 142 miles
on the Snake River, one day longer than the Expedition.

We paddled a short distance upstream on the Clearwater but drifted
back to Clarkston paddling only when necessary to avoid the many
fishing boats. In this, our first time to relax on the river, we admired the
steep hills to the north, the Snake River bending from the south to the
west and the free-flowing Clearwater River sweeping us downstream
from east to west. The Old Spiral Highway, with its tight 180-degree
switchbacks, climbs 2,000 feet in only 7.3 miles. The newer, much less
curvy U.S 95/195 takes motorists and bicyclists from the valley bottom to
the top of the high plateau, a testimonial to the engineers and contractors
who built the road and to the Missoula flood that carved the valley.

We took out at the Corps of Engineers Greenbelt boat ramp just
downstream from the Lewiston-Clarkston Blue Bridge. I felt a little
guilty that I didn't have small bills to pay the three-dollar launch fee
for the ramp. Bob contended that we needn't pay because we didn't
launch the kayak at the ramp. When I later asked a Corps attendant,
she agreed with Bob. Maybe he should have become a lawyer.

When leaving a river at the end of a long trip, I envision the first
fish that left the water for land. Everything must have seemed different
for the fish and for those who observed it. So, it was for us when we
arrived in Clarkston. We pulled Whisper past the shops on Bridge
Street and Port Drive about a half-mile to the Quality Inn. Since it
was Sunday morning, there wasn't much traffic, but people stared, and

two teenagers snickered at two old men drying their red life jackets by wearing them in the morning sun.

Knowing that it is easy to steal a kayak secured only by a lock and chain, I had made arrangements with Danielle, the hotel manager, to store Whisper at the hotel while we retrieved my vehicle. She said we could keep the kayak in a vacant conference room on the lower level. I realize that it is difficult for non-kayakers to understand kayaking, but I was still surprised when I spoke with the desk clerk, a young woman who didn't appear like the type who spent time outdoors. "Just carry your kayak through the lobby, load it in the elevator and take it downstairs," she told me.

"But our kayak is eighteen feet long."

"No problem, our elevator will hold hundreds of pounds."

I had already checked the elevator and knew it wouldn't hold a kayak longer than ten feet, but I didn't have the heart or the energy to discuss solid geometry or the difference between mass and length with her.

Eventually, I found a young housekeeper who, as fate would have it, was also a kayaker. She wasn't surprised to learn of my conversation with the desk clerk. "Just carry your kayak through this vacant room. It leads directly to the storage room." So, it did.

Postscript IV

During lunch of blackened prime rib sandwiches at the hotel restaurant we tried to figure out how we would get Whisper back to Kennewick, where I had left my Volvo. The logistics got sticky when we confirmed that there was no direct public transportation, and the car rental companies wouldn't allow us to place a roof rack on their cars. I suppose we could have walked or paddled downstream, but the next best option seemed to be to rent a car to take us to Kennewick where we would pick up my Volvo with its roof rack. One of the hotel staff drove us to the Lewiston Nez Perce County Airport, where we rented a car for less than forty dollars. We then drove to Kennewick, taking the same route Mike and I had taken on our bikes. We arrived in Kennewick in time for dinner. Bob finally had the big juicy steak he craved, the prime rib sandwich for lunch having served only as an appetizer. After dinner we drove back to Clarkston, Bob driving the Ford Mustang rental car and me driving my Volvo station wagon. As with our lifestyles, I couldn't keep up with him on the road.

On this penultimate day of August, Bob woke at 5:30 a.m. to arrange for his boarding pass. I woke soon after. We loaded our gear in the Volvo, had breakfast, strapped Whisper on top of the Volvo, checked out of the hotel, and returned the Mustang rental car to the airport. We then drove three hundred miles back to Seattle in my Volvo, opting for the scenic route that took us through the historic towns of Uniontown, Colfax, Washtucna, Othello, Royal City, Vantage, and Ellensburg, with a brief stop at Ginkgo Petrified Forrest. The old towns in Eastern Washington suggest images of the Old West. Seattle is more like the old east. We went our separate ways at the Holiday Inn near SeaTac Airport. In parting, we spoke about our next adventure with some enthusiasm. I headed home to Woodway, arriving just in time for dinner.

The end of this leg of my voyage across the country was unlike any of the others. Nothing had gone wrong. The near mishap with the rocks was just another misadventure. We ate well, didn't lose any noticeable weight, and arrived relaxed, healthy and with hearty appetites.

Palouse Falls

Lower Granite Dam

Snake and Clearwater Rivers from old highway

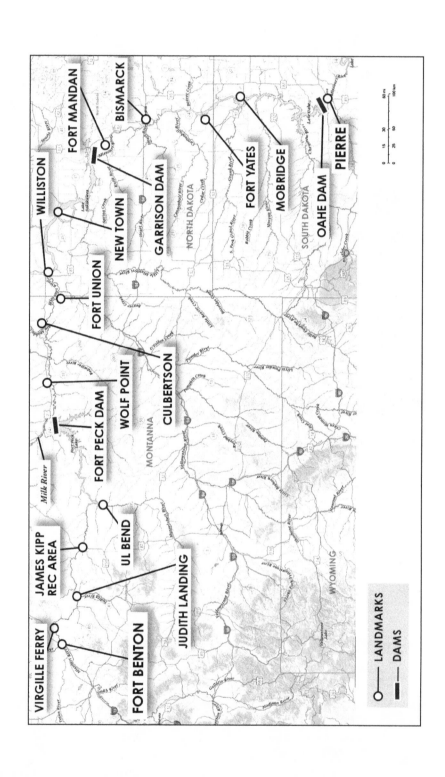

V

The Upper Missouri River

2012

Shoving off at Fort Benton

Wild and Scenic

As my seventieth year bore down on me, I still fantasized completing the Expedition's eastward journey before age swamped my ambitions. Success depended on good planning, conditioning myself physically and mentally, and stemming the health problems that had plagued me on previous trips.

I hadn't paddled the Missouri River in 2011 due to extreme flooding and reports of rattlesnakes congregating on high ground campsites. On a sunny Monday morning in early June 2012, I rumbled out of Woodway in my old Volvo station wagon with Whisper strapped to the roof rack. I headed for Fort Benton, Montana, where I would try to resume my Lewis and Clark journey, finally heading downstream.

I stopped in Wallace, Idaho, billed as the silver capital of the world. It became even more famous when The Great Fire of 1910 burned much of the town to the ground. The fire took eighty-seven lives, and blackened three million acres, making it the largest single fire in US history. The next day, after arriving at Fort Benton, I walked by the old fort and the historic Grand Union Hotel on Front Street, once known as the Bloodiest Block in the West. I had planned to stay overnight at the old hotel, but I became impatient to see what the Missouri River had in store for me.

While I set up a trip plan at the Missouri Breaks Interpretive Center, a friendly ranger told me that not only do rattlesnakes swim, but they also sometimes try to climb into low boats when they become tired of the water. Soon after hearing this disturbing news, I began my travel on the "wild and scenic" portion of the river. I put in at Canoe Camp upstream from town, rather than the paved put-in farther downstream. Canoe Camp is at US Bureau of Reclamation mile zero and US Army Corps of Engineers mile 2,074, roughly the daunting distance to the Mississippi River. There was scarcely any room for me in Whisper's cockpit, her hatches filled to the brim.

Despite benefiting from a modest current and little wind, my left shoulder hurt from the very beginning, and muscles in both arms soon ached. My body told me that it should be broken in more slowly than in the past. I stopped after only twenty miles. At Black Bluff primitive camp, two friendly canoeists told me that Wood Bottom Camp had facilities and was only a mile and a half ahead. They added that yesterday they met a man paddling to St. Louis. I looked for him around every bend.

Arriving at Wood Bottom (River Mile (R.M) 2054), just upstream of Loma Bridge, I realized why paddlers used Black Bluff. Unlike most pullouts, which are almost always in eddies—including Black Bluff—a strong current swept through the pullout at Wood Bottom. With a pair of artificial hips and age-related loss of balance, it isn't easy for me to exit a kayak quickly, especially from the left. I almost asked for help from a couple camping on shore, but my ego got in the way. Instead, I quickly went over my check list—unhitch my spray skirt, secure my gear in the event I capsize, and spin a quick U-turn to permit me to exit on the starboard side in shallower water.

While I struggled to get my legs out of the cramped cockpit, the fast-moving current began to sweep Whisper away. After several unsuccessful attempts, I was able to gain footing on the steep bottom slope in thigh-deep water. I took a firm hold on Whispers bow painter. The current pulled me back into the river. Using all my strength, and what little agility I still possessed, I lunged for shore and climbed up the low bank.

Wood Bottom was worth the risky landing. After setting up camp, I met fellow campers, Doug and Marge from Auburn, Washington, and Fort Benton, Montana, and their dog, Sarge. They were older (like me), gracious, and unassuming and shared their dinner of fresh caught catfish and sturgeon. After dinner, we sat by a blazing campfire eating the chocolate chip cookies my son Mike made for me. Doug spun some yarns while Sarge waited under the picnic table for his share of dessert.

"I used to live up the hill in Loma when I was young," Doug said. "In those days we drove cattle along a dusty trail all the way to Great Falls. I wanted to see more of the world, so I got a menial job with now-defunct Eastern Airlines. I took some courses and ended up piloting the biggest jets. Early on, I would return to Loma on a steam-driven passenger train on a now abandoned line along the left bank of the Missouri River, the remnants of which you followed as you paddled today."

Marge added that those of his high school classmates who remained in Loma couldn't believe how much Doug had accomplished. The way they smiled at each other, it was obvious to me that Marge and Doug had made it together. Before bidding them goodnight and while remembering all the help I was getting from my family, I said that I was sure Marge deserved a lot of credit for Doug's success. Doug smiled and nodded in agreement.

When I awoke at 5 a.m., it was drizzling. The forecast was for a chance of rain and thunderstorms and the afternoon wind was supposed to be 13-to-18 knots with gusts to 35 knots. I debated sleeping in but decided to take a chance with the weather. Packing too quickly, I left a pair of socks behind, hanging on a bush. From then on, I took much greater care. Other than the overboard loss of my weather radio the day before reaching the Yellowstone River, I only left behind the two socks and two tent pegs on the Missouri.

By putting in at Fort Benton, Montana, I was returning to the route Meriwether Lewis and his crew traveled after portaging the Rocky Mountains. My goal for this leg of the trip was to spend up to forty days on the river, during which time I hoped to navigate at least two of the three very big reservoirs—Fort Peck Lake, Lake Sakakawea, and Lake Oahe. The length of the three reservoirs varies with water level but they total about 540 miles at normal pool elevation. Lake Oahe, the longest reservoir at 220 miles, is twice the length of Long Island, where I spent my youth, and twice the length of Puget Sound in Washington, whose sparkling waters I see from my window while I write.

Howling wind, waves, and the sheer remoteness of these reservoirs had ended the travels of many paddlers. I knew I would encounter frequent thunder and lightning storms but hoped the extreme high water and tornados common in early spring had ended. I was anxious to put this part of my trip behind me. Traversing all three of these reservoirs and the freely flowing segments of the river that unites them, would add 1,000 river miles to the 1,136 miles already traveled since leaving Fort Clatsop. I made no attempt to find anyone to paddle with me. Other than the wild and scenic reach of the river, facing the challenge of the reservoir trio convinced me that this would not be a trip any, but the hardiest kayaker could possibly enjoy.

Less than an hour after shoving off from Wood Bottom, I paddled past the mouth of the Marias River on my left, almost hidden from my view by a wooded bluff. It was here that the westbound Lewis and Clark Expedition paused for ten days while they scouted far upstream and debated whether the Marias was the true source of the Missouri. Proceeding downstream past this convergence zone, I faced no such quandary, but wondered how history would have been changed if Lewis and Clark had taken the other fork in the river, the one that would have presented fewer physical obstacles than the Missouri headwaters route that President Jefferson had suggested. Perhaps the Marias River would now be called the Missouri. Perhaps the Blackfeet Tribe, the warlike Tribe living along the Marias River, would have turned the Expedition on its heels, and the West would still be Indian Territory. It fascinated me that history could be so altered by one seemingly minor decision.

The early morning was cool with only a slight wind while I paddled past cattle resting in the shade of cottonwood trees. I stopped at Coal Banks boat ramp and campsite where I filled my water jugs with a pale-yellow fluid that may have been water. I spoke to a friendly young ranger and a group of four trim young canoeists, two women and two men, leaving for Judith Landing, forty-seven miles downstream. As I munched on beef jerky and dried fruit, the canoeists told me that they saw a big rattlesnake hiding in the reeds at the water's edge the previous night. Forewarned, I watched where I stepped and carefully checked inside Whisper before climbing back into her cockpit. Later, on those occasions when I failed to check for snakes hiding in Whisper,

I decided that without hesitation I would jump overboard if one of those creatures slithered between my legs.

As the beauty of the river unfolded before me, I soon entered the White Cliffs where the ivory white Virgelle Sandstone is invaded by dark igneous dikes and plugs. These distinctive rock formations were made famous in Lewis and Clark's journals and have lured photographers and explorers for more than two hundred years. This remote reach of the river offers few stops for drinking water, almost a complete absence of cell phone coverage, and no food resupply options for 300 miles. Given the extreme isolation, my health issues, and my fear of being snakebit, I had added an emergency locator beacon to my equipment.

While approaching Eagle Creek, my intended campsite, a tailwind helped push me along. Not knowing what wind I might encounter the next morning, I decided to continue on to the muddy and marginal Hole in the Wall undeveloped boat camp (RM 2010). With lightning in the distance, I rushed to set up camp. In my haste, I bent an aluminum tent pole. I had brought only one spare. I needed my tent, not only to keep warm and dry but to keep crawly animals from cuddling up with me during the night.

Unable to get any weather channels on my weather radio, I relied on AM channel 1150 to provide dinner music and limited--usually threatening--weather information. With the heavy rain pelting my tent during the night and because of persistent pain in my left shoulder and both arms, sleep did not come easily. I was the one lonely camper tucked into this remote site.

The Wild Missouri

I was now in one of the wild segments of the Upper Missouri Wild and Scenic River System, which begins at Fort Benton and ends at the Kipp Recreation Area. The other two official designations are "recreation" immediately behind me and "scenic" to be found downstream. It was difficult for me to distinguish one segment from another. All feature the sights, sounds, and feel of a river that is both wild and scenic.

Paddling along, I entered the White Cliffs, often cited as the most memorable section of the Upper Missouri. It was for me too, though I failed to spot some of its most remarkable features. I never saw Hole in the Wall, an eight foot almost square hole in a cliff far above the river, perhaps because I was looking down while the hole was above me. There was no excuse for my missing Seven Sisters, the seven towering sandstone columns high on the left bank. That geologic formation inspired explorers, visitors, and artists for years. It is featured in one of Karl Bodners' most famous paintings, and, at most, I caught only a glimpse. I wondered if I had been daydreaming. Often, I was distracted searching for bighorn sheep on the cliffs, deer and antelope on lower ground, and rattlesnakes in the river. I was embarrassed when I compared Lewis and Clark's ability to observe and document over 170 plant and 120 animal species with my inability to spot a few massive geological features.

Mid-morning, I passed under a bridge that was not where I expected it to be. A ranger standing near the shoreline told me we were at Judith Landing—exactly where I intended to stop for water and river information. I knew there had been a strong current and a slight tailwind but was surprised that I had arrived before noon. Immediately past the bridge there is a boat launch where I aimed to pull out. The swift current swept me past the launch. I tried back-paddling, but that was next to useless. I struggled to turn back upstream but wasn't able to do so until I reached an eddy a quarter mile below the boat launch. By that time, I dreaded fighting the current back upstream. I moved on.

The combined impact of missing the much-anticipated White Cliffs geologic features, my inability to predict my arrival time at Judith Landing, my inability to stop where intended and my fear of the rapids which I would soon encounter, shook my confidence. I would have to plan better and be far more observant to avoid disaster.

In his memoir *Floating on the Missouri*, James Willard Schultz, aka Apikuni, the name given to him by the Pikuni Tribe of Blackfeet Indians, wrote in November 1901, "the swiftest part of the navigable

Missouri is a twenty-six-mile stretch east from the Judith, the water is all swift and there are 13 rapids in the course."

My limitations as a paddler began to haunt me. I had never learned the barrel roll, and even if I knew how to do it. I didn't have the courage to roll in the shallow water where I could hit my head on the bottom, get knocked out, and probably drown. Just when I imagined myself capsizing and my body washing ashore, the current swept me into Holmes Rapids. I was surprised and pleased that I had sufficient skills and was strong enough to avoid the rocks as Whisper sped downstream with the river bottom clearly in view. This was like a giant water slide. I was having fun.

I remained outwardly calm, though my heart was racing, when I paddled the ominously named Deadman Rapids, actually little more than shallow fast-moving water with a few boulders to keep me on my toes. But my blood pressure rose, and perspiration dripped from my forehead into my eyes when Whisper approached Dauphine Rapids, known to have stopped many steamboats. I heard the ominous rumbling of the fast-moving water, like a drum roll preceding a parade, even before I saw the rapids. I looked ahead and saw a thin blanket of clear water cascading from one rock to another over a rocky bottom. The current almost carried me into a big rock, but by paddling hard so I could steer better, I only scraped Whisper as I swept past. Just passed the rock, Whisper hit the hard bottom. I felt her undulate while she bobbed over the contours of the rocks below. With each crunch along the river bottom, I thought I would see and feel cool water spurting through a crack in Whisper's fiberglass hull. With no idea how to find my way to safety if my kayak was destroyed, I breathed an immense sigh of relief when I saw that Whisper remained dry.

A few hours after leaving the rapids behind I arrived at the Nee-Me-Poo Trail where, in 1877, Chief Joseph and his band of the Nez Perce Tribe crossed the Missouri while fleeing the US Cavalry. The Cavalry caught up to the Tribe just forty-five miles south of the Canadian border, beyond which the Tribe hoped to find asylum, and slaughtered more than three hundred men, women, and children in the battle of Bear Paw.

I had come to honor the Nez Perce during prior segments of my trip. Feeling the pull of history, I wanted to camp near their trail, so I pulled into what I believed to be Lower Woodhawk Campground (RM 1,940).

Stepping out of Whisper, I sunk in the mud up to my knees, and my apprehension morphed into fear. I had a vision of the well-publicized account of a woman in Alaska who sank to her thighs in loose watery sand along Turnagain Arm. She struggled to free herself but sank lower into the soft sand as the tide rose higher. How terrified she must have been in the hours she waited to be pulled free. Despite multiple rescue attempts, and the use of a breathing tube supplied by her husband, she drowned when the water rose above her head.

I couldn't let go of the fear that gripped me. Alone, and with no one within miles to help, I gradually worked myself toward shallow water. Fighting to keep my kayak from floating downstream, I struggled out of the mud and up the low bank. My imagination went wild. Had I let go of Whisper, the next river traveler might have been surprised to find a scavenger-riven skeleton planted in the mud bottom, a monument to my foolishness.

If conditions in 1877 were anything like I experienced, this would have been an extremely difficult portage for the Nez Perce who knew much more about the Missouri than I did. Although the tribe approached the river at this location, they wisely moved a couple of miles upstream to portage.

After pitching my tent in the damp grass at the Lower Woodhawk site, I reluctantly gave in to the need to learn how to cook my first hot meal on the Jetboil stove purchased in 2010. I had creatively avoided preparing hot food after leaving Fort Clatsop, Oregon, until 2010 when my friend Bob spoiled me with his cooking while we traveled on the Snake River. On this night I prepared an Indian dish of spicy Jaipur vegetables, beef jerky, nuts and treated myself to mandarin oranges in syrup for dessert. Preparation of the Jaipur vegetables fell within my limited cooking skills because they came in a pouch that had only to be dropped into hot water. Although well known for my ineptitude in the kitchen, I was proud of myself.

While trying to sleep that night, I dwelled on the fact that our nation treated the Nez Perce like criminals in1878. Seven decades earlier, it was this same Indian nation who befriended and saved the Lewis and Clark Expedition from starvation during their portage over the Bitterroot Mountains. Chief Joseph is especially well known in Washington State, having been brought into focus for the white public's attention by Edwin Curtis, one of Seattle's most famous photographers. According to Timothy Egan, author of *Short Nights of the Shadow Catcher,* a book about Edwin Curtis, Chief Joseph was deemed in 1903 "the most noted Indian" living at that time.

That night, while cozy in my tent, I planned for the next day by reading *The Complete Paddler,* a detailed account of a multi-year kayak trip on the Missouri River by David Miller. Miller rated river reaches with respect to degree of difficulty and provided a time range for completing each reach at paddling speeds that varied with river conditions. When applying Miller's time ranges, the forty days I allocated would see me at either the upstream end of Lake Oahe—if I made good time—or the upstream end of Lake Sakakawea if I did not. In contrast, Lewis and his crew (rejoined with Clark's group after the confluence with the Yellowstone River) traveled the 1,000 free-flowing miles from Fort Benton to what would become Pierre, South Dakota in twenty-nine days. I would find Miller's assessment to be overly conservative for the conditions I encountered, even for an old guy like me.

I was alone at Lower Wood Hawk Campsite. I had paddled 68.4 miles in one day, the most ever for me, although less than Lewis and Clark did on their best days. I couldn't get reception on the weather radio or the VHF but was able to dial into the AM channel in Cut Bank, Montana, where I got a taste of what was to come. The forecast for the next couple of days was for falling temperatures and winds gusting to 25 knots.

As the sun set over my lonely campsite, the wind died down and the bugs came out. The publicized campsite privy was nowhere to be found. Zipped into the cocoon of my sleeping bag to get warm, I loathed to crawl back out to investigate the snuffling animal whose padded footsteps snapped dry twigs in a series of pops like firecrackers, inches from my head. The animal, maybe a cougar, maybe only a camp rat, was looking for food and following scents, the strongest of which were right here. The tent's nylon fabric seemed a flimsy barrier, but it was all I had until the animal's footsteps receded in the distance.

After waking at sunrise, I used the disposable biodegradable bag for my toilet with only moderate success. Primitive pooping is the most disagreeable part of wilderness travel, especially with bad hips and when concerned about sitting on a snake.

The sky threatened with closely spaced dark gray clouds overhead. Where the sun found its way through gaps in the clouds it cast yellow rays on the ground, like a painter running his or her brush down from the sky. By mid-morning, I arrived at Kipp Landing where I was finally able to obtain water and where Amber, the camp host, allowed me to use her satellite phone to call Joyce and tell her all was well.

My maps for the next few hundred miles left much to be desired. Amber was unable to provide me with much information on possible downstream campsites or river/reservoir conditions, probably because few paddlers proceed beyond Kipp Landing. Somehow, I figured out how to use the "go-to" function on my new GPS to find points stored in its memory. This provided some help, but the level of detail was less than desired. This was the most remote country I would encounter, and I was worried.

I saw my first turtles and frogs along the shore at a campsite near CK Creek but did not see any sign of a cougar as Miller had observed near this location. For dinner, I cooked freeze-dried Louisiana red beans and rice, left over from 2010. Despite the pain in my left shoulder, my arms were definitely getting stronger although they appeared skinnier. I had a painful blister on my left heel and blisters similar to what I get each year on my hands.

I slept well until I woke to what sounded like a shotgun. It was too early for hunting season. I heard a second bang no more than twenty feet away. Not hearing any human voices or footsteps I relaxed a little. In the middle of the night, I was more fearful of a human than a well-fed bear or cougar. That sound, I realized, was probably the noisy tail smack of a beaver foraging in the stream nearby. I went back to sleep.

Shoving off about an hour after sunrise, the air was cold with a mist hanging over the water. While the sun rose, it reflected on the slight ripples. They glistened like a sea of diamonds, brightening the start to my day.

The Multiple Missouri Rivers: First Impression

One hundred and thirty miles above Fort Peck Dam, I reached the headwaters of Fort Peck Lake. David Miller referred to the reservoirs as the "dammed" or "damned" reaches. They offered both the best and worst of the river. The sparsely vegetated but beautiful country consisted of brown, green and muted yellow hills as far as my eyes could see. Early explorers poling their boats over shallow reaches of the river or pulling them from the shore, had little time to appreciate the scenery. All too often they had to clear snags and dense shoreline vegetation while fighting mosquitos and avoiding rattlesnakes. By contrast, I found myself singing the Coast Guard anthem to an audience of one lonely traveler, me.

The current ended as the river widened. I could make no progress without paddling, reminding me that the Missouri is many rivers. The free-flowing reaches of the river exist in stark contrast to the large reservoirs. During my week on the flowing river, I had camped at or very close to Lewis and Clark's campsites. On the flowing river, I found little evidence of civilization on the shore and few boats on the river. It is where the river flows like a pleasant memory that a traveler is closest to the Lewis and Clark experience. The reservoirs were a different story.

I was about to learn that the most difficult portions of the reservoirs are the upstream ends, where the river dumps its silty sediment load, forming braided channels, and willow choked marshes. At low water, these reaches are impassable to powerboats and barely navigable by kayak. At moderate water levels, such as I encountered, it was difficult to select the braided channel that remained deep enough to paddle. All too often, I would choose the wrong route when wind-driven currents obscured the river current. Even during calm periods, it was difficult to navigate through the willows without getting snagged or running aground. However, the reservoirs provided spectacular long-distance views, especially at sunset. It was also on the reservoirs that I finally found some amenities. Every four or five days I encountered a marina or lodge with hot showers, real beds, good food, and best of all, the pleasure of meeting people, as I would soon find at the Fort Peck Marina.

Fort Peck Lake and Fort Peck Dam

About a half hour after rounding UL Bend, a strong crosswind began to blow. I sought protection from the high bank on the west shore. A herd of about a dozen sleek pronghorn antelope were grazing on the east shore, accompanied by a flock of gulls reeling and circling overhead. From the time I first saw pronghorn in the wild, I had considered them to be among the most majestic of God's creatures. I attributed their ability to survive to their speed, agility, and the gamey taste. They are not popular prey with those who hunt for food. This herd allowed me to approach within the distance I could throw a rock and grazed long enough for me to observe females nurturing their young while the males stood sentinel duty, although apparently ignoring me.

Fatigued from paddling into the wind, I took it easy and reduced my cadence. It was very late in the afternoon when I finally found a landing in a cove covered with gumbo mud at RM 1,855. I set my tent on sloping ground, but it didn't stay put long. A gust of wind picked it up and blew it into the water. I was barely able to wade into the cove and retrieve my tent before the river carried it away.

Camping without a tent where the weather is good and where rattlesnakes and other dangerous animals don't visit during the night might be okay. Without a tent, and with the conditions I faced, I feared I would lay awake all night in a raging storm anticipating an unfriendly creature joining me in my sleeping bag.

Fort Peck Lake widens after the UL Bend. Wind and waves have stopped many a paddler. Karl Adams almost lost his life when he paddled the reach that I would attempt on this Father's Day. In 1987, Adams left Crooked Creek in calm weather only to find that conditions got nasty near the middle of the reservoir. Waves began to break over the top of his boat. He was losing control. He finally made it to shore at Devil's Creek Recreation Area. He thought the weather couldn't get worse, but it did. He was hit with hurricane force winds. Not able to pitch his tent, he was extremely fortunate to find refuge for two days in an abandoned truck.

My day on the water began just like Adams.' It was calm when I shoved off and, like Adams, I decided to cut across the lake to save distance. When I was near the center of the lake, the sky to the north blackened, the wind and waves increased, and the waves broke across Whisper. This was beginning to frighten me. I was barely able to control my kayak, her direction changing with each wave, each gust of wind. I feared conditions would get even worse. I searched for the nearest landing. The highly convoluted coastline, and the difficulty of determining distance when so close to the water's surface, made it impossible to fix my location. The spray made my paper maps useless, the waves made it risky to put down my paddle to use my GPS, and my GPS made my deck compass point everywhere but north.

After taking a wrong turn into Timber Creek, the wind died down. Greatly relieved, I continued paddling, thinking I was still on the main body of the lake. When I encountered a dead end in a forest of willows, my earlier adrenaline high collapsed into a depressive low. What I thought was a campsite beyond the willows existed only in my imagination. I had to turn around and paddle back out into rough water.

It was then that I saw a lone fisherman in a small boat with an oversized macho outboard motor. His grizzled face, dirty clothes and small size contrasted dramatically with his spit-shined boat and enormous motor. I paddled up to him.

"Can you tell me where I am?" I shouted.

"You're in Montana," he grumbled as he cast over my head.

"Could you be more specific," I added while I tried not to drift into his fishing line.

"I could be if I wasn't fishing."

"I'm headed to Fort Peck Dam. I want to find Bone Trail."

"Didn't you bring a map or GPS?"

Only after I apologized for my ineptness did he reluctantly point in the direction I needed to travel.

A thunderstorm was fast approaching when I unloaded Whisper at Bone Trail (RM 1,824). I rushed to raise my tent. Rain and wind arrived but were short lived. After sweating all day, and with gumbo mud from the night before covering my clothes, a bath was a necessity if I were to sleep. I was thoroughly relaxed for the first time in days while I swam in the clear warm water. My relaxing swim ended when I realized I needed to keep on the lookout for swimming snakes. After my swim, a purple sky and a lone brilliant yellow daisy growing along the shore and glowing in the setting sun complemented and contrasted with the stark hills and, again, lightened my mood.

When I awoke to a sun barely above the horizon the next morning, there was a light wind blowing from the southwest. The forecast was for winds of 10-to-20 knots with gusts to 30. I decided to shove off and see how far I could get. Staying close to shore is the safest way to travel. For the first twelve miles, I hugged the north shore. While approaching a bend, I took a risk to save distance and cut a corner and headed to a point jutting far out from the south shore. After the point,

I crossed the reservoir again, all the time worried that the gusts would again hit me when far from land.

Ominous black thunderclouds to the north of me sped eastward but the big wind at lake level held off. I leapfrogged from the tip of one peninsula to another. Had I taken the safer route hugging the shoreline of the five large bays I crossed, it would have more than doubled the distance.

I stopped at the end of a mounded peninsula (RM 1,787), just past The Pines Recreation Area. Trees had been sparse until coming upon this forest of tall pines filling the mound, not as tall as the great Douglas fir trees next to my house in Washington State, but close enough to remind me of home.

About an hour before sunrise, I woke to the sound of a big downpour. The rain gave me a good excuse to stay in bed, but rainwater was seeping into my tent, turning the lower end into a wading pool, and soaking my sleeping bag, and the books, maps and food wraps I had left scattered around the tent floor. I also worried that the longer I stayed in camp the greater the chance I would be hit by the afternoon storm. Since my feet and legs were already soaked, I decided to pack up my soggy gear and start paddling in the lingering rain.

With about fifteen miles to go before reaching the dam, I was confronted with more wide bay mouths and a strong tailwind. I debated paddling around the perimeters of the bays where it would be safer but again opted for the shorter, albeit anxiety ridden, routes cutting across each bay mouth. Had thunder and lightning arrived, I planned a difficult but potentially safer route, portaging on a dirt path that would likely be turned into gumbo mud by even a little rain.

The 250-foot-high Fort Peck Dam is hard to find when approaching from upstream. At first the dam looks like a featureless horizon. Next, the cars and trucks crossing the dam appear to be riding on water, like bugs scooting across a pond. Fort Peck Dam is the largest hydraulic earth fill dam in the world and the most famous of the six dams on the Missouri River. Construction of the dam provided much needed employment for more than 40,000 workers during the Great Depression, but the lives of eight workers were lost when a large portion of the upstream face of the dam slid into the reservoir as the dam neared completion. Somewhere, buried in the 126 million cubic yards of earth, are the bodies of six of those men. Engineers, like me, still take heed from both the failure of the dam and the inadequate safety procedures.

I was more than ready to relax with a hot shower, a good meal and resupply when I reached the Fort Peck Marina (RM 1,773) just above the dam. Tara Waterson, the owner, put me up in a rental trailer with a shower, and her staff fed me well. I ordered a hamburger and fries and was on my second helping when Daryl, one of the locals, kindly offered to take me the thirteen miles to Glasgow, Montana, to pick up desperately needed supplies. In addition to staples like peanut butter, beef jerky, cheese slices, baby carrots, and dried fruit, I bought three navel oranges, two apples and one banana, the numbers being proportional to the length of time fruit keeps in a hot kayak.

Soon after returning from Glasgow, and after cleaning mud from Whisper, she looked her best and satisfied state agricultural inspectors looking for invasive species. I entered the marina's cafe and joined Duane, a retired railroad engineer, Jerry, a retired phone company worker, and another man. The third fellow owned a ranch and two hotels that the trio referred to as railroad hotels, apparently because they were used primarily by Burlington Northern and Amtrak personnel. The men were initially rather reserved and stood with their backs toward me until I offered to buy a round of beer. I actually drank two beers, which tasted rather good and tied my record. Perhaps to make up for their initially cool reception, Duane gave me an informative booklet about the construction of the dam and the lives of the workers and their families living in the shantytowns.

Late in the afternoon, Thom and Tyler, two young men searching for adventure, entered the cafe. They intended to travel by canoe to New Orleans, a remarkable goal given their lack of experience and equipment. In response to my questions, they told me that they were in the canoe I had approached the night before and, yes, they had no life jackets, no spray cover and only a road map. They left Fort Benton without much forethought and with very little money. When they told me their only major problem was that their bag of marijuana got wet in the spray, I concluded that before they lost their supply of weed, they might have had other problems that they were oblivious to. What, me worry? They were the only other kayakers or canoeists I encountered during the rest of my lonely journey of 2012.

Thom, Tyler, and I weren't the only ones to experience dangerous conditions near what became Fort Peck. On May 11, 1805, the white pirogue, with Charbonneau, Sacajawea's husband, at the helm, was hit by a sudden squall. Instead of heading into the wind and thereby dumping it, Charbonneau loaded more wind in the sail. When Charbonneau cried out for mercy, Cruzatte, the boat captain, forced Charbonneau to do his duty by threatening to shoot him instantly if he did not. The canoe was righted and reached shore with its gunnels barely above water. Sacajawea proved invaluable in preventing capsize and rescuing equipment so important that Lewis remarked that he would have valued his life "but little" if it was lost. Lewis wrote, "The Indian woman to whom I ascribe equal fortitude and resolution with any person on board at the time of the accident caught and preserved most of the light articles which were washed overboard . . ." and all the while caring for her infant son. I didn't have to look beyond Sacajawea to find inspiration.

I slept late in order to take advantage of the comfortable bed. After eating a couple breakfast bars in the trailer, I prepared a much cleaner Whisper for portaging. Daryl had offered to haul Whisper and me to the put-in below the dam, but I declined, still stubbornly not wanting to accept motorized assistance. There are no navigation locks on any of the Missouri River dams, so onto the wheels Whisper went. All was well when I pulled Whisper up and over the dam, until I missed the last turn for the launch at the Winter Haven ramp. Fortunately, three biologists in a pickup truck stopped me about a hundred yards beyond the turn to redirect me. They must have forgotten to tell me that although locals refer to two closely spaced boat ramps as Winter Haven, the ramp at the Winter Haven sign is not actually on the river. I had just finished unloading Whisper from its portage wheels when a park ranger stopped by with the embarrassing news that I was about to launch in a giant fishpond.

After repacking and pulling Whisper another half mile, I again redistributed my stored gear and launched at the correct ramp late in the morning. Poor GPS coverage and a strong headwind made it surprisingly difficult to find my way past the many islands and ponds—excavated during dam construction or formed by recent flooding—especially when the wind and waves made it impossible to discern the river flow. On more than one occasion I had to push Whisper off the mud.

Eight miles below Fort Peck Dam, I paddled past the confluence with the Milk River. Lewis and Clark and Least Heat-Moon and his crew observed the milky white water of the Milk River blending with the Missouri, which appeared brown to the Expedition and blue green to those of us who passed after the dam was built. The Hidatsas knew the Milk, a sometime vigorous watercourse, as "The river that scolds all others." To me it appeared incapable of scolding the Missouri.

Free Flowing Again

Once on the cold, fast flowing water below Fort Peck Dam, I again picked up speed, traveling the 190 miles to the confluence with the Yellowstone River in just four days, at a gratifying forty-five miles per day. The left bank is nominally to the north but the river twists and turns so much that it could be in almost any direction. The river is almost as crooked as some notable politicians, taking 224 river miles to go a straight-line distance of 130 miles between the dam and Williston, North Dakota. Tailwinds soon became headwinds. My attitude changed as abruptly as the river direction and the relative direction of the wind.

The Fort Peck Indian Reservation, home to about six thousand Sioux and Assiniboine people, extends along the left bank for much of this distance. No camping is allowed on the tribe's side of the river without tribal permission. I had been told that local youth sometimes shoot over the heads of kayakers. I heard no gunshots while I paddled long and hard each day and hid my tent along the right bank each night.

The Expedition, while heading west, Least Heat-Moon and his crew (traveling in an outboard powered canoe) and I had similar experiences between the Milk River and the Yellowstone River. We all encountered frequent sandbars and often ran aground—although with the shallowest draft, I undoubtedly had it easiest. We all encountered boils or mini whirlpools that threatened to capsize us unless we powered through them, and we all encountered fast moving water that impeded the westbound Expedition and Least Heat-Moon and his crew while it pushed me along. Lewis and Clark were the only ones to encounter grizzly bears, the first one being killed near what is now Blair Station.

For the next several days a strong current carried me to North Dakota. I camped near Oswego, MT, a town with the same name as the college where Joyce obtained her undergraduate degree. The next day I made Poplar, MT where, in 1999, I was befriended by the owner of T J's Quick Stop when a sudden thunder and lightning storm caught up with me during my cross-country bicycle ride. The third night I camped near Blair Station, MT where the Empire Builder, Amtrak's historic train between Chicago and the West Coast passed close by and where I capped off a twelve-hour paddle with my first attempt at fishing. The only bites I got were from some pesky mosquitoes.

Below Blair Station, the steep bluffs, often struck through with a black band of coal, glowed pink in the low sunlight. It reminded me of the pink and black colors worn, and considered cool, by high school students in the 1950s. The main rail line along the left bank is so close to the river that erosion threatens to undermine the tracks. Several trains carrying large boulders waited in line to dump their loads of riprap intended to protect the railroad embankment from erosion. I hugged the right bank in order to stay clear of construction equipment and falling boulders. I chuckled when I remembered that in Brazil, where my family and I have lived, and where the letter *r* is silent, the dam construction workers referred to riprap as "hip hop."

A couple of miles above Fort Union sits the rarely used Snowden railroad lift bridge, constructed in 1913 when riverboats still plied this reach of the Missouri River. It is one of only a few bridges in the US that once allowed road and railroad traffic on the same roadbed. After consulting Wikipedia, I learned that the bridge was so dangerous that it was safe because motorists used extreme care when crossing. It is now used only for rail freight traffic. With only small boats now on the upper Missouri River, there is no longer any need for the lift bridge to be raised from its resting place.

Upstream from Fort Union, I saw my first oil well of the trip, a sign of the Bakken Shale oil and natural gas boom that was about to benefit—or plague—this area. Old time residents on limited incomes might choose one descriptor while new arrivals looking for well-paid work might choose the other.

The journey continued to be a lonely one. From just below Fort Peck Dam to the border with North Dakota, a distance of more than 200 miles, I encountered only one boat on the river, a speedy fiberglass runabout carrying two biologists, and saw two run down wooden fishing boats tied to shore. The first boat I encountered in North Dakota, near the Montana border, was a grossly overloaded small outboard runabout with six large unhappy people crammed aboard jostling for the limited available space.

As I approached the Yellowstone River, I passed reconstructed Fort Union, the most famous fur trading post on the Missouri, where Charles Larpenteur, the great uncle of a friend of mine, spent many years in the mid-nineteenth century. His book, *Forty Years a Fur Trader on the Upper Missouri, The Personal Narrative of Charles Larpenteur 1833-1872*, presents a vivid account of life along the Missouri River during this time and may be a little more realistic than the Hollywood production *Revenant*. I would have stopped to explore the fort but could find no access from the river. It is ironic that Fort Union, like so many places that relied on the river, now seemingly turns its back on its benefactor.

I spent the night at the Confluence Campground (RM 1,582) near reconstructed Fort Buford, the site of North Dakota's Missouri Yellowstone Confluence Interpretive Center. The name confluence could apply both to the joining of the Yellowstone and Missouri Rivers and to the location where Lewis and Clark planned to meet after the Corps of Discovery divided at Travelers Rest near Missoula. Confluence is also close to the location where the nearsighted Private Cruzatte shot Lewis in the backside.

Clark had arrived at the mouth of the Yellowstone about a week before Lewis. He left a note, the remnants of which Lewis found attached to a piece of elk horn. Lewis proceeded downstream for four more days, making camp near what is now the Four Bears Recreation Area, where he spotted a herd of elk on a thick willow bar. He and Cruzatte went hunting. Lewis killed one elk and wounded another. While stopped to fire on the wounded elk, a bullet struck Lewis' left thigh about an inch below his hip joint. At first Lewis thought Indians shot him. He later concluded that Cruzatte probably fired the shot, mistaking him for an elk. The next day Lewis' party caught up with Clark's. Despite his injuries, it wasn't long before Lewis resumed his duties, providing encouragement for me to endure far lesser mishaps.

A Night in the Marsh

Almost every day of this trip had offered at least one reason to quit, but the days before and after my stay at Confluence Campground offered several, although none as bad as Lewis getting shot. The day before I arrived, I dropped my weather radio in the drink at about the same time the battery to my back-up VHF radio failed. It appeared my wife, Joyce, was correct in her prediction that I would lose at least one piece of equipment—the reason she refused to lend me her digital camera. Tackling Lake Sakakawea (the official spelling used in North

Dakota) and Lake Oahe, the Missouri River's two biggest reservoirs, without a weather radio made me very nervous.

I shoved off from Confluence campground in early morning with partly cloudy skies, little wind, and a chilly 65 degrees F. After two hours, the temperature was a comfortable 80 degrees F. Suddenly, a storm hit. The temperature rapidly plunged to the shivering point and the sky darkened as if someone had pulled down the shades. When the rain began to fall, I remembered having stuffed my rain jacket behind my seat. While twisting in my seat to free my jacket, a bolt of lightning hit less than one hundred yards away. My heart missed a few beats as I almost jumped out of Whisper's cockpit. To keep from being dumped into the river, I grabbed hold of the nearest thing, a branch from a tree trunk floating next to Whisper. Heavy rain driven by cringe-worthy gusts pelted me. The fear of being struck by lightning kept me hunkered down. Even with my rain jacket on, I sat shivering in Whisper among the trees waiting for the storm to pass. Thirty long minutes later it was over. After another two hours and still thoroughly drenched, I pulled up at a boat ramp and park at the Hwy 85 Bridge. It was early in the day, but I pitched my tent, cooked some chicken noodle soup, crawled into my sleeping bag to get warm and pondered how to get to Williston, North Dakota to purchase a desperately needed weather radio.

Williston is the only town of any notable size on the river between Fort Benton, Montana, 475 miles upriver and Bismarck North Dakota, 230 miles downriver. While at the Fort Peck Marina, Duane, the retired railroad engineer, warned me that it would be risky to leave my kayak or gear unattended near Williston or anywhere near the Bakken shale oil patch. I didn't know if Duane was being dramatic, but I was about to find out. After warming myself, I left my tent with the goal of hitching a ride into Williston to find a weather radio. I looked back at a group of sleazy looking men obviously dealing drugs near my tent. Uncomfortable leaving my kayak and gear, I decided to heed Duane's advice and move on. I collapsed my tent, packed my gear, and returned to the river.

My goal was to reach a sporting goods store near the river in Williston by weaving Whisper through the fifteen-mile-long by three-mile-wide willow marsh at the head of Lake Sakakawea. I was learning that the physical condition of the river varied with both location and time. Annual flooding changed channel locations from those shown on my maps and created braided channels and willow-covered mud flats even worse than those present before the UL Bend. When travel writer Least Heat-Moon arrived at the Williston marsh while motoring upstream, all he thought he saw was a wall of trees. Approaching the marsh from the other direction, I thought I could see a path through the trees.

Lake Sakakawea is the largest USACE reservoir in the US, both by area and volume, and the willow marsh is correspondingly immense. The wind and waves made it difficult to navigate using my GPS and maps. The directions obtained from the lone boater I met were off the mark. I was tired, mad at myself and more than a little worried when I missed the channel leading to Williston. When the sun began to set over the hills, I put all my remaining energy into reaching the left bank of the Missouri less than one mile ahead but was driven backward by a strong headwind. I was getting cold. I finally gave up in despair and ended the day seven miles downstream of Williston near RM 1,543. I paddled Whisper into a desolate willow swamp along a narrow channel. The land was only a few inches above the river and could easily flood during the night, but I was too discouraged at this point to worry about that.

I longed for a hot meal and a warm bed but had only enough time and energy before the sun set to gobble down some beef jerky and dried fruit, change into long underwear and dry clothes and attempt to arrange my kayak for the night. Despite being late June, the day's rain and wind had chilled me to the core. I shivered and couldn't stop. With no hope of finding a place to pitch my tent I made a hard choice. I stuffed myself into my sleeping bag and wriggled like an inch worm into Whisper's small cockpit. Stuffed in, I pulled the sleeping bag over my head to form a windbreak. Sleep didn't come easily that night. The river I had set out to conquer was conquering me. Exhausted, cold, hungry, I was close to giving up.

Tobacco Gardens Refuge

After spending a miserable night hunkered down in Whisper's cockpit, I emerged in the shape of a twisted pretzel, but I was finally warm. Yesterday's desolate and depressing campsite didn't seem so horrible in the sunshine and calm air. Still without a weather radio, I had about fifteen miles more to paddle to get through the maze of willow marshes. To avoid getting lost in the willows possibly for days, as had recently happened to a local family in a canoe, it would be necessary to avoid the blind sloughs and follow the main channel, which, on my maps, swung from one bank to another several times on the two-and-a-half to four-mile-wide river. Easier said than done. I was deeply concerned that the 2011 flood had caused major changes to the channel location. Following David Miller's advice, I called the USACE office in Williston where I was told that the convoluted river channel was no straighter than it had been prior to 2011. The bad news was that a strong wind was expected that afternoon.

When I finally shoved off, I encountered a moderate headwind. As my direction changed, the relative wind direction also changed. The increasingly gusty wind made it impossible to go where I wanted and blew me ashore on a willow marsh island. Fearing another night sleeping in my kayak, I struggled through the sticky mud while pushing and pulling Whisper along the shore until the wind was no longer abeam and I could resume paddling.

Later in the day, an even stronger crosswind blew me onto the rocky left bank. Standing between my kayak and the shore, I pushed Whisper while trying to keep the breaking waves from filling her cockpit. After struggling for about an hour and getting nowhere, I placed more ballast in the bow compartment. This gave me better control and allowed me to resume paddling. I tried to reach the Tobacco Gardens Marina but didn't quite make it before sunset, and my strength gave out. So close and yet so far. I spent another depressing night, this one on a sandy, fly-infested beach at RM 1,513, only a mile from my destination. I tried to focus on the positive. At least I wasn't sleeping in Whisper.

Soon after waking the next day, I called Tobacco Gardens Marina. I listened to a message saying that they were closed Tuesday due to a water problem but would reopen on Wednesday. This was Tuesday. When I shoved off, I debated bypassing the marina, which I believed to be closed. But I needed a decent rest, good food, and a weather radio. I decided to take the short detour one-half mile up an unnamed bay leading to the marina. To my very pleasant surprise, the marina was open. The phone message was intended for the previous week. Staying at Tobacco Gardens, and avoiding a violent storm, saved my trip—and maybe my life.

After settling my gear at the marina, I feasted on a breakfast of bacon, eggs, toast, and jam. I asked Peg Hellandsaas, the marina manager, if it would be possible to hitch a ride with anyone traveling to Williston. She told me that Myron Smith had volunteered to run some errands for her and could take me with him. Myron, a very big man with one arm, had worked in the oil fields, driven trucks, been a disc jockey, and run a convenience store. He seemed much more interested in telling me about his life and the changes the oil boom has brought than hearing about my trip during our 130-mile roundtrip to Williston. That was fine with me. I'm a good listener.

"All this traffic is because of the darn oil patch. A few years ago, you would find hardly any cars on this road," Myron lamented, while we waited for the one traffic light between Tobacco Gardens and Williston to turn green. "Prices have skyrocketed, the locals can't afford to live here anymore, and the new people bring with them drugs, crime and prostitution."

Myron took me to Walmart where I stocked up on food, batteries, and a headset radio (the store didn't carry weather radios), and to the US Post Office for mailing gear that was no longer needed. He also took me to the sporting goods store in Williston where I had planned to purchase the weather radio. Had I attempted to hitchhike, my trip would have been wasted. The store sold hunting and fishing gear but no radios or batteries for my VHF radio.

Upon returning to the marina restaurant, I devoured a juicy steak cooked medium rare, just the way I like it, and a tossed lettuce and tomato salad. I sat alone while a rather mild thunderstorm rumbled through on its way east. Just about the time I started on a dessert of cherry pie and vanilla ice cream, Peggy joined me. Myron told her about my need for a weather radio and Peggy had a solution. She ordered one on the internet and arranged for it to be sent to a marina farther downstream.

After dinner, while working on my equipment in my cabin, an intense thunder-and-lightning storm with gale-force winds hit the area. The storm followed a day of record setting temperatures, 110 degrees in nearby Miles City. I watched the trees outside my window toss and bend in the onslaught while the horizontal rain pounded the windows. Storms like this put an end to river travels of many paddlers. Had I been in my tent I would have been soaked and my tent probably destroyed. If I had been on the river, I might not have survived. If I had survived, I might have done as many others have done and just given up.

The next morning, I said goodbye to Peg, Myron, and the staff after eating a hearty pancake breakfast. I had hoped to trade tales with the other breakfast patrons, but they were rather taciturn. There was an extra seat at the table they occupied, but they quickly closed ranks so I couldn't join them. I expect they were tired of all the new arrivals working in the oil fields. I was just one more new face. Before leaving, Peg, the only person who seemed interested in my trip, presented me with a Tobacco Gardens Marina T-shirt, which I treasure.

Leaving Sakakawea

Soon after shoving off, a strong tailwind shot me forward while I paddled past numerous oil and natural gas wells. The wells spewed fire, smoke, and greenhouse gases as if the devil in his subterranean lair was belching and stinking up the world. If this transition from prime prairie land to an industrial site marked progress, it was "progress" gained at a greater price than I wanted to pay.

The wind remained almost directly astern until past the Highway 23 Four Bears Bridge, very close to where Cruzatte shot Lewis. Swells exceeded four feet and the occasional breaking waves could have broached Whisper if I had not paddled hard. After a day of rest, my body behaved well.

As I have noted, almost every day brought at least one reason to quit. There were a few exceptions and this penultimate day on Lake Sakakawea was one. Soon after shoving off from my riverside campsite downriver from Highway 23, the mild crosswind that greeted me changed to a tailwind and increased to the point where it propelled me along while not being so powerful as to threaten to broach or capsize Whisper.

After turning the "corner" to head south at Independence Point, the northwest wind was no longer directly astern, but still helped enough for me to extend my goal for the day and cross the wide mouth of the Little Missouri River. The land in the distance was farther away than it seemed when I started the crossing, but this crossing was worth the risk.

I finished the day at RM 1,436 in a sandy cove with a gradual beach and unobstructed views, which made the lake seem boundless. The lake water was clear and warm. I lay down in the shallows and looked up at the wispy cirrus clouds floating by and the images of people, places, and things they portrayed. It didn't take me long to imagine a fox giving chase to a rabbit. My mind and my many pains eased. I could not remember enjoying another beach more.

The only sign of potential trouble was the many cattle hoof prints. I hoped a big bull wouldn't threaten my tent in the morning as one did with Miller. I had traveled over forty miles, my highest mileage on Lake Sakakawea. I called Joyce that evening to tell her of the good day and that I had seen not only cattle tracks but also the paw prints of what appeared to be a cougar. Thankfully, neither cougar nor bull visited me on my sandy beach in the cove.

Occasionally on this trip I would count the number of paddle strokes per minute and found that that they averaged about fifty-five with some bursts up to eighty, and some relaxed moments below forty-five. Using fifty-five strokes per minute and multiplying by the number of hours I had paddled (303 by the end of this day) would mean that I should exceed a million strokes the next day. No wonder my shoulders hurt. My first-time kayaking, several decades ago, my arms became so tired I was ready to quit after only twenty minutes. Now I could paddle more than ten hours without stopping for anything more than guzzling water or shoving a snack into my mouth. Was I stronger, more stubborn or both?

The next morning the lake was flat calm. In the afternoon, I had a mild headwind from the southeast which formed foot-high waves. The wind and waves were manageable but because both my shoulders now hurt, I steered a course that minimized the distance to my next intended destination at the Dakota Waters Resort. This course took me to the middle of the four- to five-mile-wide reservoir. Somewhere below the surface was Like a Fishhook Village built by the Mandan and Hidatsa tribes in 1845. They were later joined by the Arikara. The three tribes banded together in defense of the Lakota and Yanktonai Sioux after the numbers of the three peaceful tribes were greatly decimated by the smallpox epidemic of 1837. The village, named Like a Fishhook, and its symbiotic neighbor Fort Berthold supported each other until the Army constructed Fort Stevenson, fourteen miles away in 1867. It was abandoned in the mid-1880s and was lost to history when Garrison Dam flooded many tribal villages and much of the three affiliated tribes productive agricultural land in 1954.

There is an infamous photo of eleven men at the signing of the agreement, which took 155,000 acres of tribal land for the construction of Garrison Dam and reservoir. Ten men seem smug or uncaring. George Gillette, Fort Berthold tribal chairman, is pictured with his hand to his face weeping. As a former dam engineer and officer in the Corps of Engineers, the shame I felt looking at the smug faces, and the contrasting sorrow on the tribal chairman's face, overwhelmed me.

When offshore from Beaver Creek Bay my new radio predicted increasing wind and a 30 percent chance of thundershowers sometime that afternoon. Even though I couldn't yet see any dark clouds, I had experienced enough rapid changes in the weather that my heart began to beat faster, and I forgot about the pain in my shoulders while I rushed towards the south shore where the resort was located. Near the center of the reservoir, a game warden idled up to me in a high-powered patrol boat to see if I needed help. I told him I hoped to overnight at the Dakota Waters Resort. That meant only seven more miles of paddling, and I was really looking forward to an early arrival. Sensing I wouldn't be happy to hear this, he looked away toward the distant shore. Still without looking at me he said, "That place closed a couple years ago. Darn shame, too. I liked their food." The warden suggested a couple of alternatives on the south shore. I thanked him for his trouble. He gave me a look like he envied me when he sped away.

I headed for Hazen Bay, the closest option. Three days after leaving Tobacco Garden Marina, I camped at a beautiful rocky campsite on a small peninsula jutting out into the lake that offered expansive views. The site (RM 1406) was protected from the wind by rock ledges on three sides and was only fifteen river miles above the 210-foot-high Garrison Dam.

When I began paddling the next morning a strong headwind and strong pain in my left shoulder forced me to stop. I took out at the Hazen Bay boat ramp only about a mile past my campsite. I had been unable to decide whether to paddle or portage. The headwind made the decision for me.

I began a portage of unknown distance on rural roads. It took me five hours pulling along the narrow shoulder of State Road 1806, named in recognition of the date of the Expedition's return voyage, to reach Pick City, North Dakota at the top of the dam. Although tempted to accept the multiple offers of help from people who passed me on the road, I remained determined to continue this trip without any motorized support. Had the portage distance been thirty miles, as one boater informed me, I would have camped along the side of the road.

I was so dehydrated and tired when I finally reached the air-conditioned convenience store above the dam that I struggled to stay on my feet. I staggered as if I were drunk when I entered the store. Another customer helped me to a chair. When it seemed like I might collapse, the proprietor looked at me in sympathy and handed me an ice-cold energy drink. After sitting outside in the shade of a cottonwood tree for a half hour, I felt my strength return and was on my way again.

While camping at Garrison Dam, I had time to reflect on my progress. I had paddled two of the three big reservoirs and was well within my forty-day plan. I began to think of revising my goal so that I could get home in time for my 47th wedding anniversary, which might improve my odds that there would be a 48th. I decided to try for a thousand miles, hoping I could make it that far before forty days. My shoulders still hurt, my butt had begun to hurt, and I was flat-out afraid of Lake Oahe. I didn't tell Joyce of my fears and pains. She might have tried to convince me to stop.

I woke early to try to beat the mosquitoes but didn't succeed. They blanketed my bare skin as I shoved off down a steep slope shortly after sunrise. I encountered a river as smooth as the stride of an antelope. It was a warm, sunny day with almost no wind in the morning and a very slight headwind in the afternoon. In order to ease the pain in my shoulders I took it easy while a moderate current pushed my speed up to about 5 mph.

Approximately fifteen miles below Garrison Dam, I paddled past the confluence with the Knife River, just upstream of the camp where the Expedition spent the harsh winter of 1804 to 1805. Lewis noted in his journal, "This place we have named Fort Mandan in honor of our Neighbors," the Mandan and Hidatsa tribes. Throughout the bitter winter, the Native people visited the explorers to trade corn, beans, and squash, and shared information crucial for the success of the Expedition. It was also here that the Expedition hired the French-Canadian Charbonneau as an interpreter. Along with Charbonneau came his sixteen-year-old pregnant wife, Sakakawea. She soon gave birth to a son, Jean Baptiste, who Clark nicknamed "Pomp." In the eyes of many, the Expedition would not have succeeded were it not for the knowledge and bravery of Sakakawea. Little is known of Sakakawea after her return to the Knife River Villages in 1806. She may be buried at the Fort Manuel (Lisa) Trading Post, now below the waters of Lake Sakakawea near Pick City. After being weaned and at the end of the eastward journey, Jean Baptiste, was raised by Clark with the consent of both Sakakawea and Charbonneau.

I was again on the freely flowing river where sandbars often interrupted my peaceful paddling. On most occasions I could work my way past them without exiting Whisper. However, shortly after passing the original Fort Mandan, I ran aground, an offense punishable by court martial in the naval services. I had thought myself smart when I attached my new radio to my deck bag with a lanyard, but the lanyard got snagged on my life jacket when I exited Whisper and my radio tumbled overboard and started bouncing over the bottom. What a relief when after a few minutes in the hot sun the radio made a weak humming sound. Several hours later, as I pulled out to camp on a wide sandbar on a treed island (RM 1340) near the town of Price, North Dakota, I heard rock music coming from my revived radio.

My search for a campsite near Bismarck had been unsuccessful. After pitching my tent and before cooking dinner I called my daughter Amy and enlisted her help finding a place to stay and a place to buy a backup radio in Bismarck. To an Internet novice like me it seemed magical that in only a few minutes Amy and her husband, Sean, had names and numbers. However, for the first place I called, the Southport Marina, the phone was disconnected. I still had no place to stay anywhere near Bismarck. I hoped Abraham Lincoln State Park would have room, but by the time I called the office it had closed.

Bismarck is hard to find when traveling by kayak. There is almost no development along the riverbank between the city's four bridges. To convince yourself this is really the state capital, you must leave the flood plain and hike up to the higher plateau.

I tied up at Captain Freddie's floating dock. I approached a group of realtors to ask for directions. The loud obnoxious woman leading the group looked me up and down, disdainfully. She apparently came to the conclusion that this sweaty guy in grubby clothes fresh from the river was not in town to buy a home. She let me know they didn't have time to talk.

I was grateful to meet Gene, Gretchen, and Dave just before ordering lunch. After devouring a prime rib sandwich while visiting with them in the restaurant, they gave me a lift to the Kentwood Mall, where I purchased a wind-up radio as a spare, got a haircut, went to Dan's Grocery, and had a McDonald's strawberry shake.

After returning to Captain Freddie's, my server told me that I would probably be able to find a campsite about four miles downstream from Bismarck at Fort Abraham Lincoln State Park. So, back to the river I went. At the campground at the confluence with the Heart River, RVs and a few tents nestled among the trees and close to the site of George Custer's residence, before his last stand at Little Big Horn. When my campground neighbors, the Allens, stopped by with leftovers from their filet mignon dinner, I had absolutely no trouble wolfing the food down. I slept well, despite the fact that the next day I would be entering Lake Oahe, the longest and reputedly most dangerous reservoir on the Missouri River.

Wind and Rattlesnake Country

Lake Oahe is 231 miles long. To illustrate some of what was on my mind, here are some of the warnings offered by David Miller in his guide on navigating Lake Oahe:

"This lake has a well-deserved reputation for being the most dangerous for small craft of all the Upper Missouri's reservoirs. . . . Winds from the northwest or southeast can come up quickly and blow hard for days at a time. . . . To get to a suitable campsite (at low-water levels), you may have to slog through several hundred yards of mud. . . . This lake will test your skills, conditioning, judgement, and patience like no other body of water I've paddled upon."

My second day on Lake Oahe, the Fourth of July, was like my

first when I sought temporary refuge from high wind and waves at the appropriately named town of Huff. After spending the night on a sandbar near Fort Rice (RM 1,275), I shoved off on day two about one hour after sunrise into deceptively flat calm water.

It was still early in the morning when the sky suddenly turned dark gray. The wind blew hard, bunching two-to-three-foot-high waves. Last night during a check in phone call, Joyce had advised me that high winds were expected, but I never dreamed the transition from placidity to fury would be so abrupt. When two rogue waves, each about four feet high, slammed into Whisper like a pair of cannonballs, we tipped. We were precariously close to being dumped when I braced to return Whisper to an even keel. Fearful of more close calls, I sped towards refuge on a beach near a town with another memorable name—Cannonball.

As I had done the day before, I walked the beach searching for a way to climb the bluff to the highway. Seeing no reasonable egress, I waited. When, after an hour and a half, the wind didn't subside, I pulled Whisper along the shore, finally finding a protected cove where I could launch my kayak. With a tailwind and a diminishing current, I re-entered Lake Oahe. Eight hours and twenty miles later, bone tired from the battle with waves, I hauled out at a marginal riverside campsite near Fort Yates, North Dakota. Just before falling asleep, I read that Fort Yates, named for an officer killed along with Custer at his last stand, was where Chief Sitting Bull was imprisoned and buried until his people stealthily came in the night and took his body away.

Cannonball, North Dakota, went on to notoriety in late 2016 as the focus of the protest over the Dakota Access Pipeline (DAPL), intended to transport Bakken crude to the US Midwest. Various news media reported that the protest was the largest gathering of Native Americans and their supporters in more than 100-to-150 years. *Underground Construction* (Robert Carpenter, November 2016), an industry newsletter, reporting on the DAPL, wrote, "circling environmental buzzards swooped down to feast on the potential carrion of another defeated pipeline project," an article that went to press before the election of Donald Trump. Although both sides exaggerated their causes, I found that the Standing Rock Sioux Tribe, whose reservation is located just downstream of the proposed Missouri River pipeline crossing, had some legitimate gripes. Among them was the rerouting of the pipeline from just upstream of Bismarck to just upstream of their land because of concerns expressed by Bismarck's predominately Anglo residents, and the failure of the Corps of Engineers to consult with the tribe regarding water quality and the destruction of burial and sacred sites. To the tribe's concerns I would add the broader issue that fossil-fuel projects frequently pass on so-called legacy costs such as climate change, to future generations.

This area will remain an iconic place for me. I revisited Cannonball and Fort Abraham Lincoln with Joyce in mid-2016, in part because I developed a strong interest in environmental and racial justice. The plants, animals, and people I had already observed on this trip were a strong reminder of all we have to lose.

My third day on Lake Oahe began with the low wind and calm water I now knew was typical of early morning. By noon I had crossed into South Dakota. Facing a strong headwind, I moved to the shoreline. At every break in the bluff, the wind coursing down the side canyons blew me farther out into the lake. Whisper's bow, lacking sufficient weight, kept weather-vanning, making it difficult to steer. Exhausted after struggling against the wind for several hours I finally gave up and pulled ashore in a small cove twenty-five miles above Mobridge, South Dakota, just downstream from the Point of View community at about RM 1,215.

Once again, sticky mud made it difficult to get to shore and set up camp. To add to the challenge, it rained during the night, the accumulation of mud making it equally difficult to break camp the next morning. By the time I finally finished loading, most of my gear and I were coated with sticky slime.

It was a great relief when I was able to end that day at Bridge City Marina south of Mobridge (RM 1,191). I cleaned my gear with a hose, washed myself in a long shower and slept in a clean, comfortable cabin.

Mike Norder and his family, the proud new owners of the Bridge City Marina, treated me royally and took me to Mobridge for fried chicken and to replenish my supplies. In addition to the fried chicken, I gorged myself on two microwave pizzas in the marina's cafe.

The next morning, I called my son Mike. He told me that the light wind and mild temperatures expected for the next two days would change to stormy weather on day three. With only 120 miles to Pierre, South Dakota, I was anxious to finish before the storm hit. I paddled for 12 hours, finishing the day just downstream from the East Whitlock Highway 212 Bridge (RM 1,152).

For the first time in four days, I found myself among other people, but not the type I wanted to be near. Their loud voices and coarse language suggested that many were well on their way to being drunk, and if they were crude now, it was only going to get worse. I hid my tent among the low bushes near shore and tried to keep out of view. The revelers kept me awake until well after midnight shooting off their leftover fireworks and singing—or was it yelling? Only when I thought they had packed up and gone home was I finally able to fall asleep.

After my restless nights' sleep, I shoved off onto a flat calm lake. I soon saw dozens of expensive fishing boats speeding south. The previous night, Mike Norder told me the lake is a fisher's paradise, home to northern pike, bass and even salmon, with the most popular game fish being walleye, the South Dakota state fish.

While paddling the calm waters, on what would turn out to be my last paddling day on Lake Oahe, I spotted something long and slender winding its way toward Whisper like a torpedo bearing down on its target. I remembered being warned that rattlesnakes are capable of climbing into small boats when they are tired of the water. Without waiting to confirm whether this speeding missile had a rattle on its tail, I paddled as fast as I could. I spent the next hour frequently looking over my shoulder and wondering what my fate would have been if the snake had joined me in Whisper's cockpit.

Approaching Little Bend, about forty river miles from Oahe Dam,

I had three options. Traveling around the bend by kayak would expose me to the predicted strong adverse wind and waves at the confluence with the Cheyenne River near the tip of the bend. Portaging across the half-mile-wide neck would save twenty miles compared to the river route, but the terrain is rough and, according to Miller, rattlesnakes abound. One tried to crawl into his tent. With my shoulder hurting and wanting to avoid rattlesnakes, I decided to take the third option and portage by road. First, I had to get Whisper out of the valley. The 300-to-400-foot rise from the river was so steep I had to pull Whisper with all my might while facing downhill to avoid being dragged back to the river. Even so, I stumbled twice, each time taking a short slide downhill on my butt. While pulling Whisper, a friendly game warden approached me and offered to reserve a place for me at the West Prairie Resort, a large, well-equipped, and very busy fishing resort.

When I finally arrived at my destination drenched in sweat, the Nelson family, owners of the resort, and their hostess, Jessica, had a pitcher of ice water waiting for me. I celebrated with a dinner of fried chicken, salad bar, and ice cream for dessert. It helped remembering that in a day, or two at most, the trouble would be behind me.

I pulled out Miller's guide before going to sleep and read that after reaching Oahe Dam, I would "have the satisfaction of knowing that (I had) successfully negotiated the most difficult obstacle to making a complete passage down the Missouri River." I still had to get there, but it was a huge relief to know I was close. It would be disingenuous to suggest that I wasn't proud of what I'd accomplished so far. Here I was, age seventy, and held together by artificial body parts, but I felt like Odysseus, or how I imagined he felt. I could conquer anything this long lake had to throw at me.

A Long Portage

The next morning, I loaded Whisper on her wheels and again started pulling. The portages at Fort Peck and Garrison Dam were four and fourteen miles, respectively, but this one was about twenty-four miles, three miles from the river to the resort and then twenty-one miles down the road. Between West Prairie resort and the dam there was little traffic and only one steep hill, but people, water, and shade were scarce. I again encountered Western hospitality. Larry, a local farmer, invited me into his farmhouse for water and a rest and several motorists stopped to offer me the thing that became more precious as the day wore on, water. By midafternoon, I feared heat stroke and, despite nearing the end of my journey, felt like giving up. A long drink of water, and a short rest in the shade of one of the rare trees along my route, helped. After nine-plus hours of pulling, I arrived at Oahe Visitor Center. There, two women stopped by to congratulate me. One was Jessica, my hostess from the night before. An hour after touring and resting at the visitor center, and drinking water like a thirsty camel, I rolled my kayak down the road to the bottom of the 245-foot-high Oahe Dam, and arrived at my final destination, the Oahe Marina (RM 1,072).

Steve Rounds, owner of the marina sat with me while I ate the fried chicken dinner prepared by his staff. He expressed genuine interest in my trip similar to the interest I showed when he described almost losing the marina in the 2011 flood. I don't know if Steve told the staff to be nice to me or if, as I suspect, that was normal for them, but I was treated like royalty. When I asked Steve to recommend a storage facility where I could keep Whisper until next year, he offered to let me keep my kayak at his marina.

Postscript V

The next day, I spent visiting the state capitol in Pierre, where Steve Round's brother recently served as governor. As the second smallest state capital in the United States, after tiny Montpelier, Vermont, I found Pierre to be the perfect size for me. People were friendly and proud of their quiet and historic downtown. The sound and smell of the river along with the lush green parks and the tree-lined streets contrasted pleasantly with the brown of the surrounding hills. It reminded me of Boise, where my daughter and her family live. After lunch, I spent a relaxing two hours at the below-ground Visitor and Cultural Center where I learned, among other things, that South Dakota was the first state to generate power using nuclear energy.

After returning to the marina on Pierre's convenient and inexpensive public transportation system, I had my first taste of walleye, prepared by Dar, Steve Round's chief assistant and cook. The white, flakey, and mild tasting filets, somewhat like flounder, were pan fried with melted herb butter and served with French fries and a lettuce and tomato salad. I now understood why walleye are so sought after.

After preparing Whisper to winter at the marina, all that was left was the long trip home. I took two buses to Great Falls, where I got a lift from Bill Maris, a river guide to Fort Benton. My Volvo was just as I had left it. Driving home via the Little Big Horn battlefield, I arrived just before Joyce's and my 47th anniversary, and in plenty of time for Greg's birthday.

I was never bored on this reach of the river, but I was often very lonely. I had paddled too many hours a day, had eaten too little, and lost more than twenty pounds. The 1,003 river miles on the Missouri took me the same number of days it had taken Lewis and his crew. Of course, the Expedition had heavy boats and much more to carry, the need to care for Lewis' gunshot injury, and the need to hunt or bargain for their food. I, on the other hand, had those dam reservoirs. For an old man, I felt that I acquitted myself rather well. Sure, I would have liked to have been greeted by my family, or really by anyone who might have understood the hardships I'd faced. Someone who might have corroborated my desire to pat myself metaphorically on the back and say, "Hank, that was some pretty tough going!" For an old guy, you did rather well. Of course, no one showed up. It was just me there at the end. Funny thing about success and desire. Having achieved this difficult goal, already I started worrying about next year.

White Cliffs

White Cliffs at McClelland Ferry

Confluence of Yellowstone and Missouri Rivers

Campsite below Little Missouri River

Highway 212 Bridge at East Whitlock

Out of the valley after a long kayak pull

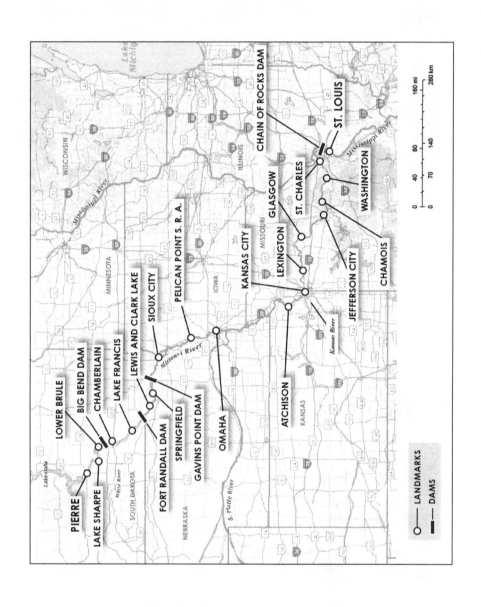

PIERRE
LAKE SHARPE
LOWER BRULE
BIG BEND DAM
CHAMBERLAIN
LAKE FRANCIS
LEWIS AND CLARK LAKE
SIOUX CITY
FORT RANDALL DAM
SPRINGFIELD
GAVINS POINT DAM
OMAHA
PELICAN POINT S. R. A.
ATCHISON
KANSAS CITY
GLASGOW
LEXINGTON
ST. CHARLES
CHAIN OF ROCKS DAM
ST. LOUIS
WASHINGTON
JEFFERSON CITY
CHAMOIS

Missouri River
Mississippi River
Kansas River
White River
S. Platte River
Lake Oahe

SOUTH DAKOTA
NEBRASKA
MINNESOTA
WISCONSIN
IOWA
MISSOURI
KANSAS
ILLINOIS
Lake Michigan

○── LANDMARKS
▬▬ DAMS

0   40   80   160 mi
0   70   140   280 km

VI

The Lower Missouri

2013

Shoving off from Oahe Marina

Self Confidence Ebbs and Flows

The sun was setting below the hilltops when I drove down the long grade into the valley of the Missouri River near Pierre, South Dakota. There was still enough light to see whitecaps being pushed by a southerly wind on the mile-wide reservoir known as Lake Sharpe. The thought of paddling into a strong upstream wind combined with pain in my left shoulder and elbow made my mood as dark as the approaching night.

A day and a half later, the rising golden sun lifted both the morning fog and my spirits while I said goodbye to the kind folks at the Oahe Marina (RM 1072) who had agreed to let me leave Joyce's 2005 Volvo station wagon with them while paddling south down the Missouri River. My mood improved even more when the horn at the massive Oahe Dam, signaled the welcome early morning release of water. Somewhat like riding the crest of a small wave, I rode the dam discharge over forty miles past brown prairie grasslands and green groves of mostly cottonwood trees before pulling ashore at an unofficial remote campsite replete with evidence of two unwelcome campsite visitors—party going humans and cattle.

The partiers left scattered trash among the scrub vegetation, and the cattle left scattered cow pies and water filled footprints close to the river. I was on the left (east) bank and knew permission from the Crow Creek Tribe was needed to camp on their side of the river. Despite repeated attempts, I was unable to contact the tribal offices on my cell phone, and the strong afternoon wind made it risky for me to cross to the other side of the river. I picked up trash to compensate for trespassing. Fortunately, the deteriorating weather discouraged both revelry and tribal wardens, and the cattle were off visiting their friends, or doing whatever cattle do.

The Teton (Lakota) Sioux

Awakening to heavy rain and a howling onshore wind shaking my tent, I saw two to three-foot-high waves breaking on the low-banked shore. It would be difficult to buck the wind, and the waves crashing on the beach could easily capsize Whisper. After the rain stopped, I took down my tent and packed my gear, except for a ground cover and the sleeping bag that I crawled back into while I waited for the wind to abate. Not being able to get a weather report, I soon began to worry that it might be necessary for me to spend the entire day and the next night at this isolated campsite, far from a paved road and with only an overgrown dirt path for access and egress. Hanging out for one day wouldn't be bad, but I had no idea how long the wind would last. Three hours after first awakening, I opened my eyes again and peaked from beneath my sleeping bag hood to see that the wind was much reduced. I rushed to shove off before the wind picked up again.

I had yet to decide whether to paddle around Big Bend, a twenty-five-mile loop that returns to within a mile and a half of its starting place, as opposed to portaging overland. Warned by several people in Pierre not to portage the loop on the Lower Brule Reservation, home of the Teton (Lakota) Sioux, I called the tribal office and spoke to Sheldon Fletcher, a tribal fish and wildlife agent. "You don't need anyone's permission to be on our land," Sheldon said. "Can I help you bring your kayak to the village?" The warmth of Sheldon's welcome made me wonder if the tribe that almost put an abrupt end to the Discovery Expedition would prove to be a much kinder host in this century than it was in the 1800's. I could only speculate that Anglo residents of Pierre who advised me not to stop at the reservation did so for a reason that is all too common—fear of people you don't know.

I decided to portage the bend. I was afraid to cross the rugged-rattlesnake-ridden terrain at the neck where nineteenth century steamboat captains allowed passengers to stretch their legs while the boats labored around the loop. I preferred pulling Whisper on paved roads. According to Steve Rounds, my host at the Oahe Marina, the first stretch of road after my pull-out at the Iron Mountain boat ramp went straight up. Steve exaggerated—slightly. The climb was so steep that it was necessary for me to stop to wipe the sweat from my eyes and catch my breath every fifty-to-one-hundred paces. Several people offered help. The first Samaritan was a teenage boy driving a car that had seen much better days. He slurred his speech and appeared disoriented. The next two motorists I met were sober and sincere in their interest in helping me. I declined their offers. Connie Badhorse recited a little of her family's history. There were tears as she told me about her grandfather being killed by white settlers. I wanted to ask her about the many run-down homes scattered among those that were well cared for, but I couldn't think of a respectful way to express my curiosity without seeming critical.

Thunderstorms threatened soon after pulling Whisper into Lower Brule (RM 993), the tribal community. After pitching my tent, Shorty, the only other camper in the tribal campground, warned me that a major storm with wind that could shake his RV and blow my tent down was to arrive that evening. "Don't pay for this campsite," he told me "They don't take care of this place." It was an easy decision to seek better shelter and dinner across the road at the comfortable Golden Buffalo Resort where a deliciously tender prime rib and baked potato for only $8.95 waited for me at the casino restaurant. My pleasant stay on the reservation belied the dire warnings I had received.

The next morning, downstream from the dam, on 107-mile-long Lake Frances Case, I passed many smiling fishermen, most of them reeling in the walleye they prized. While paddling past jumping fish that had so far eluded the hook, I relaxed to the music of cattle lowing along the distant shore. Midafternoon found me greeted by the friendly folks at the crowded, full service American Campground in Chamberlain, SD. Soon after pitching my tent at a shaded campsite close enough to the boat ramp that I could see Whisper, I struck up a conversation with an extended family of ranchers who planned to kayak for the first time.

"You are now in the best cattle country in the United States," they told me. They were the only kayakers I had seen since leaving Portland, and the only ones, but for two more, I would encounter on or camping along the Missouri River. In exchange for some tips from me on river kayaking, they agreed to watch Whisper while I walked into town.

While crossing a side street, two grizzled old guys (like me) on an all-terrain vehicle came screeching to a stop just short of hitting me. "My buddy told me to do it," the driver said. I didn't know if "doing it," meant aiming for me or stopping. After my walk, I enjoyed a strawberry shake and an extra-large Sprite at a McDonald's. Returning to my campsite and finding my possessions in order, I prepared a dinner of Indian vegetables in a pouch, with a fruit cup for dessert.

The next day saw me paddling over forty-six miles to reach my next campsite at Snake Creek State Park (RM 967). Just downstream from Chamberlain, SD, at the confluence with the misnamed White River, the shallow water became so muddy that it was impossible for me to distinguish the bottom mud from the river water. I feared it was due to a submerged mudflow entering the Missouri River from the White River. I steadied myself to avoid capsizing, not knowing if the bottom would support my weight or if it would even be possible to swim in the muck. Like Mark Twain, I pondered whether the Missouri River is too thick to drink and too thin to plow.

I relaxed a little after paddling past the shallow water and mud banks at the confluence. Had I run aground, I don't know how I would have freed Whisper. The bottom was too soft to allow me to pole Whisper off the mudbank, and the current was probably running too fast for me to maneuver back upstream into deeper water.

Despite a slight tailwind, it took eleven long hours to reach Snake Creek. For the final three hours, pains in my arms, shoulders and left heel plagued me. During a period of still air shortly before reaching the campsite, mosquitoes and biting flies harassed me in the middle of the mile-wide reservoir, the first-time bugs had attacked in force so far from shore. After finally pitching my tent at Snake Creek, I jumped into the tepid water at the swimming beach to shed the bugs and ease my pains, remaining there until a rising wind drove the bugs away.

The next day, high wind and waves threatened, but I no longer feared these conditions as much as in past years. During one straight stretch of river, a modest tailwind allowed me to do a little kayak surfing. It was exhilarating, but when the wind and my adrenalin level plummeted, I found myself dragging and counting the miles to North Wheeler State Park (RM 896). It was early afternoon when I pulled up at the park's sandy beach. The fish must have been biting because flies were eating the many fish carcasses for dinner and the campsite guests for dessert. Amy and Marty Slaughter and their sons were camped nearby while on their annual fishing-camping vacation. The Slaughters shared a feast of steak, walleye, striped bass, fried potatoes, and fruit. Amy is an art teacher. Marty is the principal of a primary grade school with many students from the Winnebago and Omaha Tribes. With thoughts of Lower Brule still fresh, this delightful couple told me about the difficult conditions faced by the tribes.

"These are two tribes who never fought against the United States, and where did it get them?" Amy lamented. "Contentious treaties kept taking more and more of their land, and efforts to assimilate them in white culture deprived them of their heritage and language."

Marty added, "Unemployment is at a critical level. It recently hit 82 percent, and with no jobs and severe drug and alcohol use in the homes, it is difficult to motivate students. But there is reason for optimism. There are always some children who rise above their conditions and the Winnebago recently opened a casino that provides some jobs. The Omaha are further behind, but the competitive nature of the two tribes may soon elevate them both."

The next morning, I paddled past expensive fishing boats and hundreds of fish swimming below me in clear water, contrasting dramatically with the water at the mouth of the White River, before arriving at Fort Randall Dam (RM 880) shortly before noon. The two-mile portage at Fort Randall provided some relief from the aches and pains of paddling. That night I camped across from the Yankton Sioux Reservation on a sandy beach with scattered low bushes (RM 864). Seeing human and dog footprints led me to believe that I was on private property, something I tried to avoid both for my own safety and in consideration of property owners. At this campsite, I was not bothered, nor do I think I bothered anyone.

While paddling Whisper under partly cloudy skies on the approach to Lake Lewis and Clark, my thoughts turned to the unusually good weather I had encountered this year. Except for the morning of the second day, headwinds were not strong enough to discourage me, and I had not yet seen any lightning close enough to threaten me while on the river. As if to even the score for three days of good weather, the sky quickly darkened to a chorus of thunder while I approached Springfield, South Dakota.

This was definitely not a good place to get caught on the river during a storm. Like the upper reaches of other Missouri River reservoirs, the river near Springfield was clogged with mud flats and low islands and rapidly changing channels. They offered little protection from the wind, waves, lightning, and hail predicted to arrive that afternoon. David Miller, in his guide, noted that the approach to Springfield is one of the most difficult sections of the Missouri River. Things might have gotten even worse since he paddled the river in 2004. Flooding in 2011 had created new sandbars and dead-end channels not shown on the route recommended by Miller.

I paddled into one channel only to find it was a dead end. Losing ground only to have to paddle the distance again was something I dreaded. My spirits dropped until desperation replaced dismay. I realized that I had to get into high gear to beat the approaching storm. My spirits sank each time I was confronted with an uncertain path. I began to doubt I would make it to Springfield until I saw the homes and other buildings on the left bank.

After miles of searching for a safe exit from the river, I pulled into the Sand Creek campground (RM 829) just when the wind began to blow. Even in the park-like setting, surrounded by many trees, the wind was too gusty for me to pitch my tent and the rain was too cold for me to remain outside. Without warning, a heavy branch from a cottonwood tree suddenly fell within several yards of where I had planned to pitch my tent. The only available refuge from the rain, wind, and killer trees was an almost new concrete block privy that smelled better than me. I spent over an hour huddled in the cleanest outhouse I had ever encountered, while waiting for the wind and rain to stop beating on my refuge.

The next morning, I emerged from my tent to find two fishermen at the water's edge. They told me they had to abandon their fishing because of gale force wind on Lewis and Clark Lake, the smallest of the six Missouri River reservoirs in both storage volume and shoreline length and only two miles downstream. "You are crazy if you go out there," they ventured. Not in the mood to sit still and suspecting that the fishermen exaggerated (after all they were fishermen), I shoved off. I remained surprisingly calm. I could have sought refuge at several protected coves along my route, but it wasn't necessary. Soon after arriving at the open water reservoir above the dam, the wind dropped to well below gale force for the two hours it took me to reach Gavins Point Dam (RM 811).

The portage at the dam was more complicated than most because of construction related detours. Corps of Engineers personnel offered to haul Whisper across the dam to the put-in ramp. I thanked them but declined, still bent on doing the trip without motorized assistance. Downstream from the dam, the current gave me a nice boost. I was making good time and soon found myself overtaking a father and daughter paddling together. David, an experienced kayaker, was obviously much more enthusiastic about the trip than his college-aged daughter, Michelle. David and I conversed while paddling. Michelle said very little.

Paddling together, late in the afternoon we reached a very wide level sandbar (RM 793) where we decided to camp together. I hoped we would all eat together, but when they didn't suggest it, I prepared a rather spicy lentil dinner in a pouch with peaches in syrup for dessert.

While I said goodbye the next morning, father and daughter were trying to decide whether they would end their trip in Vermillion SD as Michelle preferred or continue to Sioux City, SD, sixty miles farther, as originally planned. David smiled while Michelle looked very unhappy. I couldn't remember having similar experiences with my children, but it was easy to remember the dirty looks I got from Joyce when I suggested going "just one more mile."

The Multiple Missouri Rivers: Second Impression

The Missouri is many rivers, free flowing, dammed (or damned) and channelized, with each segment being roughly one-third the total length. Gavins Point Dam is the farthest downstream of the Missouri River dams and the fourteenth dam I portaged since leaving the Pacific Ocean. While in the free-flowing reach below the dam, I again felt much closer to the Discovery Expedition. On my first full day on the free-flowing river, some bottom grabbing sandbars slowed me while I paddled past gray cliffs capped with a band of yellow rock shining like a golden crown in the morning sun. Timid deer and a shy coyote came down to the river along woody ravines lined with oak and cedar to drink and stare at me while swarms of swallows defended me by voraciously attacking the insect population. A rare golden eagle complemented the gleaming bluff while it soared gracefully in the upward thermals.

Late that afternoon saw Whisper and me entering the 735 miles of channelized river beginning upstream of Sioux City, Iowa. There were many more people, and more boats on the river. I had my first encounter with a water skier, being pulled by a speeding cabin cruiser that passed so close it almost swamped me. I was reminded of Karl Adams encounter with a canoeist who lost a friend, and whose wife was severely injured, when a speeding power boat plowed into his boat. I wished I hadn't left my boat horn at home.

It is hard to find campsites in or near most cities, but Sioux City was a welcome exception. Although the flood in 2011 had silted in my intended landing at the city's protected boat basin, I made a U-turn and fought my way back upstream from the basin to exit Whisper in a strong current adjacent to South Sioux City Park (RM 733) on the right (west) bank in Nebraska. The lightly wooded park, perched on level land about fifteen feet above the beach, had over a hundred camping pads with utilities, a tent area, and four concrete block cabins resembling cell blocks, one of which served me well. After calling my son Greg to wish him happy birthday, I went off looking for a steak dinner and found one at an upscale riverfront restaurant. Even after changing to long pants and a clean shirt, I felt out of place amongst some of Sioux City's elegant citizens.

Upon returning to my campsite, I encountered Bill Heiman, from Ashland, Oregon, who was tent camping nearby. Other than Thom and Tyler, the two young canoeists I met at the Fort Peck Dam, Bill was the only long-distance paddler I encountered between the Pacific and the Atlantic Oceans. He was just finishing a canoe trip from Three Forks, Montana. Apparently, this was one of his shorter adventures, having bicycled around the world and paddled other rivers in the United States. I would have enjoyed staying up late swapping tales, but after padding over ten hours non-stop that day, I needed sleep. Some years later, I asked Bill if it wasn't much harder to paddle a canoe in open water than a kayak. "I can keep up with kayakers half my age," he said. I told him that a male friend and I once challenged Joyce and a female friend to a race, the women in our canoe and the men in our double kayak. The women crossed the finish line first, but they were rather upset when they saw a rope tied between the two boats and realized they had been pulling us. "No dinner for you two tonight," Joyce quipped.

Midwest Hospitality

Perhaps there is something about being an old guy alone in a kayak or at a campsite that brings out the best in people. After a long day of paddling, I arrived at Pelican Point Park, a clean wooded campground (RM 673). "How about joining us?" John and Sharon Bitter called out. The Bitters, semi-retired from their concrete products and lawn ornament outlet store in nearby Tekamah, NE, fed me an incredible chicken dinner with all the trimmings, including the most delicious zucchini bread. While we sat by their campfire after dinner, we compared my youth in and around New York City to their lives in the Midwest. "Ours is a good life," they told me. I had to agree that it seemed much better than NYC's paved canyons and pushy people. Even though we have many friends who love NYC, Joyce and I have never regretted migrating west to Washington State. I shouldn't speak for Joyce, but I don't join in singing "New York, New York, it's a wonderful town . . ." at class reunions.

After comparing the attributes of city verses rural life, the Bitters pulled out their fishing gear and demonstrated the finer art of using a trip line to catch catfish. I learned that catfish are carnivorous, one of their favorite foods being sand toads that wash into the river after storms. The Bitter's bait consisted of goldfish and frogs; one sad looking frog missing two appendages had already helped catch two big catfish.

The next morning, after enjoying more of Sharon's zucchini bread with coffee, I shoved off bearing a sack lunch Sharon had packed for me. Sharon also offered to send some of my unneeded gear back to Joyce. I gave her some money for postage. Actual postage was less so Sharon sent the excess money to Joyce along with a note that conveyed the warmth I felt while in the company of Sharon and John. After returning home, I wrote the Bitters to thank them. Sharon followed up with some photos taken of the three of us. *It's not about the destination,* I told myself, *it's about the friends you make along the way, like the Bitters.*

While camping with the Bitters at Pelican Point Park I saw the first, and only flock of white pelicans, a vanishing species, on this year's trip. Like a chicken-and-egg puzzle, it is strange that they would visit one of the two Missouri River parks named after them.

While paddling toward Omaha on July 29, 2013, which for a midsummer morning was near-record chilly, I passed the campsite where Lewis and Clark stayed exactly 209 years ago, two and a half months into their arduous upstream journey. This was the only confluence of day, month and location for their roundtrip and my trip. The expedition poled and rowed hard upstream, averaging less than ten miles per day while I was paddling downstream at forty-five-to-fifty-five miles per day. Near this location, Clark reported that they were in the land of the Otto Tribe where they encountered numerous very large catfish. Clark also noted that the one Missouri Indian he met was one of the few survivors of that tribe.

Omaha was nicer and friendlier than I remembered from past visits. Mark, the caretaker at Dodge Park and Marina (RM 580) obtained permission for me to camp at this restricted facility. City leaders seemed focused on improving the waterfront, including a graceful, curved cable-stayed pedestrian and bicycle bridge across the Missouri River connecting trails in Omaha, Nebraska, and Council Bluffs, Iowa.

Less than fifteen miles below Omaha, I began to see many more birds: wild turkeys on riverbanks, kingfishers darting back and forth among the trees, eagles soaring above and the first cormorant that greeted me east of the Rocky Mountains. Other than many blue herons, I still saw no other herons or egrets. My enjoyment in seeing the many and varied bird life changed when I came across the first evidence of direct discharge of sewage to the river, in the form of storm water combined with untreated human waste. I pulled away from shore to avoid the repugnant brown liquid pouring from the pipe. Combined discharges, now being eliminated in the US, are a legacy of communities avoiding the costs of separate storm drain and waste disposal pipes. No longer would I wash my dishes in the river or take river baths unless far from a city.

The Missouri River of the Future

While paddling the lower 735 miles on the Missouri, I was witnessing the rebirth of a river. Early in the 1900s, Congress charged the USACE with "taming" the river to reduce flooding and improve navigation.

These measures straightened the river, added levees, wing dikes and more land suitable for farming, but in the process greatly reduced habitat. The Endangered Species Act and the Missouri River Recovery Program provided incentives and the means to correct some of the unintended consequences of river taming. Under the leadership of the USACE, the US government bought at least thirty-two parcels from willing sellers. The government paid market prices for the land even though many farmers had obtained free land behind the new levees when the river was straightened. The USACE is now relocating levees and dikes to form sandbars, chutes, and deep pools conducive to habitat, while maintaining navigation and flood control. My spirits were lifted by the thought that my children, and grandchildren, if they chose to travel on the Missouri river might enjoy an experience comparable or even better than mine.

Downstream from Omaha, I had my first close encounter with a Corps of Engineers team working to restore the natural habitat. After pulling ashore on the left bank at RM 531 and driving a stake in the ground to secure Whisper, a Corps of Engineers tug and sand-laden barge approached heading downstream close to the bank. Concerned that the tug's wake would wash over the bank and dislodge the stake, I rushed from my tent to hold on to Whisper just as the tug's bow wave climbed up the bank, washing over Whisper's stern. I held my ground when the undertow tried to pull Whisper and me back into the river, all the time remembering the story of one paddler who was sucked back into the river in the path of large pleasure craft. The boat swerved to miss him.

Wanting to stretch my legs, I walked through a band of trees about two hundred feet wide bordering the river, where I was surprised to observe fields of corn as far as my eyes could see. Somewhere during the past two hundred or so miles, the best cattle land in the country had transitioned to some of the best farmland. For some reason, I continued to be surprised that there is a much different world beyond the river.

At first light the next morning another tug passed by in fog so dense and surreal it made me feel that I was alone in a hostile world. I waited to launch until the fog diminished. It soon closed in again.

With no safe place to pull ashore, I stopped paddling and drifted warily while listening for approaching tugs. It was eerily silent, but memories of my experience with the stealth freighter that sneaked up on me on the Columbia River, kept me on full alert until the fog finally cleared.

The farther I went, the more I wondered whether it was worth the cost of dredging the channel or maintaining all the navigation aids. In all my time on the Missouri River I encountered only one moving tug and barge that was not involved in dredging or dike construction. Apparently transport by barge, even though less costly than rail and truck under good river conditions, is not dependable. Very low and very high river levels impede the tugs and barges but do much less to impede road and rail travel.

Just as the river is changing in the new millennium, so too are the river towns. The loss in shipping combined with the advent of mega stores, is taking a disastrous toll. Many establishments mentioned in relatively recent guides are gone, having been supplanted by mega stores five-to-fifteen miles away from the river, especially where there is no bridge over the Missouri. The larger inland stores draw from an arc of 360 degrees, while those on the river draw from only half that arc. Other than nice people, there seemed to be little life left in the many small towns I passed. Signs of death, like rusting grain elevators and abandoned buildings, made me feel like our country was losing its history, and I was losing friends. I found two poignant reminders of both the death of institutions and the resiliency of humans 100- and 300-miles downstream during my stops at Miami and Chamois, Missouri.

There were exceptions to the decline of small towns. Atchison, Kansas (RM 423) has a well-landscaped riverfront park, excellent restaurants, and a pedestrian friendly shopping mall. A police dispatcher told me camping was allowed along the river, but a patrol officer overruled her and politely asked me to move my tent. Kelly and her partner Todd at Ruby's Landing offered to let me camp on a plot of grass next to their restaurant, where I later enjoyed a catfish dinner.

Before leaving the next morning, I approached a group of about a dozen older men gathered at the community dock. After sharing that they met every day of the year at 6 a.m. for coffee and conversation, they gave me an update on river conditions. Apparently, the river was about the same as usual for this time of year. "I can't remember when I last saw a grain barge," one older man remarked, confirming my suspicion of little commercial barge traffic.

My plan was to stop for a day of rest at a riverfront casino in either St. Joseph or Kansas City, but my intended destinations in both cities were closed for renovations. After a long period of neglect, Kansas City, like Omaha, seems to be taking advantage of the history and amenities the river offers. I spent the night at Kaw Point Park, Kansas (RM 367), about where the Lewis and Clark Expedition camped while heading west. Unsure if camping was allowed, I hid my tent in an out of the way location. There was a lot of trash along the riverbank near the boat ramp, but the park itself was clean and well designed with two creative amphitheaters, one honoring the entire Lewis and Clark Expedition with the names of all members carved in limestone blocks, the other honoring Native Americans with the names of Midwest Tribes inscribed on brass plaques. I picked up some trash to pay my camping fee. An overnight fishing tournament was about to begin, and the boat ramp soon became crowded with catfish hunters, most of them arriving with their expensive boats and equipment on trailers. The event crew had filled a large plastic pool with fresh water to keep the fish alive until they were weighed. I asked if I could rinse myself with their hose.

"This is for fish, and you don't look like a fish" one worker remarked.

"Yeah, but he sure smells as bad as a fish. Better that he rinses himself off," said another worker.

The next morning, I learned that the winner caught an eighty-pound channel catfish. A little research told me that in 2012 Rob Stanley, while fishing with Brad Kilpatrick, the president of K.C. Catfish caught and released a blue catfish weighing 102.8 pounds, more than the weight of Whisper.

The current grew noticeably stronger now that I was below the

confluence with the Platte and Kansas Rivers. Heading upstream on
the Columbia River or into the wind on the reservoirs of the Missouri
River, I was lucky to make 2 mph. Below Kansas City, where the river
flow increased, I sometimes exceeded 7 mph, not fast compared to
powerboats, but like a water slide to me.

My fear of forecast flood conditions below Kansas City was
exacerbated by my meager knowledge of this reach of the river. I had
tried to find maps and charts similar to those available for the upper
Missouri and the dammed Missouri with no luck. While at Kaw Point,
Missouri Wildlife Agents Dan Schepis and Aaron Post approached me.
"Where are you headed?" they asked. When I told them about my trip,
they gave me the very recent and very helpful USACE guide, "Aerial
Photography and Maps of the Missouri River."

Now that I was encountering tugs and barges and many wing dams,
I wanted to make sure I knew how to pick the safest route. The US
Coast Guard has the responsibility for maintaining aids to navigation,
including buoys marking the main navigation channel and daymarks
to inform when to cross from one side of the river to the other. I found
very few buoys were in place, perhaps twenty, between Sioux City and
the confluence with the Mississippi. Most were either washed up on
riverbanks or in piles on the shore. Dan Schepis told me that the last
flood swept most buoys away. Only the ones in critical locations had
been replaced. The daymarks were better maintained but the otherwise
excellent river maps and guides published by the USACE were less than
clear in describing how to interpret them. I feared crossing in the wrong
direction and getting in the way of a tug.

Floodwater Around the Bend

Below Kansas City fewer people asked about my journey and those
who did usually wanted to know why I wasn't going all the way to New
Orleans. I suspect this is because of the greater number of boaters who
either paddle or float this part of the river, and because of the Missouri

River 340, an annual event billed as the longest kayak/canoe race in the world. It begins at Kaw Point Park and ends 340 miles downstream in St. Charles, Missouri, thirty miles from the confluence with the Mississippi. While it took me six and a half days to paddle this reach of the river, the winning racers sometimes do it in less than two.

I began to encounter silver (also called Asian and flying) carp. The Bitters had experienced so many jumping carp that they appeared to be falling from the sky. These fish can be several feet long and jump very high when spooked, sometimes into or across a boat. People have died when hit in the head or knocked overboard. I read that I shouldn't worry because it was the vibration of the motors that excited the fish. Apparently, the carp hadn't read the same report.

When upstream of Lexington, Missouri, a large school began to jump all around me. Some flew into the side of my kayak like unguided missiles. They seemed to be following me. One jumped close to Whisper and hit my upper arm. No damage was done other than a large red bruise.

Upon arriving in Lexington (RM 316) I pulled Whisper well up on the riverbank and secured her to a stake before unpacking. After setting up my tent, I walked down to the river to take my evening bath. I met two fisherman, Kenneth and Raymond.

"Any rattlesnakes in the river near here," I asked.

"Don't expect any" was Kenneth's rather abrupt answer.

After taking my bath and doing some chores, I returned to the river.

"Were you the one who asked about rattlesnakes?" Raymond inquired.

When I answered yes, he suggested I broaden my inquiry.

Pointing to a place on the river not ten feet from where we stood, he added, "After you finished your bath, Ken killed a cottonmouth moccasin right about there. Cottonmouths are the most aggressive snakes around here," he added, "and this one was hanging out right where you entered the river."

Like a special present wrapped in brown paper, Lexington offers a surprise history lesson. The largest city west of St. Louis in the

1830s and 1840s, Lexington played major roles in both westward expansion and the Civil War. It was a major outfitter for westward bound emigrants. In 1852, the steamboat Saluda carried two hundred Mormons enroute to Salt Lake City. While increasing steam pressure to overcome the fast current, the Saluda exploded just upstream from Lexington, resulting in the death of about 150 passengers and crew.

Lexington was also home to two of the largest Civil War Battles of the western campaign. During the Battle of Lexington in 1861, a cannonball lodged in the city hall. After the war, a group of rebel soldiers known as Quantrill's Raiders refused to honor the ceasefire. Two months later, they entered the city under a white flag only to be attacked by Union soldiers. To even the score one of the wounded Quantrill's Raiders, Jessie James made it a point to return to Lexington and rob Lexington's Alexander Mitchell Bank in broad daylight.

Although unusual for me to leave Whisper or my gear alone, I left my campsite to do some exploring. A friendly family in an old beat-up sedan gave me a lift into town where I visited the 1861 Civil War battlefield, a monument to the steamboat Saluda, the Gothic revival Episcopal Church built in 1848, and took photos of the Civil War cannon ball still embedded in the town hall. After refueling on a trio of spicy enchiladas at Las Carretas restaurant, I became a little lost on the way back to camp. I asked a middle-aged woman with big hair pulling out of a McDonald's parking lot in her big white Cadillac for directions. She refused to answer my question or look directly at me. The expression on her face told me she was more afraid of me than I was of cottonmouth moccasins. I don't usually intimidate people, but I had to admit that my grisly beard, and muddy clothes did not inspire confidence.

Upon returning to my camp at dusk, I failed to check Whisper. The next morning, I walked to the riverbank and was startled to see that some person or persons had disconnected Whisper from her mooring stake and had tossed all my gear on the ground or in the river. My guess is that the vandals wanted to find things they could sell. With the exception of my graphite paddle almost all the gear I left in camp was of little value. They probably didn't know the value of the paddle.

Despite the rising river level, Whisper had not yet floated away, and the gear tossed into the water remained trapped in an eddy. Like a baggage claim carrousel, each item in its turn circled back to me.

There was no potable water available at the Lexington campground and none available at the two stops I made before arriving there. While paddling downstream from Lexington, I scanned the shoreline all morning for a place to refill my empty water bottles. Shortly after noon I saw something red in the river ahead of me. It was too big to be a buoy and appeared to be moving too slowly to be a fellow paddler. Nearing this strange object, I observed a young man lounging on a beach chair in an oversize red canoe. Finally, another paddler, someone I might be able to relate to. He was the first paddler I had encountered on the river since I passed Thom and Tyler above Fort Peck Dam, 1,500 miles upriver.

Bill Smith picked up his paddle every few minutes and took one or two strokes, smoked his cigarette, and relaxed in the sun. He had just quit his job in Kansas City and was canoeing and floating to an undetermined location—and future. Bill's relaxed approach to life was so different from mine, neither better nor worse, but certainly different. I doubt we figured out what made each other tick during our brief conversation. Sensing that he preferred to be alone with his thoughts and after he generously gave me enough water to get me to my next destination, I moved on.

As if to make up for the ill treatment at Lexington, gracious hospitality awaited me in Miami, Missouri (RM 263). My visit included a delicious steak and eggs dinner with Denise and David Ward who live along the main road just above the boat ramp. "Miami was a thriving town in the 1920's with a movie theater, two supermarkets, gas stations and all the other trimmings," David explained. "The only business left is the grain terminal." While I prepared to shove off the next day after the morning rain had turned to drizzle, David arrived with a cup of coffee and his wish for my safe travels.

Soon after, Pete Solomon, another neighbor who identified himself as a farmer and fisherman, arrived with his grandson Dave to check the trip lines set the night before to catch catfish. They also brought a dozen donuts. It became apparent that Pete wasn't kidding when he said the donuts were for me. While we shared the donuts, Pete lamented that his lanky teenage grandson was the only one of his grandchildren who enjoyed the outdoors. My question about different species of catfish spurred a lively debate as to whether flathead, channel, or blue catfish made the best meals.

"Flathead catfish are best, after that comes channel and then blue catfish," Pete declared.

"Grandad, you don't know much about preparing catfish. Blue catfish may be a little oily, but they taste great when prepared properly."

Their disagreement reminded me of similar discussions among Pacific Northwesterners about which species of salmon make the best eating.

I passed Bill and his red canoe once again before reaching Glasgow, Missouri (RM 226), an historic town, near the original home of the Missouri Tribe. After pulling ashore at the Stump Island Riverfront Park, I saw three small turtles lounging in the sun. They reminded me of Bill Smith's relaxed life.

While resting, Harley Gebhardt, the retired president of the town bank approached me. Looking forward to learning about Glasgow, I gladly accepted his offer to tour the town once he assured me that my kayak would be safe. Glasgow is a town in transition. Harley drove past several large industries that had closed in recent years, replaced by smaller industries. The 2013 population of 1,103 was down from 1,263 in 2000 and a high of 1,840 residents in 1880, not long after the Civil War Battle of Glasgow. "Many African Americans left when the railroad repair shops closed," Harley told me, and as of my visit, "there is only one Native American living in Glasgow."

While in historic downtown Glasgow, Harley took me to the oldest family-owned pharmacy in Missouri where I bought supplies and gulped down a strawberry milkshake while sitting on a stool at their old-fashioned luncheonette counter. After thanking Harley, I walked back to the park where I found my kayak untouched. I looked for Bill and his red canoe but didn't find him there or see him ever again. Downstream from Glasgow, I paddled for an hour and a half before pulling up on a sandbar (RM 215) to camp. Later, drifting off to sleep after taking two Tylenol to relieve the pain in my left shoulder, lightning flashes began and continued most of the night. There were more lightning strikes in any single hour than I experienced in the past forty years at my home north of Seattle. I awoke each time I heard the explosive noise but was so tired I soon fell back to sleep again.

Shortly after noon the next day, I pulled into Coopers Landing (RM 170), a haven for Missouri River paddlers and a survivor of all too frequent flooding. I had been looking forward to this visit since I began paddling on the Missouri River. When I almost capsized in the fast-moving water at the landing, I hoped no other kayakers were watching. When no one made fun of me, I assumed they were not.

Almost immediately, I felt out of my league with all the muscle and cleavage in view. The people I met were helpful, but I didn't feel the kinship I expected. No one asked about my trip. Maybe it was my age.

To be sure, the stop was worth it. That night, while a bright red-orange sun emerged from beneath the low hanging clouds and dropped below the horizon, six musicians entertained the gathering crowed with an impromptu blues jam session. I had a nice chat with David Bandy, one of the musicians, who introduced me to the Missouri River Paddlers Facebook page managed by Norm Miller. Despite my aversion to Facebook, I have enjoyed and learned from Miller's postings ever since.

I experienced a certain kinship with Jimmy Fogle, the one person at the landing who, at sixty-eight, was almost my age. Jimmy once explored much of the US on his bicycle before beginning the first of four battles with cancer. Cancer had taken a toll as Jimmy's body seemed fragile, but his mind was sharp. He now cruises the Missouri on the Swan, an innovative riverboat he designed, with creative steering and anchoring features to add to the safety of navigating in fast moving shallow water. Jimmy told me that the Moreau and Osage rivers, which converge with the Missouri downstream from us, were in flood stage and filling the Missouri. He warned that the fast-moving water made it even more important to watch for tugs, barges, and submerged wing dams.

Floods Flows

I was now encountering three-to-seven wing dams per mile. On the Missouri River, wing dams are piles of rocks that jut out from the shore. When first encountering the rock wing dams, I thought their threat was overrated. The river was low, they were clearly visible, and it was easy to paddle around them while still avoiding river traffic. Now, the wing dams were mostly or entirely submerged and not clearly discernable in the turbulent debris laden water. Fearing that the rocks lurking beneath the surface would rip a hole in Whisper, I was on full alert.

Rain was beginning to fall when I pulled ashore for the night in Chamois, Missouri (RM 118), only 118 miles from the Mississippi River. The Missouri was still in flood, but a long boat ramp located in an eddy eased my landing. I set my tent on a patch of green lawn near the river, after first checking for sprinkler heads. I was greeted by a group of teenagers racing their cars in the parking lot, and soon after by Wayne Trachsel, a local corn farmer who had driven to the ramp to check the river level. He told me the river had risen five feet in the last two days and was expected to rise more overnight, but he was relieved that the water wasn't likely to flood his land. Wayne lamented that Chamois had been in decline for some years. It had long since lost its only doctor, lawyer, and dentist. In the past year it had lost its only restaurant and supermarket and the pending closure of the nearby coal burning electrical generating plant would hurt even more. "Locals are now forced to shop at the larger towns like Hermann and Jefferson City," he told me "And young people move away after completing high school. Declining school attendance might soon mean the closure of the community's only school, but I hope to see my children graduate high school and go to college before that happens."

Somehow, I couldn't see Chamois becoming a ghost town. The nearby farms were prosperous, many people prefer rural life on the river, and some of the residents would always prefer purchasing some services locally compared to driving long distances.

"Why not join me at my home for a shower and dinner," Wayne offered, even though he was busy preparing for his middle daughter's wedding, only two days away. Remembering Lexington and thinking about the rising river, I reluctantly declined to leave my post. Wayne left, returning forty-five minutes later with a plate of grilled chicken and tomatoes and peppers from his family's garden. We exchanged phone numbers with the hope, but probably not the expectation of meeting again.

Fourteen miles below Chamois, the Gasconade River discharged its floodwaters into the Missouri, along with many logs, tree limbs and even complete trees. I successfully avoided the strong eddies at the meeting of the waters. Soon afterwards, when I became temporarily trapped in a small eddy, a large cottonwood tree passed me by. Below the confluence, the nature of the Missouri changed. The water was noticeably higher and almost all the rock wing dams were now lurking below the water surface. Moving away from shore to avoid wing dams, led to more encounters with floating trees trying to beat Whisper and me to St. Louis.

After reading about a tug-barge operation near Hermann, MO (RM 98), I paid even closer attention to my surroundings. My first two rules of the road were one, obey the rules, and two, stay alive, the second rule being more important than the first. The navigation rules require a more maneuverable craft like mine give way to a less maneuverable vessel like a tug. That rule often conflicts with the rules that human powered vessels have the right of way over powered craft, that two approaching vessels should approach port to port (left side to left side) and that favored vessels should hold their course unless a collision is eminent. The tug driver in Hermann didn't make it easy for me to obey any of the rules. The tug left the north shore and headed diagonally upstream toward me. Guessing that the tug was headed for a commercial dock on the south shore, I turned toward the left bank to avoid a collision. A few seconds after I turned, the tug also turned to head directly at me again. What was going on? I had heard of tug drivers playing chicken with kayakers but found it hard to believe one was aiming for me. What had I done to offend? I turned to the right and began a sprint to shallow water. The tug eventually changed course to avoid a collision, leaving me with nothing more than to ponder if the tug driver's actions were deliberate.

As the flooding increased, whirlpools that developed near the wing dams and tributary confluences grew in both size and number. I often heard a loud and startling *whoosh* when a whirlpool formed near me. Missouri River whirlpools have capsized many paddlers. My big test came just below Hermann. Most whirlpools were less than ten feet in diameter, but on this day a two-foot-deep crater twenty feet in diameter formed directly ahead of me. Paddling with all my strength, I propelled Whisper downstream with enough momentum and steerage to circumvent the center of the whirlpool, where I probably would have capsized. It was unsafe to relax my vigilance. By the end of a relatively short seven hours on the river, I needed a rest.

The town of Washington, Missouri (RM 68) was as inviting as Chamois was depressing. Washington is eighty-three miles from downtown St. Louis by river but only about forty-five miles by road, close enough to be in St. Louis' sphere of influence. I had both the fortune and misfortune of visiting Washington during the annual town and country fair that seems to attract people from much of the surrounding area. The fair is good for townspeople and for entertaining visitors, but not so good for a kayaker needing a place to stay. Washington does not allow camping in its riverfront park, and the river had flooded all the sandbars. My only other option was to try to find lodging at a motel or bed and breakfast in town.

My landing at Washington taxed my skills. Knowing the approach to the floating dock would be difficult in the high current and with a threatening standing wave at a wing dam only a hundred feet downstream, I didn't want to miss connecting. My approach to the upstream end of the dock was so unsuccessful as to be both embarrassing for me and entertaining for the townspeople on the dock. Drifting further downstream, I grabbed hold of a cleat at the outer face of the dock. Without letting go, I worked my way to a position closer to shore where Whisper would not be battered by the trees and other debris floating downstream.

All the motels were far from the waterfront. So, I decided to give the local bed and breakfasts a try, hoping the friendly people near the dock would keep watch over Whisper while I was away. The five B&Bs near the river either had no vacancies, or I got no response when I rang the bell. As a last resort, (pun intended) I left a note at the Glenrich Bed and Breakfast while doing some shopping. Later, when I approached the waterfront, Glenda Richards pulled up in her car. She had seen my note, and although she had not planned to rent that day, she decided to make an exception because my note mentioned that I was a kayaker and because she had a friend who was now kayaking in British Columbia. The apartment Glenda showed me was luxurious with a large living area, well stocked kitchen, king-size bed, and oversized shower. It was commensurably expensive. After unpacking, I took a free bus to the fair, visited the downtown including the historic St Francis Borgia Catholic Church, and the Gary Lucy art studio and capped off the day with a mouth-watering prime rib dinner at the Old Dutch Tavern. I slept uneasily, wondering if Whisper would still be tied to the dock in the morning.

During my last full day on the river, I stopped at historic St. Charles, Missouri (RM 29) where I visited with Daryl and Mimi Jackson at the Lewis and Clark Boathouse and Nature Center. "Why don't you call Mike Clark, the river guide, for suggestions on how to deal with the confluence and with the Chain of Rocks Dam," they suggested. I left a phone message with Mike before eating a hamburger, French fries, and a salad for lunch at a cafe close to the visitor center. After lunch I paddled eighteen miles downstream to the Pelican Island boat ramp

(RM 11) where I spent the night. Although there were many people near the ramp, there were no pelicans.

Chain of Rocks Dam

The next morning, I reached the confluence of the Missouri River (RM 0) and the Mississippi River. It was here that I expected the greatest turbulence and the largest whirlpools. Mike, whom I had contacted while on Pelican Island, suggested calling him when I arrived at the confluence, but this was definitely not the place to put down my paddle to make a phone call.

Flood waters and the resulting strong current swept me around the bend where the Missouri joins the Mississippi. Small whirlpools were all around me, new ones forming with an audible *whoosh*. I passed all too close to some whopper holes in the water that seemed capable of swallowing Whisper. Even when the confluence was far behind me, the river channel was too turbulent to put my paddle down. Finally, finding some relatively calm water below a tree covered Island, I called Mike to ask about the route ahead.

At long last, it looked like I would make it to St. Louis, but first I had to negotiate the treacherous Chain of Rocks submerged dam (diversion dam) about ten miles above the Gateway Arch. The Chain of Rocks has class III features, projecting concrete and rebar, and holes that can trap a kayak, and indeed have caused several deaths. Portaging is strongly advised, and I fully intended to do so.

Mike tried to dissuade me from portaging. "Why don't you try going over the dam," he suggested. I told Mike that I was seventy years old, not seventeen, and wasn't sure I was sufficiently skilled. "Don't worry," he said, "I will be on the old bridge just before the dam and I'll yell directions down to you on the best course to take to avoid a big wing dam jutting out from the right bank and a water intake structure near midstream." I got the feeling that he thought I was more competent than I believed myself to be. With my year-end destination, the Gateway

Arch, tantalizingly near, the exhilaration I expected to feel was consumed by fear that I would become the dam's latest victim. On the other hand, I must admit that I looked forward to one more challenge.

The river widened above the dam much like the belly of a snake trying to swallow its prey. At first, I converged on the dam slowly like a dog approaching the snake. The dam was almost invisible, its presence appearing like the drop off early explorers thought they would find at the end of the world. When the river constricted close to the dam I moved faster. I was still looking for a place to pull ashore and reconsider my options. Soon, I was past the point of no return. The flooding current had me in its grasp. While I paddled hard to maintain steerage, I looked for Mike on the bridge. I could see him and see his mouth moving but it was impossible to hear him over the river and road noise. Cresting the dam, I could see rocks below me, but not directly in my path. Mike, far above me, was waving his arms. What he wanted me to do, I didn't know. In a flash I was over the dam and beyond the rocks. Mike later told me he was worried about my route but took comfort that I would miss the wing dam and the water intake structure. Like many of life's challenges, the anticipation is as frightening as the event. I complemented my kayak, "Well done Whisper."

About an hour after running the Chain of Rocks Dam I passed under the historic Eads Bridge. I made a sweeping U-turn into the strong current and pulled ashore beneath the arch at the Jefferson Memorial. The ending was bittersweet. A voyage that began in 2008 and included five rivers, fifteen dams, 2,511 river miles, and a 676-mile bicycle portage over the Bitterroot and Rocky Mountains seemed worthy of a celebration. I stood alone on the riverbank with no one with whom to celebrate.

The end of this year's voyage was different in the sense that completing the acknowledged route of the Lewis and Clark Expedition gave me a good excuse to stop. Did I really want to stop? I would wait for my body to tell me, but I was inspired by my success so far. My mind was already contemplating going farther.

Postscript VI

It had taken me twenty-four days to paddle Whisper from Pierre to St. Louis. It took the Expedition only five days longer even with their many stops to hunt and meet with traders. I stayed with Mike while arranging to have Whisper transported back home to Washington State by truck. Then I flew to Pierre, SD where I picked up my vehicle for the drive home. While repairing damage Whisper experienced during the transport home, Sterling Kayaks in Bellingham, WA, found that the steering cable was just about to break. Loss of Whisper's rudder while going over the Chain of Rocks Dam would have ruined my day.

Big Bend Dam

Golden Cliffs

Kaw Point silhouette

Flood stage at Jefferson City

Author with Whisper I

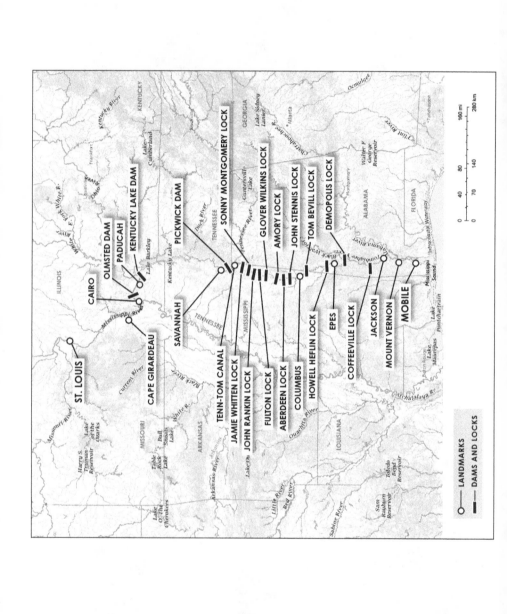

ST. LOUIS

CAPE GIRARDEAU

CAIRO

OLMSTED DAM
PADUCAH
KENTUCKY LAKE DAM

PICKWICK DAM

SAVANNAH

SONNY MONTGOMERY LOCK

GLOVER WILKINS LOCK

AMORY LOCK

JOHN STENNIS LOCK

TOM BEVILL LOCK

DEMOPOLIS LOCK

TENN-TOM CANAL

JAMIE WHITTEN LOCK

JOHN RANKIN LOCK

FULTON LOCK

ABERDEEN LOCK

COLUMBUS

HOWELL HEFLIN LOCK

EPES

COFFEEVILLE LOCK

JACKSON

MOUNT VERNON

MOBILE

ILLINOIS
MISSOURI
ARKANSAS
TENNESSEE
KENTUCKY
MISSISSIPPI
ALABAMA
GEORGIA
FLORIDA
LOUISIANA

0   40   80   140   160 mi
0   70   280 km

——— LANDMARKS
▬▬▬ DAMS AND LOCKS

VII

St. Louis, Missouri to
Mobile, Alabama

2015

The arch

Zero minus time

L ate one winter night in 2014, I traced my fingers from one blue body of water to another across a map of the eastern US. I was dreaming about kayaking all the way to the Atlantic Ocean, perhaps on a route to my roots, passing through Indiana where Joyce and I started our family, and finishing in New York, where we were born. A spirit of exploration, developed while I followed the route of Lewis and Clark, had taken hold. Pressing on to the Eastern Seaboard just felt like a natural expression of that inspiration.

I over optimistically focused on heading up the Ohio and Allegheny Rivers, skirting the shore of Lake Erie, traversing the Erie Barge Canal, and finally floating down the Hudson River with the current. Joyce was concerned about my going that far on my own. In order to get her buy-in, Joyce was not above extracting some concessions—a new sewing machine and a *real cruise* to someplace exotic in exchange for my new Kevlar single kayak and some late summer days on the river.

On the last day of July 2015, I flew to St. Louis from New Jersey, where I had been spending time with family and friends while trying to torture my body into shape. At Lambert Field, I hopped on a bus to the Alpine Shop in Kirkwood, Missouri. My new Current Design Solstice GT North American style single person Kevlar kayak and my gear, sent by my son, Mike, were waiting for me there. With a length of seventeen feet and seven inches, a beam of just over twenty-four inches, and weighing only fifty-four pounds, my new kayak should make for easier portaging. The staff at Alpine helped me select additional gear, stock up on food, and prepare my new kayak. It was a tight fit, but I was able to cram all my gear, including the wheels used for portaging, inside the watertight compartments The only items that added wind resistance were my deck bag, spare paddle, mooring line (bow painter), water pump, and me. I named my new kayak Whisper II in tribute to the Eddyline Whisper that had taken me from the Pacific Ocean to St. Louis.

That night I celebrated the start of another kayak voyage by dining on White Castle hamburgers, a food group not available in the Pacific Northwest. The hamburgers cost seventy cents per burger, quite a bit more than the five cents I remembered from my youth. On the second of August, Perry, the lead guide for the Alpine Shop, and I loaded Whisper II onto a trailer to take her to my 2013 finishing point below the arch along the Mississippi River (RM 179.6). Access to the river was blocked by construction. Perry found a way through the maze, thus avoiding a gap in my river journey. The Mississippi had dropped to just below flood stage the previous day. Small boat travel was again allowed.

Perry is a retired neuropsychologist who now spends his time guiding Alpine's customers and leading the St. Louis Adventure Group (SLAG). I was disappointed when he didn't ask about my trip, so I used my time with him to learn from his experiences. He was a good instructor and an accomplished paddler, having won the Missouri River 340, the canoe and kayak race from Kansas City, Kansas to St. Charles, Missouri. This year, he intended to make it a "pub crawl." To him, that meant finishing in the top half.

The Mississippi River

I shoved off on a sunny Sunday morning and paddled downstream close to the right bank hoping to avoid what the local paddlers call "running the gauntlet" of the busy lane of barge and tow traffic that crowds the river in the vicinity of St. Louis. I encountered seven or eight tows along the industrial waterfront. I patted myself on the back (or would have if I could reach that far) for starting on a Sunday when there was supposed to be less traffic and for bringing a very high frequency (VHF) radio to contact towboat pilots. Most reacted positively when advised of my position, and most passed the word on to other commercial traffic.

Practically flying down the 180 miles on the Mississippi River to its confluence with the Ohio River, I averaged 7 mph and sixty miles per day. I will never object to a mild tailwind, but the temperature those first three days was hot enough for me to have welcomed a slight headwind to cool off and at least ameliorate the need to frequently wipe sweat from my eyes and glasses.

I am often impatient at the beginning of a long trip, and later wish I had stopped more often. This year my regrets included not picking up more food and water at Hoppie's Marina (RM 150.5), the only facility with fuel and food between St. Louis and Memphis, Tennessee.

Late on the first day, a pusher towboat with too many barges to count rounded a bend heading directly towards me while I paddled near the Missouri bank. Doubting that the pilot saw me, I called several times on my radio. I received no response. Distance and speed are hard to judge when you are in a kayak low to the water. Hoping that I was far enough ahead of the tow, I began to dash to the Illinois side of the river where there was more room for me to maneuver out of the way of other watercraft. As the tow bore down on me, and with my heart pounding, I used all my energy to avoid being swept under the tug and barges. After the pusher tug passed, the pilot called on his radio "Orange kayak, this is Bigboy. Accompanied by a series of profane oaths, the tug operator berated me with, "You trying to commit suicide?" I radioed back that I had tried to contact him numerous times, but when he did not respond, and I was still directly in his path it seemed best to get out of his way. As far as I could tell I was following all the rules, including my own survival rule, and the rule that tows have the right of way over kayaks. The pilot didn't answer when I asked what I should have done differently.

Finally, able to focus on something other than tugs, I experienced the dramatic changes in landscape downstream from St. Louis. Massive cliffs over a hundred feet high rose along the west shoreline. The gleaming white-and-pink limestone was capped in green with oak, maple, beech, and catalpa, except where quarries large enough to accommodate multiple football stadiums had carved it away.

The flooding river meant that there were far fewer campsites than during low water when sandbars emerge below wing dams. Due to the dearth of campsites and the uncertainty of their locations, I stopped earlier than usual. My first campsite, near RM 123 in Illinois, was on a sandy slope along the left bank a few miles below the St. Genevieve and Modoc cross-river ferry, the only surviving ferry on the middle Mississippi.

While pulling over to camp, I misjudged the current. I was swept into a tree at least twelve inches in diameter grounded in deep water two kayak lengths from shore. Whisper II's rudder mechanism caught on a branch. I couldn't reach back to the rudder or break the branch. Water piled up on Whisper's upstream side and she began to take on water. She would move neither forward or backward, and the water was too deep for me to exit without capsizing. I needed to free my kayak before it was swept under the tree, a dangerous condition that has caused too many paddlers to drown. Being alone with no one in sight added to my anxiety. After trying briefly to finesse my release in the fast-moving water without success I surged forward, freeing Whisper II, and making it to shore but bending the rudder mechanism in the process. After beaching, I unbent the rudder. One small part hung loose. There was nothing I could do to fix it, so I moved on to other tasks.

After leveling the sandy slope at the campsite with a trowel, to keep me from sliding to the bottom of the tent and into the river, I dined rather well on spicy lentils, prepared by placing a sealed pouch in a container of boiling water. Following a bath in the muddy river, writing in my journal, and planning for the next day, I tried to sleep while perspiration pooled on my sleeping mat.

Waking before sunrise, I was on the river in a little over an hour. Not far downstream from Chester, Illinois (RM 110) I passed the mouth of Salt Creek on the Missouri side of the river. It was here that I first crossed the path of the Spanish explorer and conquistador Hernando De Soto, who explored for salt in this area before 1542, more than 250 years before Lewis and Clark came through. The latter camped near Chester while on their way to St. Louis, where Lewis proceeded north on foot while Clark stayed with the soldiers in the boats.

My greatest risk of capsizing on the Mississippi was near Tower Rock, a hulking limestone remnant at RM 80, about halfway between St. Louis and the Ohio River. *The River Gator*, an excellent guide to paddling the Mississippi describes Tower Rock as "dark and brooding . . . the biggest snag you have ever seen." It goes on to say that at high water, giant whirlpools that have caused the demise of many riverboats, form at the base of the rock. My fears were somewhat alleviated by Perry's and river guide Mike Clark's comments that the risk was reduced if I stayed on the Illinois side of the river. I did hit swirling water at Tower Rock, but it was less threatening than *The River Gator* suggested. Of greater concern was a very large tow that rounded a bend heading upstream straight toward me. Fortunately, this tow pilot responded to my VHF call, slowed down, and advised me to hug the Illinois shore.

Poor planning saw me running very low on drinking water by early afternoon. The chocolate-brown Mississippi river water was not appealing and would have clogged my filter. After pulling ashore at the remote community of Neely's Landing, Missouri (RM 74) and struggling across a wide muddy shore, I found only one house. I knocked at the door, but no one answered. I was reluctant to take water from the outside tap not knowing if it was contaminated but thirst won out. I wrote a thank you note on a scrap of paper and tried, without success, to contact the owners upon returning home. I didn't get sick, so the water must have been potable.

This year, unlike in past years, I would not pass close to a single Native American reservation. White settlers supported by the federal, state, and local governments forced many Natives in the states through which I would be paddling from their ancestral land. I paddled by the Trail of Tears State Park between RM 69 and 65.6 on the Missouri side of the river. Despite the blistering heat, a chill ran down my spine. I'd done my research and understood that the fate of the Cherokee and other tribes forced from their homelands following the Indian Removal Act of 1830 was deadly and demeaning.

Andrew Jackson had pushed this act through Congress. The Cherokee, one of the tribes referred to as the Five Civilized Tribes, and perhaps the only Native American culture with a written language, contended that the state of Georgia had no right to force them from their land. They took their case to the US Supreme Court in the matter of Worster vs. Georgia and won. President Andrew Jackson ignored the Supreme Court decision, thus allowing, and perhaps even encouraging, Georgia to remove the tribe to Indian Territory west of the Mississippi River. This forced exile from their lands became known as The Trail of Tears. Of the 16,453 Cherokee who began that arduous journey, approximately 2,000 to 6,000 perished. Jackson's action helped explain the push for another removal act, the elimination of Jackson's likeness from the twenty-dollar bill. Reminders of the horrendous treatment to which Native Americans were subjected occurred almost every day since leaving the Pacific Ocean.

On my last day on the Mississippi River, I was in a good mood. My map for this reach of the river was in color, a small change that brightened my day. Maybe the greater reason for my improved spirits was thinking about my daughter Amy who once competed in gymnastics at Cape Girardeau, Missouri, a town I would soon pass at RM 52.3. Approaching the city, I observed drab grey concrete flood walls pierced by several flood gates, a stark contrast to the tall sycamore, cottonwood, and oak trees in the nearby forests. My goal was to get drinking water. The one person I observed walking on the levee told me he knew of no public source of water, and because it was still very early morning no stores were open. I decided to paddle on, forgoing my chance to visit the downtown area known for its colorful murals.

Traveling on to Thebes, Illinois, (RM 44), I hailed a man working in his yard. "What do you want?" Captain Bob Wright, a retired tugboat captain asked in a not very friendly voice. His demeanor softened when I asked if I could obtain water from his hose. It softened even more when I asked him for advice on river safety and area history. As I filled my water containers, he emphasized that it could be dangerous to pronounce Cairo, the town near the confluence of the Mississippi and Ohio Rivers, like the city in Egypt. "Call it Kayro," he said. "That's what the people want." Next, he pointed to the top of the bluff on the eastern shore. "There's an old courthouse up there," that's where Abe Lincoln once practiced law.

Before we parted, Captain Bob wanted to make sure I understood two dangerous conditions. One, which I would later encounter, occurs when both a tug and a small boat find themselves close to shore and close to each other when approaching the outside of a river bend. In rounding the bend, the tug will tend to slide toward the shore and, if the small boat is between the tug and the shore, the tug could run over the small boat or force it into the riverbank. If the small boat escapes the first condition it might still be exposed to the second. When a river bend puts a small boat in a position between the stern of the tug and the shore, prop wash from the tug will bounce back from the shore, mix with the tug's wake, and create dangerous confused waves.

Later that same year, I had reason to worry about Captain Bob. He had built his retirement home on wooden piles to a height only a little above the maximum-recorded flood. In late December 2015, the Mississippi River swelled to a height of two feet above the record height at Thebes. I thought about getting in touch to see how he and his house had weathered that storm but knew that if he didn't get back to me, I would assume the worst. Rather than endure that, I chose to be hopeful.

The Ohio River Confluence

It was late afternoon when I approached the Ohio River. The last of those majestic limestone and dolomite bluffs were behind me. I was now paddling the sweeping curves of the Missouri Bootheel, the wide alluvial floodplain that stretches to the Gulf of Mexico. The valley opened up before me, exposing its many twists and turns as cypress trees replaced the oak and maple forests, in much the same way that the Bible Belt replaced the swinging jazz culture of St. Louis. The previous day I was served notice of the Bible culture as I paddled by the 111-foot, high-gleaming-white Bald Knob Cross on a distant hill in Illinois.

The River Gator Guide advises against camping at Fort Defiance State Park at the confluence because "it is depressing place, and not very friendly or safe feeling." However, the complex and colorful history of the area was too much of a history buff's magnet to resist. Lewis and Clark stopped at this location on November 14, 1803. Fort Defiance was later used by the North as a supply depot during the Civil War. In recent years, Cairo has been a city in decline. Fort Defiance Park, operated by the city, has a reputation for being poorly maintained and plagued by theft.

Having missed the last accessible camping area on the Mississippi, perhaps because the campsite was covered by high water, I considered continuing upstream on the Ohio River. When I couldn't identify a desirable campsite, I was likely to reach before dark, I decided to take a chance at Fort Defiance Park and sought out the boat ramp. Access to the ramp was partly blocked by a fleet of barges moored close to shore. The boat ramp was coated with a thick layer of gooey mud and debris. I sank in almost to my knees, when I tried to walk on the mud and had to dig down to recover a paddling shoe the mud had sucked from my foot. Spreading some drift logs to distribute the load kept me from sinking into the mud, but it still took me almost two hours to unload Whisper II and make camp. It seemed that the entire park was coated with a thin layer of dried mud, but the park was surprisingly free of trash, having been washed away by the floodwaters.

I had misgivings about cooling off in the polluted river, but the oppressive heat and swarming flies drove me in. While descending a riprap slope, I slipped and sliced my leg on the jutting edge of a large rock. During my overnight stay, biting flies persisted to land on any exposed skin. I was apparently the only buffet available.

I never saw or heard another person in the large park. Karl Adams wrote that he had never camped at a more depressing place than Cairo. I saw unfulfilled opportunities. The land had considerable historical importance and could be protected from flooding. There was ample river commerce and the present low property values could prove attractive to developers willing to take the chance that racial or other prejudices would not get in their way.

The Ohio River dominates the Mississippi. At the confluence, the Ohio River is about three-quarter miles wide compared to the half-mile-wide Mississippi. The average flow in the Ohio is about 40 percent greater than the Mississippi. At most times of the year, the Ohio has so little sediment that it appears almost black compared to the brown Mississippi. The difference in colors appears to be dependent on several factors, the most obvious being the type of sediment, minerals and organic matter in the water and differential absorption of the sun's rays. The setting reminded me of my visit with Joyce to the "meeting of the waters" where the Rio Negro (Black River) meets the Amazon River near Manaus, Brazil. Although the color (and temperature) demarcation in the Amazon basin was distinct for many miles downstream, no such difference was evident to me at the Mississippi and Ohio confluence. Both rivers had recently been in flood stage, and both remained muddy.

Long-term weather and river condition reports led me to select early August as the time of year to begin this trip. For most years, the Mississippi and Ohio are well below flood stage by then, the adverse current in the Ohio is manageable if only just, the wind is modest and generally favorable, and the chance of thunder and lightning is lower than during most other months. In mid-July, I learned that 2015 was not a normal year; the Ohio and Mississippi were still above flood stage. The average current in the Ohio was reported to be about three mph. If I encountered long stretches with a current even a little greater than 3 mph on the Ohio, I might find it impossible to paddle upstream. My initial encounter with the Ohio River showed the current to be closer to 2 mph. I decided to give it a go. At least I could tell my children and grandchildren that I had tried.

The Ohio River

Soon after shoving off the next morning, the forecast rain began as a drizzle. There was thunder and lightning behind me, seemingly trying to catch me. I paddled hard to stay ahead of the storm. Soon, the temperature dropped about 10 degrees F and driving rain made it increasingly difficult to see the many barges, much less determine if they were moving. Several harbor tugs passed close by, changing their courses to avoid me. The hard work of paddling kept the chill off my rain-soaked body. After a couple of hours, the rain let up, the wind abated, and I continued my upstream slog.

After about seven hours of hard paddling, Olmsted Lock and Dam loomed in the distance. Olmsted was being built to replace Dams 52 and 53 because age-related maintenance caused frequent river traffic delays, and because one dam (with two large locks) in place of two dams would expedite the passage of heavy barge traffic. Olmsted is a massive concrete structure surrounded by barges and cranes and visible from several miles away. Approaching it reminded me of my first view of the New York City skyline from the New Jersey Meadowlands. Both Olmsted and New York City seemed similarly out of place.

A Corps of Engineers harbor tug arrived to escort me past construction activities. For the duration of that brief escort, I felt like royalty. Schools of fish surrounded me. Small fish, unknown to me, darted up to Whisper II while large fish jumped, breaking the water's surface all around me. One crashed into the side of the kayak. I suspected that the larger fish were the dreaded Asian carp, the same invasive fish that bruised my right arm on the Missouri River.

Construction of the sixty-two-foot-high Olmsted Lock and Dam began in 1992. The dam was completed in 2018, twenty-six years later. It took China less time to construct the 594-foot-high Three Gorges Dam on the Yangtze River, even though it's the world's largest, or second largest, producer of hydroelectric power (virtually tied with Brazil's Itaipu Dam). Three Gorges includes a unique ship lift (elevator) in addition to locks and, according to the Chinese government, required the displacement of 1.3 million people. My early professional work, and lingering interest in dam construction, drew Joyce and me to visit the Three Gorges Dam in 2004, and Itaipu Dam in 2016. As impressive as is the Olmsted Dam, it doesn't rival Three Gorges or Itaipu.

Olmsted experienced funding delays and other setbacks. Perhaps the greatest was the need to modify the design for unexpected geologic conditions and potential seismic activity at the New Madrid fault located forty-two miles to the southwest. When beginning my engineering studies more than fifty years ago, I was surprised to learn about the New Madrid earthquake; actually, three earthquakes that occurred over the three months from December 1811 to February 1812. The estimated magnitude for the largest of the three New Madrid earthquakes was about 7.7, which ranks as one of the top four or five earthquakes in the lower forty-eight states. The other two New Madrid earthquakes were right behind. Even so, there was relatively little loss of life or property damage because there were so few people living in the area at the time, and because flexible one-story high Native American dwellings were less prone to life-ending damage during an earthquake. Fortunately for me, the next New Madrid earthquake had a low probability of occurring while I was on the river.

Since starting at the Pacific Ocean, I had encountered fifteen dams without going through a single lock. I wanted to negotiate the lock at Dam 53, but it's a strange creature called a wicket dam. When the water in the river is high such that there is no need to back up water for navigation, the four-foot-wide wickets (panels) spanning the width of the river are lowered to the bed of the river, thus precluding the need to operate the locks. Much to my surprise, and no small measure of disappointment, I passed over Dam 53 without even knowing it was there.

I hoped to make the Grand Chain Lodge before dark but began to have doubts. I wasn't exactly lost but I didn't know where I was. After paddling hard ten hours, I observed a building on the Illinois side of the river that resembled a picture I had seen of the lodge. Judging from the overgrown vegetation, and complete lack of any activity at the ramp and in the vicinity of the lodge, it appeared to be closed. Hoping to camp nearby, I climbed up another muddy boat ramp to check, but slipped on the mud and came down hard on my butt. My immediate fear was that I had broken one of my artificial hips, as had happened once before, but fortunately, my hip was only bruised.

A sign at the resort informed me that the highly recommended restaurant was closed. The convenience store in the lodge had little in the way of conveniences or supplies, but I could get a room. "Lock up before you go to sleep," the manager instructed. She gave me the key to the building and went home, leaving me as the only person in the lodge. What should have been a pleasant evening with good food and good company turned out to be lonely and depressing, despite the comforts of a soft bed and hot shower.

It took much longer for me to approach objects on the Ohio than it did on the Mississippi. The math is simple. For a paddler whose normal speed is 3 mph, even a 1 mph (0.87 knots) adverse current will cut a kayaker's speed by half compared to a one mph favorable current (2 mph versus 4 mph). It was especially frustrating that even when making fairly good progress at 2 mph, I was moving slower than a walking pace. I would have pulled Whisper II on land if the roads obeyed my rules—paved and level, went where they should, and had convenient access and egress. The nearby roads were none of that.

Midafternoon, approaching Paducah, Kentucky, I began searching for campsites. Fort Massac State Park in Illinois, where Lewis and Clark stopped to recruit more expedition members before proceeding westward, was a possibility. A park visitor walking near the shore told me that there were campsites at Fort Massac, but none were near the river. I didn't want to risk the theft of Whisper II or my gear, so I proceeded eastward to the Brookport, Illinois Boat Ramp. When reminiscing on my disagreeable experience at Brookport, my mind plays the Four Season's hit lyrics, "Oh what a night . . ." but not for the erotic reason envisioned by the songwriter.

Brookport's boat ramp, on this brutally hot day, was festered with the acrid smell of dead and dying carp lying amidst the wet and slimy mud-covered rocks on the beach. There was trash in the trees and flies buzzed and attacked the stinking fish—and me—from all directions. The beach sloped toward the river, but this time leveling my campsite with my trowel was impossible because of the densely packed mud and rocks. All my senses rebelled against this site. I take undue pride in my ability to rough it, but even I have limits. This was not the noble Ohio River Thomas Jefferson observed. In his "Notes on the State of Virginia" he wrote, "The Ohio is the most beautiful river on earth." Based on Brookport and discounting the mostly tree-lined banks that comforted me over the past two days, it came closer to its 2010 ranking as the most polluted river in the US. Unless the water level in the Ohio was to fall quickly, conditions would probably be much the same for hundreds of miles, and my slow progress against the current would make it tough to find decent campsites.

Discouraged that night, I pulled out Hay's *Guide* and my many maps with the hope of finding an alternate route. I rejected heading upstream on the Wabash River in Indiana or the Scioto River in Ohio. Both routes would eventually require long portages to Lake Erie on rural highways and paddling the exposed waters of Lake Erie did not appeal to me. Instead, when I reached Paducah, Kentucky the next morning, I decided to make a right turn and head upstream on the Tennessee River. Karl Adams had paddled this route as part of his cross-country kayak trip in 1987 as described in his book, *In the Wake of the Wind Dancer*. Based on Adams' account, and my experience, I would be trading mud, enormous tows, and adverse current along the entire Ohio River, for smaller tows, a variable current, and alligators, snakes and almost every species of objectionable insect. According to Adams, the terrain became increasingly remote in Mississippi and Alabama, culminating in a major concern for one's mortality in the big swamp north of Mobile, Alabama. With my goal being adventure, I chose to head south.

Kentucky

John Sullivan, a paddler who had canoed down the Ohio River, had written me that the worst tug and barge traffic he experienced was in and around Paducah, the most northerly ice-free port on the Ohio River. As I paddled past Paducah on an ice-free summer morning, the commercial traffic comprised three tows, only one of which included more than six barges. In contrast to Sullivan's experience, the traffic was less than I had found on the Mississippi River at St. Louis or at the confluence of the Mississippi and Ohio Rivers.

It took me most of the day to paddle the twenty-two miles from Paducah to Kentucky Dam, a hydroelectric dam and one of nine dams on the Tennessee River owned and operated by the Tennessee Valley Authority (TVA) and built during President Franklin Roosevelt's New Deal program. Even paddling in the middle of the river, I could easily enjoy both riverbanks. Deciduous trees were already starting to show some red, orange, and yellow, and birds flew among the trees resting on the water away from me and other river traffic.

Few rivers are perfect. The adverse current kept increasing during the day, something I should have anticipated given the greater need for hydroelectric power generation in late afternoon. A half dozen tows with barges waited in the turbulent water below the dam for their turn to enter the lock, their engines churning the water astern of them in order to hold position. Feeling very small near the large tows and below the huge dam I paddled up to two fishers in a lone heavily powered aluminum boat. As the fishers used their twin engines to keep from being swept downstream, I paddled hard to stay near them.

"How long will I have to wait for my turn to enter the lock," I yelled to be heard above the river noise.

"You are about as low priority as you can get. Better allow at least five hours," they yelled back.

A portage around the dam seemed the better alternative. After paddling over to a boat ramp on the west bank, I met Ralph Camp, a local fisherman. With his help, I secured Whisper II to her wheeled carrier. Ralph and I took a few minutes to trade war stories when we learned that in 1969, we had both been at Fort Leonard Wood, Missouri, waiting to be sent to Vietnam.

My stay at the Kentucky Dam Resort, a mile upstream from the dam, was a far cry from my lonely night at the Grand Chain Lodge. I was coddled by a large room with a firm comfortable bed and a view of the river, delectable food served buffet style, warm friendly people, and reasonable prices. Dinner was all you could eat for only fourteen dollars, and since I was very hungry, I'm pretty sure the resort lost money on me. I took advantage of my clean room to treat an infected blister on my left hand, the cut on my leg which had become infected, and to nurse my left eye which had begun to hurt badly for an unknown reason. I slept well on clean sheets. I didn't want to leave such an enjoyable spot but the next morning, after stopping at the nearby post office to send a rearview mirror and other unneeded gear back home, my curiosity of what lay ahead drove me to move on.

Guests at the resort warned me about high wind and waves on Kentucky Lake, but I had great weather when I shoved off. There were many expensive homes along the shore, reminding me of Mercer Island near Seattle where Microsoft co-founder, the late Paul Allen, and many other ultra-rich live. Not surprising, then, were the many amenities along this part of my journey.

At the Kenlake Marina, RM 43 on this 220-mile reach of the Tennessee River, I finished a huge hamburger while proprietors Scott and Donna made sure I had the best river and camping information available. I bought two water-resistant maps of Kentucky Lake and a 2005 edition of the *Tenn-Tom Cruise Guide* by Fred Myers. Unfortunately, Myers' guide was outdated and, unlike Hay's guide for the Ohio River, it was written almost exclusively for power boaters.

While setting up camp that night at a quiet bug-free riverside campsite in a small cove, Steve Hromada stopped by in his bright yellow day-use kayak. He was a biologist and herpetologist from

Philadelphia studying the venomous snakes at the Land Between the Lakes National Recreation Area. "You could easily encounter copperhead, cottonmouth, and pygmy rattlesnakes," Steve warned, "but the large timber rattlesnakes are less common, or maybe just better hidden. You will need to watch where you step, where you wade in the river and even look up to make sure no snakes drop down from the trees." While I appreciated this information, I didn't find it at all comforting. Nor was I comforted when he told me that I might as well toss my snakebite kit because it would be of little help should I suffer a bite. I kept the kit in the belief that I might need every bit of help.

Tennessee

The next morning, the river was calm, but the adverse wind increased as the day progressed. Approaching the US 79 Bridge, both increased boat traffic and a wider river contributed to choppier water and intensified my worries. Needing a break from a fight with wind and rough water, I made a midafternoon stop at the Leatherwood Marina where I met owners Jim Butkiewicz and Curtis Johnson. As I devoured their signature burger and onion rings served in their Pirates Cove Restaurant, Mr. Johnson, a Tennessee state representative, made sure I knew I was now in Tennessee. He went on to explain some of the issues the legislature had been dealing with, especially the sale of alcohol in private stores. As I prepared to leave, he gave me a sample of Hillbilly Crack, the resort's very spicy beef jerky. Although far too spicy for me, it would probably appeal to Joyce while not being spicy enough for our two sons.

The next day, while I approached the I-70 bridge, the lone occupant of a strange-looking eighteen-to-twenty-foot-long box-on-boat cabin cruiser hailed me. "Where are you headed?" After determining that the boat's skipper, Steve Thorp, and I were both headed for Mobile, we commiserated on the dearth of information we had about what lay ahead. Steve wasn't traveling very fast, but he was moving at least twice my speed and should have been able to travel longer days because he didn't have to find a campsite, just a place to anchor or tie up. When we called out "Goodbye," I never expected to see him again.

Pleasant conditions since leaving the Ohio River behind had spoiled me. That was about to change. Late in the day on August 10, near RM 108, I struggled to find a decent campsite. The west side of the river was a dark and gloomy marsh. On the east side was a heavily rip-rapped dredge material disposal area, not exactly a prime recreation site, although some realtors would probably market it as such. I explored a couple of dead ends, looking unsuccessfully for a place called Sycamore Landing before finding an area with a sandy beach not much larger than Whisper II. I carried my boat and gear up a low rocky slope, all the while looking for snakes hiding in the voids. Before setting camp at the edge of a brush-covered field, I swept the brush with my paddle hoping to evacuate any snakes but found none fleeing or preparing to strike.

My fear of snakes was soon sidelined when I came under attack by the Clydesdale version of a horsefly. At first, I mistook it for a large intelligent bee that knew it was immune from my swatting if it bit me in the center of my back. After the fly satisfied its appetite, I found that the grassy field was the home of hungry ticks and chiggers. I picked one tick off my backside before it burrowed in. The chiggers stayed hidden, but the next day I had dozens of red bites on my lower legs. They soon began itching like crazy and continued to bother me for more than a week. If I hadn't been so tired at the end of the day, the itching would have kept me awake.

A phone call to Joyce further dampened my mood. She told me that the son of good friends, a young man we much admired, was expected to die soon of brain cancer. Why should I have the luxury of spending all this time on the river while friends were suffering? Was this trip just my trivial pursuit or did it expand my horizons as aging tended to narrow them?

At the end of the day, I pulled ashore at the Perryville Marina only to find that it was closed for the day. While debating what to do, I heard someone call out, "Can I help you?" This statement often means the opposite of the words' intent, but in this case, the words had a pleasant ring. Dwayne introduced himself. He was much younger than me, but like me was thin and unshaven. He proposed that I stay with him in his trailer. His offer made me a little nervous, but he seemed nice enough, and the thought of a real bed was appealing. I agreed to the twenty-dollar price he suggested.

Dwayne took me to get a cooling shower at the campground and then to Fatman's Key Stop, the local convenience store and restaurant, where I bought us both pizza and beer. Dwayne told me he had a tough life but admitted that most of it was his own fault. "I was spoiled as a kid," he said. "I was the star player on my high school baseball team and got a free-ride college scholarship. I didn't attend class and soon flunked out." Dwayne asked about my life. "I went an entire Little League season without my bat ever hitting the ball," I admitted. "Once I realized that I had limited athletic skills and marginal brainpower, I worked hard to take advantage of every opportunity life presented. I was lucky, often in the right place at the right time."

While at the convenience store, the owners said they were surprised Dwayne wanted pizza since all he ever bought was beer and cigarettes. The owners were from India, and their body mass indices contrasted with Fatman's Key Stop, the name of their store. Dwayne bantered freely with them and made no disparaging remarks about their race or about outsiders "taking over," as I had heard others in Tennessee say.

"My hope now lies with my daughter." Dwayne told me as we drove back to his trailer home. "She doesn't live with me, but she knows that I love her. She'll soon start college. She's not like me. She has a plan for her life and is willing to work hard. She's convinced me to return to work at the lumber mill." The next morning, taking a break from preparing his fishing gear, Dwayne helped me load and launch Whisper II. "Hope to see you again," we called to each other as he cast his line into the river.

On August 13, my last day on the Tennessee River before entering the Tenn-Tom Waterway, I lost my key map. It fell into the river leaving me no way to know where I was other than my memory, very imprecise GPS maps or asking people. Soon thereafter, I encountered someone to ask—an older man doing maintenance on a grass strip along the riverbank. Desperately short of water, my two-gallon container having sprung a leak, I called out, "Can I fill my water containers?"

Jerry walked slowly with me along the narrow dirt road leading to his modest river home He told of the anxiety he was experiencing while helping his wife fight cancer. "How will I go on without her?" he mused. He gave me water, cold sodas, energy bars, and advice on how to negotiate the current at the Savannah Bridge a few miles downstream, where he swam as a boy. Because my left shoulder hurt badly, I thought I'd fare better portaging this stretch and asked him about pulling Whisper the fourteen miles from Savannah to the next dam. Pickwick Road seemed to pass my to-pull-or-not-to-pull tests. "Don't do that," Jerry said, "the road is not very safe and not as level as it appears on your map." He offered to put my kayak in his pickup and take me to the dam. I declined. As before, accepting no motorized support was an important part of my journey. I did accept his advice not to portage, though, which allowed me to take advantage of a slight tailwind while paddling against the current the rest of the day.

Despite many stops, shorter paddling days, and upstream travel, I averaged twenty-nine miles per day for the seven-and-a-half days and 215 miles I was on the Tennessee River. Even the temperature cooperated, climbing above ninety degrees on only two days. Except for my left shoulder, my pains and injuries had been minor, and my leg infection and eye pain were much improved. I was almost thankful for my many blisters, which distracted me from the attention demanded by my shoulder.

The Tennessee-Tombigbee Waterway

Paddling a largely human-made connection of lakes, rivers, and a long canal lay in my immediate future. The Tennessee-Tombigbee

206 THE MISADVENTURES OF A CROSS-AMERICA KAYAKER

Waterway, unofficially known as the Tenn-Tom, is the 234-mile reach between the Tennessee River and Demopolis, Alabama. The remaining distance between Demopolis and Mobile is the Black Warrior-Tombigbee Waterway. This nomenclature is less than clear in the literature. Maps sometimes show the Black Warrior-Tombigbee Waterway as the Tombigbee River and the Mobile River. To add to this confusion, it seems that many boaters refer to the entire 451 miles from the Tennessee River to Mobile as the Tenn-Tom or just the Waterway. The rivers and waterway I would have to navigate after leaving the Tennessee River were a dark mystery. Finding folks familiar with this leg of the journey might prove critical.

For many miles, I had looked forward with considerable trepidation to navigating my first active lock. The moment arrived at Pickwick Dam, the second and last TVA dam I would encounter. To navigate Pickwick would require being lifted sixty-three feet in the smaller of the two dam locks. The small lock measured 110 feet wide by six hundred feet long, half the size of the 1,200-foot-long larger Pickwick Dam lock. The small lock I was in had the same dimensions as the ten locks on the Tennessee-Tombigbee Waterway and the two on the Black Warrior-Tombigbee Waterway. As the only boat in the Pickwick lock, it felt cavernous and dangerous. I imagined the walls closing in on me.

The lockmaster at Pickwick told me where to hold a position. I had thought that kayaks were allowed through all the locks on the Waterway, but the lockmaster set me straight. "You had better obey the rules, I can kick you out if I don't like what you're doing." He went on to say that he had the discretion to prohibit paddlers in locks due to turbulence, and that high turbulence was most likely to occur when proceeding upstream, as I was. I had studied locking procedures but was still worried I would inadvertently do something wrong and be evicted. The lockmaster instructed me to loop my bowline around a floating bit (bollard), about the size of a fireplug that was supposed to rise and fall with the water level.

The bit was way above my head. I couldn't stand up in Whisper

II without capsizing. It took several tries with me imitating a cowboy to get the line around the bit. The lockmaster blew the horn, the gates closed behind me, and the swirling water flowed into the lock and lifted me as I held the line tight. When the water calmed, I began to relax, and as the only boat in the lock, there was little turbulence. So far so good, but there were twelve locks still to navigate between Pickwick Dam and Mobile.

I stopped for a healthy lunch of mandarin chicken salad and potato soup at the Pickwick Landing Lodge within Pickwick Landing State Park. A courtesy car took me both ways between the lodge and the marina, making me feel like a celebrity. While charging my cell phone in the lodge lobby, I bought an Atlantic Mapping Company *Recreation and Fishing Guide to Pickwick Lake,* which includes a small but important portion of the Tenn-Tom Waterway.

I had fifteen easy miles to go before reaching my intended destination for the night. First, I paddled upstream to RM 215 on the Tennessee River, which is also RM 451 on the Ten-Tom, the location where southbound travelers turn right into Yellow Creek. This marks the entrance to the waterway and my entry into Mississippi, the fourteenth state I would touch since starting my journey in 2008, more than 3,600 miles to the west at the Pacific Ocean. Had I proceeded straight ahead, Whisper II could have continued up the Tennessee River 430 miles to Knoxville. Instead, I chose the route that would take me 451 miles to Mobile, my intended destination. Entering the Tenn-Tom marked the halfway point of this year's journey and warranted a celebratory fruit cup.

At RM 449.5, I stopped at the Grand Harbor Marina with an aim to purchase maps of the Tenn-Tom but was unsuccessful in finding anything other than some old, bulky charts—not useful. Even with Myers' guide and my map of Lake Pickwick, I still managed to get lost when I mistakenly entered Yellow Creek State Inland Port. The different placement of buoys led to my confusion. While proceeding up the Tennessee River, the red buoys were always on the right and the green ones on the left. Boaters know this as red-right-returning for ships returning from the sea. Now, red buoys were on the left side, because heading south on the Tenn-Tom takes boaters to the Gulf of Mexico. The change in buoy placement implied that I would now encounter a favorable current, but the actual current depended on whether Pickwick Dam, now behind me, or the next more southerly dam and lock released more water. To my dismay, Pickwick Dam always seemed to win. I had to endure another six days of upstream paddling before noticing a favorable current.

According to the Corps of Engineers, the Tenn-Tom—not to be confused with the Tennessee Valley Authority—was intended to open up the nation's mid-section to the eastern Gulf of Mexico. When completed in 1984, it was the Corps of Engineers largest civil works project and was considered by many to be an example of exorbitant pork-barrel spending. Support for the project had been minimal until TVA projects lowered the cost of Tenn-Tom construction by providing low-cost electricity and access and increased the benefits by forming a much larger and more efficient navigation system. The project moved ahead under Richard Nixon's administration. However, even today, some question its cost effectiveness. I for one was sure glad to have an alternative to the heavy commercial traffic on the mighty Mississippi.

On August 14, I camped at a Corps of Engineers day use park just ahead of the major human-made feature of the waterway, the twenty-four-mile-long, 280-foot-wide Divide Cut. The Divide Cut slices through the topographic divide between the Tennessee River basin to the north and the Tombigbee River basin to the south. It surprised me to learn that the cut required more earth moving than the Panama Canal. There is no place to camp along the Cut, and only one location where a breach in the rip rap slope for a boat ramp would allow egress without damaging a small craft like Whisper II. I camped just before reaching the Cut to increase my chances of making it through in one day. The launch fee was only five dollars, but I deposited a twenty because the park was not intended for camping. I am writing this now in the event some official is still trying to track down the kayaker who illegally camped overnight in the summer of 2015.

Both Joyce and my weather radio informed me that a cold front was heading my way and would likely result in afternoon thunder and lightning storms. It rained as I was setting up camp. This proved a mere precursor to the thunder and lightning and downpours that would plague me on all but two of the next nine days. My clothes and gear never fully dried.

In addition to alerting me about the weather, on previous trips my radio had been a source of entertainment and news. Not so on this voyage, at least not in this stretch. I couldn't get any AM stations, and when FM was available it was usually a single station with programming that ranged from the sale of used household items to very conservative pay-to-pray religious broadcasts.

Even my radio objected to the programming. The sound shut off in the middle of the afternoon. At first, I blamed myself. I had dropped this radio in saltwater in July only to get it working again by ingeniously placing it in a pot of hot fresh water to dissolve the salt and then drying it out in a warm breeze.

Maybe the existing problem wasn't my fault. My backup radio, made by a different company and never dropped in water, also turned itself off. Both radios emitted sound again after the sun went down when it was not quite as hot. Inductive reasoning led me to conclude that my radios, like me, objected to the oppressive midday heat, almost always at least ninety degrees, until the rain brought instant relief.

While I paddled, the rip-rapped canal looked to me as straight as a new carpenter's nail. My road map showed that it was more like the nails I frequently bent on home projects, as it conformed to the preconstruction drainages of Yellow Creek and Mackey's Creek. It was much greener than shown in historic photos of the denuded strip-mine topography, visible when the waterway opened in 1985. Holcut, the only town relocated while building the Tenn-Tom, is gone, though a small, worn-wooden sign still stood on the shoreline marking the place.

I wondered if those who named the town had a premonition of its fate. Contrasting the displacement of the few residents of Holcut with the 1.3 million people China relocated when building the Three Gorges Dam puts things in perspective. Still, the Holcut folks lost their homes.

The skies clouded over, and thunder erupted in the distance while I was still well within the cut. Having passed the one breach in the riprap, I had no intention of turning around. The thunder and lightning drew closer. My adrenaline kicked in. With no high trees nearby to attract the lighting, my thoughts turned to long ago soldiers who marched in formation into battle without any cover. Was it the drumbeat I heard, or was it distant thunder? When the rain arrived and lightning did its devil's dance in the near distance, I was still in the canal, fully exposed to the weather. I paddled as fast as I could. There was no other alternative. Lightning struck ground very near the cut just as I made it to the relative safety of Bay Springs Lake. I nosed Whisper II into the shallows under some low trees. Nothing more to be done to protect me. Pulling my paddling jacket over my head, I hunkered back in the cockpit, anchored my paddle into the shoreline underbrush, and took a well-deserved nap.

Dams and Lakes

After the thunder and lightning passed, I set out again, struggling across whitecap-covered Bay Springs Lake. My destination was the Piney Grove Recreation Area, the first of many Corps of Engineers campgrounds and recreation areas in a string that I would encounter over the next two hundred miles. The proliferation of Corps sites reminded me of the well-kept Corps campgrounds along the Columbia and Snake Rivers.

While looking for a place in the heavily wooded park to check in, camp host Gary Miles greeted me. He and his wife Terressia are allowed to camp at no cost in exchange for assisting paid guests. Gary went well beyond the call of duty in helping me transport my gear from the boat ramp to my camp. He then drove me to a convenience store where I purchased a pizza dinner, and a Dollar General Store where I purchased supplies.

Joyce and Mike had done some research and provided me with locations for many of the locks and dams and other Corps of Engineer sites along the Tennessee-Tombigbee. I had complete faith in Mike's research and almost total faith in Joyce's; her only failure is reading maps. She seemed to think I was headed for Atlanta.

I was surprised at how little commercial traffic and recreational boater traffic there was on the waterway. I hadn't encountered a single tug or boat in the cut and rarely was there another craft in view. That night on a check-in call, Joyce and Mike told me why. The Fulton lock (RM 391) was under repair and wouldn't reopen until late August. This planned maintenance had cut down on the traffic and all but eliminated delays at the locks. So far so good.

During the morning of August 16, I negotiated three closely spaced locks. There was so little traffic the lockmasters seemed pleased to see me. Whitten Lock and Dam (RM 411.9) with a lift of eighty-four feet, is the ninth highest single-lift lock in the US. My trip down in the cavernous chamber went without a hitch, as did locking through John Rankin Lock (RM 394.0). The river below each lock was as I hoped, lush with vegetation and birds. It was barely wide enough to permit passage of a kayak in one direction and a tow in the other, a ribbon narrow enough for me to almost feel both shores. I saw my first nutria, an invasive beaver-like mammal known to damage crops and cause extensive riverbank erosion.

Disaster almost struck while in the Sonny Montgomery Lock (RM 406.7). My bowline became snagged around the floating pin and couldn't be paid out. Normally this wouldn't be a problem with a floating pin, but instead of moving down with the water this pin got stuck in its channel. With the water going down and the pin staying fixed, Whisper II's bow would soon be pulled out of the water, and I would be unceremoniously dumped over backwards. I frantically tried to free myself, tugging and twisting at the line to nudge the pin to move. I considered calling the lockmaster on my cell phone, but that would take focus away from my attempt to free myself. You can imagine my relief when the pin finally plopped down just before Whisper II would have dumped me. "Scared you, didn't we," the lockmaster called down to me. He told me he had seen what was happening and would have stopped emptying the lock if the pin hadn't fallen into its floating position. He cut it very close, leaving me quite annoyed. For the remainder of the locks, I made sure my line didn't get snagged.

The lockmaster at Whitten Lock advised me to portage the closed Fulton Lock by pulling Whisper II three-to-four miles through the town of Fulton, Mississippi. He didn't think the traffic would be bad because it was Sunday. The lockmaster at Rankin Lock disagreed with Fulton's assessment. "You'll do better portaging on the levee road on the west side of the waterway," he strongly advised. "You'll find a put-in after about seven or eight miles." I went with that option but soon regretted it. The levee roadway consisted of loose gravel. Pulling my loaded kayak over the rubble was exhausting.

The sun was blazing hot, and I was bombarded with flying insects and aggressive large ants that climbed onto Whisper II and then me whenever I stopped to rest or guzzle water. I knocked the ants off Whisper II and my skin before they bit and covered the cockpit to prevent them from taking up residence, but the flying insects were feasting on me. If only to defeat the biting critters, I welcomed the late afternoon arrival of thunder and lightning accompanied by a cool rain.

I never found a decent put-in to the river before the lengthening shadows signaled dusk. I waived my normal custom of bathing in the river because the rain had provided me a shower, plus, my access to the river was down a steep and muddy slope, and mosquitoes were still biting. These were not like the friendly mosquitos living in western Washington State, the kind that, had they been able to speak, would have asked permission before they bit. Instead of camping in the grass with the chiggers, I set up camp in the rain on the gravel levee road with the hope that no vehicles would drive over me during the night. Everything was drenched, but a hot dinner of rice and beans helped quell my shivering. The weather report for the next four days, according to the lockmasters, was thunder and lightning storms with a headwind of 10-to-15 knots.

The next morning, long before sunrise, I called the night lock operator at Rankin Lock for advice. He thought that there was a safe put-in about two miles beyond my campsite. He seemed knowledgeable, so I took his advice and resumed pulling. I found a location without any drop-off close to where he described and launched Whisper II without any problem other than sticky mud.

Several hours after launching, I heard a familiar voice and looked back to see the strange boat I had seen where Kentucky Lake transitioned to the Tennessee River. I hardly knew Steve Thorp, but even meeting a person with whom I had only a passing acquaintance was so rare it felt like a class reunion. This time Steve was with his stepfather Denny Laughton. Steve had arrived at Fulton Lock last Thursday, August 13, when it was closed. He found his way back to Minnesota, where he picked up his car and trailer to tow his boat around Fulton Lock. He convinced his stepfather to join him. Both were now on their way to Mobile. As they approached, I was near the riverbank, massaging pain in my left shoulder. "What are you doing, trying to catch an alligator?" they asked. They told me that a few weeks before, an alligator over eleven feet long was shot just to the north of us. I hadn't realized we were already in alligator country. After my encounter with Steve and Denny, every bumpy log looked like an alligator.

Approaching Columbus, Mississippi one day later, after a night at an oil storage tank farm, there were more signs of industry, especially those related to wood products. Large grain handling complexes sat on the riverbanks and cranes hoisted as many as thirty trees at a time into giant wood grinders. The dissonant sound of jet planes from Columbus Air Force Base rang across the miles. Because of its use as a training facility, the base is reported to have about the same number of takeoffs and landings as Chicago's O'Hare Field.

I was the only transient boater at the Columbus Marina. Jimmy, the marina manager, told me that most transient boaters travel in the spring and fall. "There's been a long-term drop off in long-distance recreational boaters and the restaurant and motel at the marina are closed because the owner failed to pay the rent." This is how the cycle begins, less traffic leads to failing services, which leads to even less traffic. There may be another reason for less traffic, the "Deliverance Syndrome," which I would soon encounter.

While at the Columbus Marina, I met another Steve sitting in a bug proof screened enclosure on another strange looking boat, this one propelled by a paddlewheel. He invited me aboard for coffee. An injured Navy war veteran, Rev. Steve had traveled the waterway several times with his wife. As we sat together in the heavy humidity, Steve's voice was barely audible. "My wife died of a heart attack two months ago. We sailed around the world twice in our sixty-foot sailboat. She was my best friend." While mourning his wife, Steve lost all interest in boating. He was attempting to sell his paddle wheel-driven cruising boat and much of his gear.

He drove me into Columbus, Mississippi in the marina's courtesy car. With a population of about 23,700, Columbus is the largest town, other than Mobile, along the waterway. At our first stop, a Walmart store, I was hit by the sensation of being in a much different world than I had become used to. On the river, the confining narrow green corridor had become home. Near the Walmart, the land stretched out for miles. The water, vegetation, wildlife, and quiet were replaced by people, buildings, commerce, and noise. Steve helped me select a machete to clear brush and for protection, more from snakes than from people, and replenish my freeze-dried foodstuffs. Upon returning to the marina, and still in need of navigational aids, I purchased Steve's Garmin 650t chart plotter.

After another two days, sixty-one miles, two locks and a pleasant stay at Pickensville Campground (RM 309) I stopped late in the day at the Southwest Taylor Access (RM 274). The owner of a nearby building met me at the landing. He warned me to watch out for poisonous snakes and, in the most disparaging of terms, Black folk. He led me to his now-closed rundown store across the road and blamed the store's closure on Blacks. He had taken over the store from his father. For reasons that would probably be obvious to an impartial observer, the local African American residents, with whom his father had been popular, stopped shopping at his store. He was not the only one I met to use the "N" word. I didn't humor him with a supportive response. I began to wonder if some of those offering me Southern hospitality did so only because I was White. I still looked forward to human contact, in part because of my fear of what lay ahead, but I dreaded meeting other hateful people like him.

Up to this point, the waterway had been so green that half of the channel markers blended in with their backgrounds. Seventeen miles below the Howard Heflin Lock and Dam (R M 267), the limestone White Cliffs of Epes transforms the landscape and reminds the visitor that the South has some vertical relief to interrupt the horizontal landscape. The cliffs constrict the river and increase the velocity of what for me at that time was a favorable downstream current. The white cliffs on the west side marched along the riverbank for more than ten miles, at one point so solid and looming, they might have been mistaken for a manmade fortress against river borne attacks.

My last campsite before Demopolis (RM 238) was on the west side of the river. It was near this location that Karl Adams encountered fire ants and was badly bitten. The ants I encountered while portaging Fulton Lock were comparatively well mannered. Adams found the fire ants to be very difficult to shed from both his tent and kayak.

The daily rains for the past week had kept everything wet including me and most of my gear. While in my tent, I tucked my cell phone in the tent-wall pocket. Although there was no rain that night, it was so humid that my cell phone got drenched from condensation and ceased to function. The instruction book clearly said to "take out the batteries and call Verizon." Bucking the irony of this advice, I tried calling, but with or without batteries, you need a very loud voice for Verizon to hear you while calling on a non-working phone from a river bottom in Alabama.

Tennessee-Black Warrior Waterway

One mile above Demopolis, Alabama, the Black Warrior River entered along the left bank. I was leaving the Tennessee-Tombigbee Waterway and entering the Black Warrior-Tombigbee Waterway, also known simply as the Tombigbee River. I arrived at the Demopolis Marina (RM 217) in the sweltering heat just before noon on August 22, and checked in, having now paddled slightly more than three-quarters of the way to Mobile. Between celebrating with guzzled water and soft drinks, I spoke with Joe, a marine police officer, and Curtis, from the Alabama Department of Conservation. "You began where and are heading where?" they asked. They seemed to welcome the opportunity to linger in the air-conditioned marina fuel dock store to answer my many questions. Curtis let me use his cell phone to call Joyce, who located a Verizon store in Demopolis, a town of about 7,500, where I bought a new flip phone.

The next day, while passing through the Demopolis Lock (RM 213.2), I spotted one lonely deer and dozens of white herons frolicking in the spray that danced in the air above the natural falls below the spillway. Less than a mile downstream, I passed moss covered trees and what may have been three stubby mostly submerged wing dams, the first wing dams I had seen since the Ohio River. I also encountered five tows, the most I had seen in one day on the Tombigbee.

I soon entered a reach with far fewer privately owned facilities and with no Corps of Engineers camping or rest areas. Up to this point, I had no regrets in picking this route compared to a long slog up the Ohio or continuing on the Mississippi to the Gulf. I still couldn't understand why I never encountered any other paddlers, or why Karl Adams was the only other paddler I could identify who paddled across the country on this route. Joe and Curtis, the state employees I met at Demopolis, referred to this area as "No Man's Land."

The river began to twist and turn like Chubby Checkers hit song. Near RM 188, Myer's *Guide* reports that the river takes three miles to progress 1,000 feet. Apart from Bashi Creek Park at RM 145, and Bobby's Fish Camp at RM 118.9, I slept at boat ramps or rare areas of higher land at the side of the river. On the plus side, rain, thunder, and lightning were less frequent, and I was finally starting to notice a favorable current.

Setting up camp on a sandbar near RM 184 late in the afternoon, my first day after Demopolis, I tied Whisper II to a stake close to the water's edge. I was unloading when an upstream tow approached from around a sharp bend. The tug slid toward the bank as Captain Bob from Thebes, Illinois said it would. I seemed to remember Captain Bob telling me something bad could happen. Suddenly, the water receded from the bank as the barges pushed it out of the way, leaving Whisper high and dry. Soon after, waves, from the tow's wake, crashed against Whisper II. I was in no physical danger, but I was at risk of losing my kayak and my gear out here in No Man's Land. With a surge of nervous energy, I grabbed Whisper II's bow painter and quickly gathered up my gear before things floated away and left me stranded. The tug soon disappeared around the bend and the waters edged back to the natural riverbank.

That night in my tent, I read in Myers *Guide* about the killer flood of April 1979. The river at Demopolis crested at the lofty height of 72.4 feet—an unbelievable 59.4 feet above the normal pool level. The tugboat *Cahaba* was working its way downstream below Demopolis when it lost steerage in the powerful current and was swept underwater and under the now-demolished Rooster Bridge. According to Myers, "eyewitnesses feared the worst as they saw the tug disappear into the muddy water and heard the sound of it being banged and scraped along the bottom of the bridge." Miraculously, no one was seriously injured, and the tug was later repaired.

I was beginning to feel the darkness and danger Karl Adams encountered as he entered this area. After paddling past many miles of eroded slopes, I arrived at Bashi Creek Park (RM 145) late in the afternoon. While preparing to land, a large snake, similar to one I had seen at the Demopolis Marina, swam between Whisper II and the shore and disappeared in the undulating darkness of the river. On sandbars snakes are openly visible. No sandbar here. I examined reeds at the shoreline and the grass and brush in the park for a snake-free place to land. While I saw no movement, I was still uneasy. I knew that the absence of movement didn't guarantee the absence of a reptile.

In my focus on the grasses, I startled as I heard someone call out. It was Buddy Rush, a local man known to all who told me that he came to the park just about every day. He declared no fear when it came to snakes. He seemed quite familiar with the river as far as Jackson, Alabama (RM 93).

"You should find more civilization downstream than your guidebook reports," he told me. His quirky sense of humor cheered me as he taught me about the river I would soon paddle, but as the sun got low in the sky, he said it was time for him to return home. I asked Buddy if I could purchase a cold drink from him. He said no. He then walked away and returned a few minutes later to give me three ice-cold colas and three bottles of water. My fear of snakes was replaced by appreciation for Buddy's friendliness and generosity.

The next morning while shoving off, Ricky, a scruffy and remarkably thin middle-aged man of medium height, approached me. He didn't say much but he did tell me that boaters should slow down. "If you bother local fishers or riverside landowners with your wakes, you should expect to be shot at." Why was he warning me? Whisper II didn't leave much wake.

Myers *Guide* reports that the more common, and much more civilized, response is for the boater or homeowner offended by someone's wake to drive ahead to the next lock where they are usually successful in having the police give the boater a ticket.

It was on this morning that I had my first close encounters with alligators. The riverbank now had the look of a subtropical jungle with cypress trees and gloomy Spanish moss. I had been paddling close to the right bank in order to see wildlife, while still trying to stay alert to what I might find. Rounding a sharp bend, I saw several alligators on a mudbank. The first two were maybe eight feet long, if that, and appeared docile. They lulled me into a false calm as they casually slid into the water. I may have startled the third, one that was at least ten feet long. It charged me on its stubby legs, like a wiener dog and lunged at me as it slid into the water. It then took several powerful strokes towards me with its massive tail before submerging within a few feet of Whisper II. I'm not highly proficient in psychoanalyzing gators, so I didn't know what its next move would be. I tried to remember how to defend myself. Nothing came to mind. It was no comfort remembering that the gator was likely to drown me before eating me. I was scared stiff that it would come up beneath my kayak and capsize me, so I paddled away as fast as I could. I was extremely grateful when the alligator gave up the chase.

No Man's Land

What might await me in the reach of the river below Jackson was a concern. Karl Adams got lost in the swamp, had his boat bumped by an alligator, and ended up sleeping on a jury-rigged platform. I had found no reports by anyone else traveling by kayak or canoe and no evidence of any campsites for the final ninety-three miles. The last paddler I had met was Bill, in the red canoe on the Missouri River, so I certainly didn't expect to find any company in the next hundred miles. The Mobile swamp was home to pitcher plants and other flesh-eating plants. Their diet was usually limited to insects, tadpoles, and small fish, but that didn't stop me from imagining I would encounter plants with appetites for bigger prey. Would I be making a big mistake trying to tackle this part of the river? I went as far as to ask Joyce and Mike, to look at the feasibility of my pulling Whisper II the sixty-five road miles (ninety-three river miles) from Jackson to Mobile. The drawback was that we couldn't be sure how safe the road was, or where I would find food and water.

As the day wore on, both the favorable wind and the favorable current increased. A large cabin cruiser, whose full wake would have swamped me, slowed while passing. Soon after, two angry fishers told me the cruiser hadn't slowed for them. I didn't hear any shooting, but I suspect that angry yells from the fishers had something to do with the cruiser slowing for me.

Shortly after noon, I arrived at Bobby's Fish Camp (RM 119) the last stop for food and fuel before Mobile. I was reluctant to forgo the benefits of the current, wind, and cooler than usual temperatures, but wanted better information before proceeding. I also craved a warm shower, a soft dry bed, and a filling meal that included vegetables, a salad, and fatty meat. I was more than a little disappointed when a note on the restaurant door read that it was closed for the day. However, I was relieved to see that the note gave a number to call for other services.

Bobby's daughter Lora Jane McIlwain soon met me. She was one of the most helpful people I met on the trip. As I moved my gear to a small but neat and modestly priced cabin, Lora Jane began to sort out maps and other information needed for the river ahead. While her husband, Randolph, took me into town for a late lunch and supplies, she marked up two topographic maps and the pages from an old chart book to show me the way.

The next day found me downstream from Coffeeville Lock and Dam (RM 117), the last of what boaters refer to as "the dirty dozen," While navigating the river's increasingly sharp bends, I became even more concerned about tows and being forced into their path. Other than tows, I wouldn't encounter much activity along the river; it was seventy-four miles to the next bridge.

I can't say that I had any death-defying close calls, but I know I unintentionally irritated at least one tow driver. As I approached the appropriately named Horseshoe Bend near RM 72, I hugged the right bank. I may have been overly focused on looking for alligators along the shore because I didn't notice the approaching tow until the lead barge was fully in view. As successive barges came into view it seemed as if the tow was heading directly toward me, but it was hard to gauge the angle of approach because I couldn't yet see the pusher tug.

I tried to raise the tow captain on my VHF radio but got no response until the tug was in view. My presence seemed to surprise the captain. "Pass on the one whistle," he called out. I had heard that term before but wasn't sure what it meant. "Does that mean to pass port-to-port?" I asked. I was very relieved to hear him say that it did. Otherwise, I would have had to cross the river in front of him. Our passing was otherwise without consequence, the obliging pilot having slowed the engines. The tow's long, rolling wake left me fighting turbulence, but I'd experienced worse, much worse, from passing cruisers.

Proceeding downriver, the many creeks and sloughs converged with the main river like the veins leading to a heart, while cypress, tupelo, and gum trees on the riverbank transitioned to endless seas of swamp grass. The area became more remote and the current stronger. I benefited from both the river current and sometimes, to a lesser extent, from an outgoing tidal current. Lora Jane had told me of a fishing village on Bates Lake near RM 54. I arrived there at 1:15 p.m., way too early in the day for me to stop. Myer's *Guide* noted that I could expect to encounter friendly people at Bate's Lake. A guest at Bobby's Fish Camp had offered contrary advice, suggesting in no uncertain terms that I avoid Bates Lake because, "Blacks who live there will steal you blind." I was a visitor to Alabama, so I kept my mouth shut; what I heard unfortunately confirmed stereotypes.

I pushed on, but only because it was still early. Two hours later I passed the confluence with the Alabama River at RM 45. I never actually saw the confluence since I was focused on avoiding an approaching tow that didn't answer my radio call.

In late afternoon after a long day on the river, I arrived at Mt. Vernon Boat Ramp (RM 41). Arnell Scott, a Black fisherman, befriended me at the ramp as he had when we passed each other near the confluence with the Alabama River. I greedily drank the iced cold water he offered. He told me to be cautious around the ramp. He said that his two sons had recently been sitting on the dock eating their lunch when a ten-foot alligator spied them. They bolted back to land while the alligator devoured the remainder of their food. When he came to pick up his sons,

Arnell found them sitting on the roof of a pickup truck in the parking lot. While taking my evening bath at the bottom of the boat ramp I entered the water very cautiously, looking for pairs of large eyes poking above the surface and praying there was nothing lurking below.

I let the river soak my tired body as I took stock of my health. I had constant discomfort in my back and often got cramps in my feet that I could only alleviate by removing my feet from the rudder controls. The bruise I developed on my right leg after slipping at Cairo was still present, but the infection was gone. My left shoulder often seemed on the verge of disintegrating.

The river north of Mobile flows through the Mobile River delta and ranks second to the Sacramento River delta in terms of plant and animal diversity. The Tombigbee splits into the Mobile and Tensaw Rivers. The Tensaw then transitions into the Middle River and the Tensaw. I wanted to remain on the Mobile River, but I may have ended up paddling in a circle for days had it not been for the buoys and other aids to navigation operated by the US Coast Guard. My only objection to the Coast Guard's otherwise excellent navigation system was the difficulty I had locating the buoys. From the waterline perspective of a paddler, the green buoys were almost invisible, disappearing into the background of green vegetation. I once asked a high-ranking Coast Guard officer, if the Coast Guard ever considered adding bright yellow marking to the green buoys. He didn't seem to take me seriously, a possible sign he had never been lost in a swamp.

I had been very concerned that there would be no place to camp between Mt. Vernon and Mobile, although Arnell Scott and some other fishers I met along the way said there was a small marina a short distance up a creek called the Dead River near RM 17. I arrived at what I thought was the Dead River at about noon on August 28 and called the marina on my cell phone. As with my previous experiences, the person in charge didn't know whether I was at the correct creek and didn't know how far up the creek the marina was located. I thought it best not to get lost going up the creek, even if I had a paddle, so I moved on.

Even professional river pilots get confused in this maze of channels, sometimes with disastrous consequences. Very early in the morning on September 22, 1993, the towboat *Mauvilla* took a wrong turn in the fog at RM 10 on the Mobile River and struck a fixed railroad bridge on the un-navigable Big Bayou Canot, which connects with the Dead River upstream of the bridge. Less than ten minutes later, Amtrak's *Sunset Limited*, traveling at about 70 mph with 220 passengers and crew on board, derailed while crossing the damaged bridge. The lead locomotive plunged into the far bank. The next two locomotives, the baggage car, dormitory car, and two of the six passenger cars plunged into the water. Forty-seven people lost their lives, most by drowning, and 103 were injured. It was, and still is, the deadliest train wreck in Amtrak's history. Amtrak has since discontinued this route.

The delta consisted of an enticing blend of cypress trees, marsh grass, and wading shorebirds. The pungent primeval odor of decaying vegetation was even pleasant. Unfortunately for me, terrain that is the perfect habitat for wading birds is not good for camping. To make matters worse, I was bucking a strong headwind and the tidal current was running against me. Two fishers motored near and suggested that there was higher ground just upstream from a railroad trestle on Catfish Bayou near RM 8.6. I scoped out the area they suggested, but it appeared far better habitat for snakes and alligators than it did for me.

Reluctantly, I returned to the wind and adverse current on the Mobile River. Like the long-distance runner I once was, I caught my second wind. An hour later I saw the tops of the tallest buildings in downtown Mobile.

River observations while kayaking are the opposite of objects seen in auto mirrors; distant objects seen on the river are farther away than they appear. I kept paddling and watched the sun sink lower in the western sky. It wasn't until I was underneath the US 90 Cochran Bridge near downtown Mobile that I found some higher ground. Keeping a wary eye for snakes and using logs as cross ties, I hauled Whisper II up a rocky slope and found a place to pitch my tent near the river.

Other people were camping under the bridge, but I didn't advertise my presence and never met anyone. I was now very low on drinking water but didn't trust purifying the brackish water from an industrial waterway. I cooked Jaipur vegetables, the one remaining dinner in my pantry that didn't require the addition of water and went to sleep.

Since this was to be my last day of paddling, and I was exhausted, I was really looking forward to sleeping in. However, the wind was supposed to pick up throughout the day and Mobile Bay can be dangerous, the wide expanse offering no obstruction to block the wind. Learning that five sailors had died earlier that year during a windstorm, I reluctantly decided to wake up at my regular time, which had been extended from 5:00 to 5:20 a.m., as the days got shorter. In my haste to get going, I left my life jacket behind. Joyce thinks that kayaking causes memory loss. After less than five minutes without my life jacket, I felt almost naked, realized what I had done, and returned to find it still at my campsite. When I shoved off again at about 6:30 a.m., the river was dead calm. By the time I reached the bay, there was a quartering east wind (sidewind) stirring up a mild chop.

My final destination was the Dog River Marina about ten miles south of downtown Mobile. When Joyce called the marina the week before to ask about storing my kayak, Bob Swartz, the manager, offered to do so at no cost. I stopped to ask several fishers for directions. I was feeling spent and grateful for the wind-driven waves pushing me along to the marina. I paddled under the AL 193 highway bridge and sidled up to the floating dock.

From the smile on his face, it seemed as if Ricky, the fuel dock attendant had been looking forward to my arrival. Ricky called Paul the marina guard who helped me pull Whisper II onto a floating dock for inspection and cleaning. Linda, the marina manager who had been communicating with Joyce, greeted me warmly with words that made my voyage seem important. "You made it. What a heroic journey"

Postscript VII

The remainder of the day was spent cleaning and storing Whisper II and arranging for a motel in Tillmans Corner with the aid of the Dog River Marina staff and Joe, one of the marina's moorage tenants. I spent the next few days shipping most of my gear home, visiting Mobile and the battleship Alabama, and driving to Biloxi where Joyce and I had helped in the post-Katrina cleanup. I flew back to Seattle on September 3, about twenty pounds lighter than when I began paddling.

While paddling this year, I kept close tabs on notes I'd made after reading Karl Adam's book. Like me, Karl made the trip from St. Louis to Mobile Bay as part of a longer journey. Unlike me, Karl took no annual breaks between trip segments. As the first paddler attempting to kayak from the Pacific to the Atlantic Ocean, he stopped frequently to give interviews. He did his trip in 1987 at age sixty. I was twelve years older when I arrived in Mobile but wasn't hampered by the need to stop for publicity. I often used his progress as a guide for predicting my arrivals at destinations. I would complete this year's journey of 901 miles in twenty-eight days, paddling an average of eight-and-a-half hours per day and averaging 3.8 mph. This was a few days faster than Karl had done it, but just about the same if you accounted for his stops. He still had many miles to go to Miami, his final destination. I could stop, at least for this year.

Approaching the Mississippi River / Ohio River confluence

The Olmsted Dam

Pickwick Lo**k** & Dam, Tennessee River, September 1937.   33,471

Lock at Pickwick Dam

Tenn-Tom Waterway Divide Cut under Construction

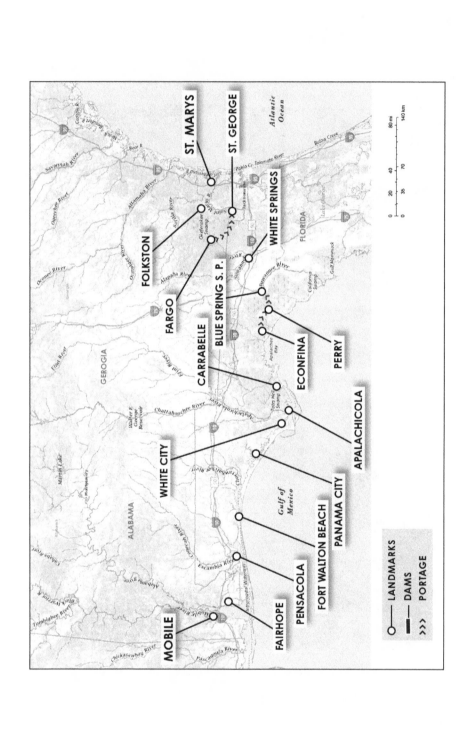

VIII

Mobile, Alabama to the
Atlantic Ocean

2017

Big Lagoon

Shoving Off

My heart wasn't keeping pace with my ambitions. It had begun to beat irregularly and fast, and a heart valve was giving out. An ablation helped with my heart rate, but my surgeon said there was a risk of reverting to pre-procedure conditions if I didn't take care of myself, whatever that meant. I was planning to kayak many hours each day, so I couldn't afford to be running out of breath or shortening my paddling day due to overwhelming fatigue. Despite my cardiac status, I was most concerned that my left shoulder might give out. Quitting was an option. Not an attractive one.

In the spring of 2017, my doctors finally gave me the green light to kayak. If they hadn't, I probably would have looked for other doctors. Kicking my preparations into high gear, in May Joyce and I traveled to Ocean City, New Jersey, where I began my on-water training. I dug into a rigorous regimen of rowing and kayaking on the Intracoastal Waterway (ICW) and back bay, just one hundred yards from our backdoor. By late June I was able to paddle up to five hours before pain in my left shoulder warned me to stop.

The Atlantic Ocean was my ultimate goal, but I was still unsure of my route. In 2015, I was forced to reroute to Mobile, Alabama when flood waters held me back on the Ohio River. This year I was unsure what route I would take after the "Big Bend" in the Florida coast at the eastern end of the panhandle. It would be a learn as you go experience.

A severe nor'easter hit Ocean City just three days before I was to leave for Mobile. Sitting at the kitchen table watching the rain and tidewater flood the backyard and the wind attempt to free the boats from their moorings, my mood turned as dark as the heavy black clouds hanging over the bay. I feared encountering similar dismal conditions in Alabama, Florida, and Georgia, the last states I would encounter. Adding to my downward spiral, my friend Bob, who had kayaked with me on the Snake River, wrote to say he would be unable to join me. I dreaded failing to reach my goal but sensed that at my age and with my heart condition it was now or never.

As the rain continued and as the lights flickered, my son Mike called to say that he was sending three boxes of gear and food supplies to the Dog River Marina where my kayak had been stored for two years, the marina having steadfastly refused my attempts to pay for storage. Soon after Mike's call, a fully soaked Joyce left a puddle of water on the floor when she returned from walking to and from the bank. She had arranged for me to obtain a debit card in the event I needed more cash while traveling.

I still had concerns about logistics in Mobile, and major worries about crossing the ten-mile-wide Mobile Bay, which has the reputation of chewing up small boats and spitting them into the wind. A phone call to Tracy Lannie of the Mobile Bay Canoe and Kayak Club lifted my spirits. Tracy and her husband, David, offered to pick me up at the airport, let me stay at their home, then take me to my kayak.

It wasn't hard for Tracy and David to recognize me in the airport. I was the only one carrying a duffle bag and a dry sack and wearing a shirt adorned with a picture of a kayak. Tracy and David impressed me as a pleasant and handsome couple several decades younger than me. Both exuded Southern hospitalities, although David's was subdued while Tracy's was vibrant.

While driving to their home in Bayou La Batre, first settled by David's ancestors in 1786, Tracy checked her smart phone and told me that the wind predicted for the next day might prove treacherous on Mobile Bay. David offered to take Whisper and me to Meaher State Park on the east side of the bay. He said it was ten miles farther north than the marina so I would paddle the same distance I had planned to cover but would be close to shore. Tracy and David then asked if I would speak to their kayak and canoe group after completing my first day of paddling. Hoping to share my experiences with my new friends and learn more about the Gulf Coast in the process, I readily agreed.

After a restful sleep and a hearty breakfast of bacon, eggs, and toast suited for a day of high-energy expenditure, David drove me to the Dog River Marina on the west shore of Mobile Bay. The incredible staff had laid out Whisper II, and my gear, all neatly presented for my inspection and use. While I thanked the marina staff, David loaded Whisper on his roof rack. About an hour later, now coated with sunscreen, I waved my paddle in farewell to David and shoved off at Meaher State Park. Whisper II's bow pointed south towards storms, dehydration, dangerous waters, and dangerous wildlife that would make this the most challenging segment of my cross-country trip.

The day was sunny and hot. I joked to myself that the many fish I saw jumping were doing so to cool off, but that wouldn't help. The air temperature, in the mid-90s, was even hotter than the water. I didn't seem to be sweating as much as usual, perhaps because of unseasonably low humidity, or because I was reluctant to stop paddling to drink enough water. Shortly before noon, my lower arms locked up with painful cramps. I would have been more concerned that the cramps revealed I was in poor condition except, curiously, arm cramps occurred on the first day of each leg of my cross-country voyage and didn't return until the following leg. Backing off on the effort I put into my paddle strokes and drinking water with electrolyte even before I was thirsty, the pain soon went away.

Although I probably could have cut across the bay, now blanketed with only a slight chop, paddling near shore allowed me to take in the scenery, and offered an easier escape route to shore if the wind did pick up.

Given the poverty I had seen in Alabama in years past, I was surprised at the many expensive homes and watercraft dotting the shoreline, especially near the upscale village of Fairhope along the northeast shore of Mobile Bay. I learned that one of Fairhope's claims to fame is Ecor Rouge, which I caught a glimpse of from the water and which, at 115 feet, is the highest point of coastal land from Mexico to Maine. Now that I have lived in the Pacific Northwest for more than forty-five years on an unnamed bluff two hundred feet above Puget Sound, it seems so strange that a hill just 115 feet above sea level would be considered high.

I drank in the luxurious views, but when shorelines are developed to such a degree, finding a place to come ashore and spend the night is tricky. There were surprisingly few boaters on the water who I could ask about camping, and the two jet skis and one sailboat I observed didn't approach close enough for me to hail them. By midafternoon, I was far more tired than expected, and grateful that the plan to meet up with Tracy and David for the club meeting gave me an excuse to stop paddling early. I had covered only eighteen miles—nothing to brag about but not so meager that it would be embarrassing to tell fellow kayakers if they were to ask.

The farther south I paddled, the fewer people I saw on shore or on their docks, and the only creatures on the water were hundreds of brown pelicans and me. Approaching Week's Bay and the protected wildlife habitat that surrounds it, my options for camping were fast running out. When only a few hundred yards from Week's Bay's wetlands, I spotted two people somewhat younger than me relaxing with iced drinks in a gazebo at the end of a long pier. Although reluctant to interrupt their tranquility, I asked if they knew of any nearby place to camp. They asked where I was headed and when I told them the Atlantic Ocean, they invited me to camp overnight on their back lawn. I could get used to the famous Southern hospitality.

Rick Horsley and his friend Kathryn helped me come ashore and stage my gear for the night. That evening, while writing in my journal about my meeting with the Mobile Bay Canoe and Kayak Club, one of Rick's granddaughters stopped by to invite me to join their large family for breakfast in exchange for my telling them about my trip. I couldn't pass up an offer like that.

Soon after an extravagant breakfast of eggs, pancakes, sausage, sweet rolls, coffee, and juice with Kathryn and the Horsley family, they waved goodbye to me from the end of their pier. Two months later I read that Hurricane Nate, which hit Mobile on October 8, 2017, destroyed or damaged 90 percent of the piers on the east side of Mobile

Bay. I tried to contact the Horsley's to find out how they had fared but was unable to reach them.

A warm breeze caressed me on my way south to the ICW. Other than a fishing boat far in the distance, I was almost alone on the clear bay water for more than two hours. My senses soon jolted into focus on a tight group of fins cutting across my peripheral vision in the distance. I recalled David Lannie's caution about bull sharks. Known to be aggressive, the stocky bull shark has gradually moved into the brackish water in Mobile Bay and even some rivers that empty into the bay.

I was reminded that Joyce and I were once thrilled when a male orca much longer than Whisper passed directly beneath us, the animal's bent dorsal fin brushing the bottom of Whisper as the whale's wave lifted us. More afraid of sharks than orca, I began to prepare myself for an uncomfortable—and possibly risky—encounter in Mobile Bay. When I finally spotted the unmistakable spray bursting from a blowhole, I relaxed and smiled. For the next twenty minutes, a pod of seven or eight bottlenose dolphins escorted me south while cutting across Whisper II's bow and rising and diving alongside. Their sleek two-tone grey bodies gleamed in the sunshine. I felt as if my new friends were playing a game with me.

Luxury Living Along the Intracoastal Waterway (ICW)

At the southeast limit of Mobile Bay, I entered the ICW. From here to Carrabelle, Florida, I would be on the western segment of this 3,000-mile-long waterway that stretched from Boston to Brownsville, Texas. The ICW comprises inlets, bays, and artificial canals, and protects recreational boaters and commercial traffic from the risk of offshore travel. The trade-off? Longer travel distances, running aground on shifting mud flats, and crossing dangerous inlets. A trade-off I was, nevertheless, willing to make.

The first ten miles of the waterway, here a narrow canal, was all anyone could ask for: multiple variants of green with pine, live oak and southern magnolia draped in Spanish moss on the nearby banks, the sound of hundreds of jumping fish splashing when they hit the water, flapping pelican wings and squawking egrets, the feeling of warm Gulf water on my arms, and the smell of the sea, which, of course, is the smell of the land near the sea. To top it off, there were few noisy boats to mar my enjoyment. Being close to heaven, I sang "America the Beautiful."

After reaching the end of the canal in the vicinity of Orange Beach, Alabama, the glorious cooling shade from the water-loving trees whose branches draped over the narrow waterway disappeared. The sun beat down in full force, and I started dripping sweat and drinking so much water I was afraid of running out. The presence of offshoot bays made navigation difficult. My rhythmic paddling lulled me into not paying proper attention and I almost took a long detour into a bay that would have lived up to its name, Perdido Bay (Lost Bay).

Late in the afternoon I pulled ashore on a white sand beach at Big Lagoon State Park. I was now in Florida, the sixteenth state I had touched since leaving Fort Clatsop, Oregon in 2008. I was pleased to have made it this far on a trip that had far exceeded my expectations.

While walking the beach looking for the primitive shoreline campsite reserved for non-motorized boats, I met Craig McDonnell. Owner of a mobile concession stand, Craig rents kayaks and serves such delicacies as the great American hot dog. I settled for two ice cold root beers and a chocolate fudge ice cream bar. Craig tried to convince me to purchase a sail so Whisper II could take advantage of what he said would be a prevailing tailwind. I told Craig I didn't want a sail. I had to do this under my own steam.

Later, I checked NOAA Climatic Data Center reports, which confirmed what I expected—and dreaded— the prevailing wind in the month of August near Pensacola was a headwind averaging 7 mph from the east-southeast. After my conversation with Craig, I paddled Whisper II a half mile farther east to a secluded campsite along a slough and not far from a clean rest room and a gazebo. I was rewarded with an expansive view of Big Lagoon with its broad marshes and numerous tidal creeks surrounded by the remnants of twisted oak and pine coastal forests, bonsai like due to high wind and storm surges.

Having paddled about thirty miles in nine hours, I was pleased that I had little shoulder pain. The most annoying pain was in my feet, apparently resulting from reduced blood circulation caused by my tight paddling socks. For the next day, I decided to limit my footwear to my Keen sandals. After a dinner of freeze-dried beef stroganoff with noodles, and peaches in syrup for dessert, I took a cool shower at the rest room and went through my normal routine of writing in my journal, calling Joyce, planning for the next day, and reading a book that was intended to ease me into a restful sleep.

Development along this reach of the ICW is disturbingly similar to New Jersey. Small homes on the barrier islands were being replaced with luxury homes and condominiums. As in New Jersey, few of the boaters seemed to realize that the steep closely spaced wakes they leave behind their powerful boats threaten kayakers, especially when their wakes combined with wind-driven waves. Even so, the only time I felt seriously threatened during my first week was just ahead.

The next day while crossing Pensacola Inlet south of the Pensacola Naval Air Station, and between historic Fort Barrancas on the mainland and Fort Pickens on Santa Rosa Island, I failed to account for the rapidly moving outgoing tide and northeast wind. I was being swept out to sea, or at least was on my way, something I only realized when I observed that I was approaching a red buoy in the inlet very rapidly. Whisper II was amid blue-green rollers towering high above me as they careened toward ominous white breakers that formed where the waves curved around the point at Fort Pickens. Afraid that it was too late to avoid broaching, capsizing, and either being pounded by the breaking surf or cast adrift somewhere in the Gulf of Mexico, my heart started beating so fast I feared it would trigger my arrhythmia. A small Coast Guard patrol craft heading out through the inlet slowed to observe me.

Apparently more satisfied than I was that I was not in great jeopardy, it moved on. Even paddling with all the energy I could summon, I sensed I was moving in the wrong direction. Just when I was about to give up, turn around and attempt to run through the inlet to the Gulf, I realized that I was finally moving slowly away from the breaking waves. Ten long minutes later, I rounded the point and headed away from immediate danger, paddling as hard as my fading strength allowed to keep from being sucked back into the inlet.

To prepare for this trip I had downloaded a collection of annotated Google photos called Visit Florida by the Florida Paddle Trails Association, and a set of more traditional maps and narrative published by the Florida Office of Greenways and Trails. I also had my GPS, pages from *DeLorme's Atlas & Gazetteer: Florida,* and a set of topographic maps.

Over the next two days, I experienced the non-sunshine side of the Sunshine State. Places to camp were few, as David Lanie and members of the kayak club had cautioned. On the first night I accidently stumbled across a primitive campsite near Big Sabine Point. My first encounter with Florida rain was nothing more than a short-lived shower that fell when I was making camp. Able to capture some of the rain in my cockpit cover to add to my rapidly dwindling supply of drinking water, I filled one water bottle.

From Joyce's weather reports, I knew that rain accompanied by thunder and lightning was soon to arrive in force. What I didn't yet know was that the rain would be my companion for almost my entire stay in Florida. The next day, the rain was so intense I lost sight of land and had to use my compass to make sure I didn't turn around. Seeking relief, I paddled to shore at Opal Beach on Santa Rosa Island. I waded across the ankle-deep water covering the main road and tried to find someone who could provide a reliable weather forecast. The one resident camper in the park, who seemed about my age, didn't want to open his door or window to talk to me while Perry Mason, his favorite TV show, was on.

When about to again cross the main road in the driving rain, I asked a couple of police officers sitting in their SUV if I could wait out the rain in the park's clean rest room. They told me it was okay to sit out the storm, good news until they added that I might be sitting for a long time. The same weather pattern was supposed to linger for a week. When rain subsided, I decided to move on.

By midafternoon, I entered a reach known as the Narrows. While struggling against a tidal current, I found a camp site on a human-made sand island near the town of Mary Esther, and across from Hurlburt Field and Eglin Air Force Base. Composed of dredge material, the island is one of many signs of the USACE's efforts to maintain the channel at the twelve-foot depth intended for most of its length.

During the early morning hours, I heard thunder roiling close by and a loudspeaker from the air base warned that a lightning storm was approaching. I stayed in my cozy sleeping bag until an "all clear" was announced. About an hour and a half later, while paddling and choking down breakfast, I heard another announcement. Another warning? An all clear? Didn't matter. I was on my way.

The Emerald Coast

That morning, not long after the announcement, I paddled past the Fort Walton Beach Indian Temple Mound, a twelve-foot-high ceremonial mound along US 98, built by the Pensacola Indians long before white settlers came to this area. It is one of three surviving ceremonial mound complexes in the Florida panhandle, although there are many more middens containing shell residue. I chuckled at the memory of a question asked by another tourist while Joyce and I visited Pueblo cliff dwellings in Arizona: Why did the Indians build their community so close to the main road?"

A few minutes after passing the Temple Mound, I approached Destin Inlet. Even armed with advice from the kayak club, it wasn't clear which route to take when past the inlet. There were three options. The one offshore route involved passing through Destin Inlet, known as East Pass, into the Gulf of Mexico and following the Emerald

Coast to Panama City. I could also choose between two moderately protected routes, both across Choctawhatchee Bay. My maps showed two State Parks on protected offshoot bays along the northern option. The southern option was shorter, but my maps showed no campsites.

I stopped at the Adventure Marina on the southwest side of the Highway 98 Bridge to buy more electrolyte drink, snacks, and a butane lighter. The morning's storms, coupled with a weather report of more storms on the way, convinced me to avoid the offshore route. I also decided on the shorter southern route across the bay when I remembered David Lannie mentioning that he and a friend had been able to find a place to camp.

The Emerald Coast is a long shoreline marked by stark white fine quartz sand and emerald-green water. Although the clear water normally allows swimmers and boaters to see the bottom, I doubted the likelihood of good water visibility if the wind was blowing, and the waves were high. The water on the inland side of the long peninsula—where Destin is located—was usually clear, but it has the weak-coffee or tea brown color associated with low levels of tannins. Despite the tint, when the water was calm, the bottom, with an almost hypnotic hue, was clearly visible. Schooling mullet milled about, pursued by speckled trout, which according to my expert fisherman friend Chet, is a trout in name only.

Steering well away from the narrow part of Dustin Inlet, I crossed it without incident. While paddling along the southern shoreline of Choctawhatchee Bay, thunder and lightning threatened. By noon, the storms had passed, and lingering cloud cover kept the temperature in the mid-80s. With plenty of time to think, my mind turned to the history of the Native American tribes in the age of exploration here in the US. In the eighteenth and nineteenth centuries, this was the land of the Creek (Muscogee), a tribe whose land once included almost all of Georgia and Alabama. Most Creek were forced to flee to Oklahoma after the Indian Removal Act of 1830, but some of those who sided with the US in the war of 1812 were allowed to remain. If you examine

a map closely, you may find three small dots in Alabama, two of them
just north of the northwest corner of the Florida panhandle and only
about twenty-five miles from the Mobile River where I paddled in
2015, and the third near Montgomery. These dots mark the last
remaining 172 acres of Creek land in Alabama, a grotesquely small
residue of the millions of acres of land the Creek occupied at the time
of the Discovery Expedition.

On November 21, 1984, the land depicted by these dots was finally
declared a reservation for the Poarch Band of the Creek Nation. As I
observed while on the Mississippi River, and much to my dismay, I
would not pass close to a single Native American reservation between
St. Louis and the Atlantic Ocean.

After paddling more than nine hours, I was beat. I had been
searching for a place to camp for more than two hours but had seen
only the low-lying marsh of the Choctawhatchee River Wildlife
Management Area. Soon after, while passing ominously named
Alligator Point, I came upon a few houses. Most appeared unoccupied,
but when I saw a young, smiling man in his backyard, I asked him
about camping. Chris Flow was rushing to get to a job site in Destin,
but before he left, he showed me where to pitch my tent, take a shower,
find a toilet, and help myself to cold drinks. Having been prepared to
sleep in Whisper II, I considered myself very lucky. The next morning
an intense thunder and lightning storm blew in just before I'd broken
camp. While I waited under Chris' deck for the storm to subside, even
a little, he arrived and offered me a cup of hot coffee.

Underway again, a couple of hours past Chris' home I came to
the town of Port Washington and entered a narrow reach of the ICW
known locally as the Ditch. Much of the Ditch, built by the Corps of
Engineers, comprised near-vertical side slopes of sand over gray shale
or limestone. Majestic live oak trees arched over the waterway while
long-leaf pine stood more vertical on the canal banks. During the eight
hours it took me to paddle through the ditch I found absolutely no
place to camp, few places to pull ashore, and almost no wading birds

because there was no place to wade. There were few tributary streams, the porous sand above the rock allowed most of the rain to infiltrate. Nearby agricultural use of the land was evidenced by a half dozen or so pipes that returned what appeared to be agricultural runoff to the ICW. I didn't see any fish, but there must have been some because there were a few kingfishers trying to live up to their name while also trying to evade me in their mysterious way of repeatedly flying ahead of Whisper II and waiting for me to catch up before alighting again.

It was dark and dreary until midafternoon, when clouds lifted, and the sky became bright and clear. I began to see a few boats including one obnoxiously noisy airboat, a sign that the end of the cut near the community of West Bay was near. After spotting the Highway 79 Bridge, I began to look for a campground, known to me only by the acronym BFE. I came upon a rather lumpy and grumpy man fishing in a rubber raft as raindrops fell on his almost nude body. He had no idea where the BFE campground was located.

Less than a half-mile farther, I stopped at a small cafe just before the bridge to ask about BFE. The waitress who greeted me started to say she didn't know, and then interrupted herself to exclaim, "Wait a minute . . . that's us, BFE is Best Food Ever, the name of our restaurant!" Needless to say, they don't get many campers at BFE, but that didn't stop Suzette, Stacy Lee, and Paulann from treating me like a real adventurer and serving me a nice dinner of brisket of beef, baked beans, potato chips, and watermelon. It may not have been the best food ever, but it tasted great to me. My host's hospitality added additional flavor.

For the first two hours after leaving BFE, with Panama City my next waypoint, I traversed a bay that was so wide I couldn't see both shorelines, although the morning haze may have had something to do with sight distance. I had been concerned that crossing this bay in high wind would be dangerous, but the early morning was so calm that Whisper II lived up to her name while she glided smoothly along. The downside of having no wind: it soon became very hot and humid with no breeze to relieve my discomfort. Although I didn't have a thermometer, a good indication of temperature was the condition of my jellied fruit drop snacks. They simply melted so the temperature must have been in the low to mid-90s. If they melted and congealed into the shape of a giant dead amoeba, as they did once on the Columbia River, the temperature was over 95 degrees.

By early afternoon I had paddled 8 hours without resting. After passing under Tyndall Parkway on the FL 98/U.S. 30A bridge, I spotted a boat ramp on the northeast side. I pulled over to look for drinking water but ended up staying the night. There was a large sign near the bridge warning, *no trespassing beyond this point,* so I pitched my tent on what I thought was the legal side, without realizing the same message was also on the other side of the sign.

I had been following the story told by Karl Adams in his book *Wake of the Wind Dancer.* Like me, Karl started at the Pacific Ocean and finished at the Atlantic. Although we traveled different routes, we both paddled the ICW along the Florida Panhandle. Karl was an accomplished kayaker and suffered few mishaps of his own doing, but there was one exception. While a guest in the home of a family living in Panama City, the town I had just passed, he failed to secure his kayak. The next morning it was missing. Fortunately, the local authorities found it and returned it to him.

Karl was traveling a little slower than me, due in part to his frequent publicity stops, and because "Redundant Roy," (the nickname Adams gave to the man then accompanying him in an outboard powered canoe), kept having mechanical problems. When Karl was on his own following the ICW, as he was when Roy stopped for repairs or moved too far ahead, he pushed himself to make up for lost time, covering as many as forty miles in a day. I was averaging twenty-five miles per day since leaving Mobile. For his entire trip from the Pacific Ocean to the Atlantic, Adams reported averaging thirty miles on actual travel days. My slightly higher daily average since leaving the Pacific Ocean (excluding my bicycle portage across the Rocky Mountains) could probably be attributed to Adam's frequent stops for interviews and his travel with Redundant Roy.

The Forgotten Coast

When I shoved off the next morning an hour after sunrise, cloud cover made the morning slightly less hot than the day before. I paddled through scenic bays until noon when I entered a twenty-mile-long dredged cut that would eventually take me to Lake Wimico and Apalachicola, Florida. When the cloud cover lifted, the sun bore down, and I began to doubt that I would make it through the canal without finding more drinking water. I had doubts that there would be drinking water at the two primitive campsites along the canal as shown on my maps. I recalled the advice given to me by Harriet, a health care provider friend of David and Tracy, that dehydration could trigger my arrythmia. Within one mile of entering the cut, I came upon the only boaters I would see in the cut, Kelly, and Gina, who were on their way to Destin. They were familiar with the canal and after giving me a bottle of water, told me there might be more water at a cluster of houses just ahead. They added that they were unfamiliar with the two primitive campsites I was seeking, but camping might be possible at the FL 71 highway bridge in White City, about seventeen miles ahead.

Approaching the cluster of about ten houses, I saw that some of them had low docks, and decided I'd ask for water. After trying to find someone at home, with no success, I pulled up to a dock with a hose and filled my water bottles, not knowing for sure if the water was potable.

By midafternoon I stopped every few minutes to drink the little water I still had and to toss brackish water from the canal on my head. Pine trees lined the canal, but they were not dense enough to block the sun. I finally picked up a slight favorable current, which was headed for a cut-off canal that led south to Port St. Joe, Florida, and the Gulf of Mexico. After passing the canal, the favorable current flowing eastward changed to an adverse westward current. This flow, combined with a headwind, slowed my progress. I had paddled close to nine hours with an aching left shoulder and lingering congestion and wasn't sure how much farther I could go. Late in the afternoon, just when I was about to pull over and take on the risk from alligators and snakes if I slept in Whisper II, I heard road traffic, an almost sure sign of a nearby highway bridge.

I found a clean and compact park with dual boat ramps next to the bridge. Several boaters were preparing to head out for the "evening bite." A man living in a floating home tied to a dock adjacent to the park walked up to me and told me I might not be allowed to camp in the county park, but he thought I could camp on state property underneath the bridge. As I set up my tent under the bridge, first a woman and then a couple asked if they could take me to a store to resupply. The couple also invited me to dinner at their home after they returned from fishing. I thanked them profusely but told them that even though I was hungry I was so tired from the day's paddle that I needed to rest. Knowing that we were near a transition in time zones, I asked the couple which time zone we were in. They replied in unison, "Both."

After leaving the next morning, I kept my eyes peeled for the second primitive campsite, but like the first, I never found it. In the entire length of the canal, the only possible place I found to camp–other than the FL 71 Bridge–was the corridor for an electric transmission line. The rest of the canal either had high, steep banks, or was bordered by low marsh with standing water, and the likely presence of alligators and snakes.

Two hours after shoving off, I entered Lake Wimico, a shallow body of water about five miles long in the direction of my travel and one-to-two-and-a-half miles wide. It was a glorious morning with sunshine, little wind, and a still moderate temperature. I had feared that Lake Wimico, as described by Karl Adams, would be dark, dreary, and intimidating, but I found it to be refreshingly welcoming. Perhaps the sunny weather and the comforting presence of other people helped. I spoke to several fishers who were after catfish, and who confirmed that the small fish jumping all around us were probably mullet. Somewhere near the center of the lake, a lone tree growing on an island—smaller in diameter than the length of a full-grown python—reminded me of my relative isolation in a land little known to me.

Exiting the lake and proceeding down the Jackson and Apalachicola Rivers, the favorable current was neutralized by an unfavorable wind. I encountered my first house of the day on the outskirts of Apalachicola. The homeowners seemed to take better care of their flag display than their home. One flagpole had a Confederate flag mounted above the stars and stripes. I wondered if that was legal, and even though I wouldn't display the two flags in the same manner, I hoped there was no law that prevented such free expression. Another flag displayed *Make America Great Again* with an image of Donald Trump, and a third had a message reminding people not to forget our soldiers missing in action.

The flags made me think that the freedoms we have today were earned at the expense of many Americans, including Blacks and Native Americans. I was approaching the dominant village of the Apalachicola (Creek) Indians. At the time of the Lewis and Clark Expedition, their numbers had already been reduced to a few hundred by disease, slavery, and war. The even fewer remaining in 1834 were forced to flee to Oklahoma in their own Trail of Tears. In 2000, the census reported that 0.17 percent of the 2,334 residents of Apalachicola were Native. That equates to four people.

I still didn't know where to stay in Apalachicola, a name that rolls off my tongue now that I can pronounce it. About a mile before town, a small tour boat broke boating rules and cut directly in front of me from my left before nosing into a sandbar. I was glad I didn't complain because the operator, his wife, and son were all very nice. They told me of two hotels on the water in town.

Although prepared to pay more for an on-the-water location to keep Whisper II close by, I was surprised that the Water Street Hotel on Scipio Creek cost $206, admittedly for a moderate sized family apartment. I couldn't help comparing the cost to the five dollars charged for my overnight stay at the campsite with the similar name—Scipio's Marina—on the Columbia River.

While securing Whisper II to the dock in a tidal current that was attempting to carry her downstream, a welcoming committee of two young and very friendly women bicyclists helped me unload. I tried to impress them with my athleticism, but I only embarrassed myself when I almost lost my paddle in the fast-moving water.

"Where are you from and where are you headed," they asked. Their jaws dropped when I told them I was trying to get from the Pacific to the Atlantic Oceans. Maybe I redeemed myself a little in their eyes.

The town of Apalachicola remains delightfully in the past, with restored buildings and fishing boats moored along its shore. Apalachicola Bay is famous for scallops, although a sign posted on a billboard said that scallop harvesting was temporarily closed due to an algal bloom. After a shower, a nap, and lunch of yogurt, orange juice and a breakfast roll provided to me at no cost by the motel housekeeper, I looked at my watch, and was surprised to see that it was already 3:15 p.m. Rushing to the post office, I mailed home a package of mostly unneeded clothes just before the 4 p.m. closing.

After wandering the downtown area and stopping to enjoy a pint of chocolate ice cream and a soft drink at a brightly painted cafe, I entered the Apalachicola River Keepers office to see what I could learn about the water path ahead. "Oh, you'll want to speak to Dan Tonsmeire. Sorry he isn't here now," the friendly young woman at the front desk told me. I made a mental note to call Dan at the number she gave me.

Before returning to my room, I stopped at the Chamber of Commerce. I admit that I wasn't dressed like a rich tourist, but the manager was unhelpful to the point of being rude. He put my request for information on hold, in order to speak about an upcoming gun, show with a woman who had arrived after me. The woman said the event was to feature gun-toting locals dressed in cowboy and cowgirl outfits, an inducement for children to learn about guns. I support gun education and weapons used for hunting, but after my experience in Vietnam, I didn't feel comfortable listening to this discussion. I excused myself but received no response in return. It was as if I was invisible.

Craving contact and friendly conversation with people, I went to dinner at the riverside Up the Creek Raw Bar. I ordered a hamburger and salad; the hamburger was the diameter of a 45-rpm record. Am I showing my age again? While enjoying the view on the restaurant's back deck I met a young couple seated next to me who appeared to be on their honeymoon. I tried not to bother them but was pleased when the young woman turned to me. "Look at the manatee eating its evening meal," she said, as she pointed to the river below us. More than half the length of Whisper II and easily weighing more than my vintage '66 VW bug, this ungainly greyish-brown mammal with a whiskered face and paddle tail seemed to propel itself by walking on its forelimbs while using the same appendages to shove plants into its mouth. It was the first manatee I had seen in the wild.

First Dunking

The next morning, I prepared for the almost twenty-five-mile paddle to Carrabelle beginning at Apalachicola Bay and continuing along St. George Sound. The first five miles was parallel to the John Gorrie Memorial Bridge and Causeway. The bay and sound in this area are partially protected by St. George Island, but because the barrier island is about five miles from the mainland, the protection is minimal. I was glad to have fastened my spray skirt before leaving. While struggling to attach it, Mike, a gentleman of about my age who was taking his four-year-old grandson on an auto tour of the Forgotten Coast, appeared out of nowhere to help.

A sharp pain soon emerged in the gap between my thumb and index finger on my right hand. Doubling up on the kayak gloves my granddaughter Kyla had given me for Christmas provided welcome relief and reminded me how much I missed my grandchildren.

Nearing Eastpoint, I saw two clusters of boats, a pod of ten, and another numbering sixteen. At least one occupant of each boat was probing the bottom with long handled tongues. This area is well known for clams, oysters, and scallops. I didn't interrupt the fishers to ask, but my guess was that oysters were the shellfish choice that day.

I hoped to reach Carrabelle, Florida before the post office closed to pick up a care package. After arriving at the downtown boat ramp, I hustled to the post office, getting there just in time. My eagerly anticipated package included more freeze-dried dinners, Top Ramen soup, beef jerky, nuts, dried fruit and most importantly my luxury fare of fruit cups with syrup.

After my stop at the post office, I returned to Whisper II and paddled upstream on the Carrabelle River about a half mile to The Moorings. The dock at the inn was at least a foot above my head. With reduced mobility that comes with artificial hips, I decided to ask a man resting on the dock to help me exit Whisper II.

"Can you give me a hand getting out of my kayak? Can you catch my line?" I asked.

"Not now" he grumbled.

I decided to try without his help. That was a mistake. Whisper began drifting away from the dock in the tidal current. As the distance to the dock increased, I reached out to grab a piling. Oops! Too far. I was going over. There was little I could do other than twist my body to avoid hitting my head on the piling. After awkwardly extracting myself from the cockpit, I managed to pull myself to a ladder. Somehow, I was able to climb onto the dock while holding Whisper II's bow line in one hand and my loose gear in the other. The grumpy man made no effort to help me out of the water or secure Whisper.

"You're not very good at this are you?" he said with a sneer.

It was all I could do not to respond to his rudeness with an ugly comment. Not only was I embarrassed and annoyed, but I lost my floppy hat, my glasses, and, worst of all, killed my weather radio. An attempt at resuscitation by soaking the radio in warm, fresh water before drying it only slowed its demise.

While searching for the post office and motel, I walked through Carrabelle's small downtown area. Like Apalachicola, it is a fishing village transitioning to tourism. Needing time to care for my gear, I cooked dinner in my motel room instead of eating out. I called Joyce and confessed to having capsized and losing a pair of glasses. I bragged, (prematurely) about my foresight in bringing a second pair.

The next morning, without any shame, I asked for help from one of the staff when getting into Whisper II from the high dock. After compiling the information from multiple sources, especially the recommendations from Dan Tonsmeire, who I had reached by phone, I decided to take the outside route around Alligator Point rather than the roughly sixty-mile-long and appropriately named Crooked River route. Even though I had been looking forward to possibly seeing black bear and cougar along the Crooked River, uncertainty about the availability of campsites, the abundant bugs, and the fact that the outside route was about half as long, convinced me to risk paddling along a fully exposed part of the Gulf Coast. The tradeoff included open water on the southern horizon and a scenic coastline where the wind and waves could quickly build to dangerous levels.

Soon after leaving Carrabelle, I paddled on the mainland side of Lanark Reef as Dan Tonsmeire suggested. The water was very shallow. I could easily see the bottom and the disturbance my paddle caused to the sand ripples. I scattered many fish including a two-foot-long speckled trout. Near the terminus of the reef, the water was still shallow, so I steered toward a pod of dolphin assuming that they needed deeper water than Whisper II. The wind remained calm. I kept my eyes closed most of the time to avoid temporary blindness from the glare but opened them full time when the wind picked up while rounding Alligator Point, one of three Alligator Points encountered this year. The wind whipped up two-to-three-foot breaking waves, high enough to capsize Whisper if caught broadside. While near shore I paddled between two lines of breakers, hoping that the apparent convergence of the lines in the distance was fake news caused by the same phenomenon that makes it appear that railroad tracks converge. I was again glad to have fastened my spray skirt, a safety measure I sometimes skipped on very hot days like this.

Even when past the breaking waves, I was kept on edge as a

following sea threatened to broach Whisper II. I moved faster and so did time. I reached Ochlocknee Bay almost an hour before I expected. My trip guides warned about crossing the bay in high wind, but Bald Point partially protected me from the now-southerly wind.

After pulling ashore at Mashes Sands Boat Ramp and Park, I asked the attendant if camping was allowed. He said no, but told me how to reach a sandy beach north of the park where I was less likely to bother anyone or be bothered. Not finding the location he described after paddling more than the distance he said would be necessary, I pulled ashore. My campsite was less than a quarter mile from a park outbuilding where I was able to fill my almost-empty water containers and take a shower before going through my evening routine. Dinner was rice and chicken, one of the freeze-dried dinners picked up at the post office in Carrabelle. For dessert I treated myself to another cup of peaches in syrup.

The Big Bend

The next morning, I entered Apalachee Bay and the Big Bend, noted for bugs, shallow water, and the largest scallop industry in the country, one now threatened by red tides. There was little wind, so instead of hugging the shore for protection, I took a more direct route toward St. Marks Light House on the north side of the bay. When I stopped to ask two men and a woman in an outboard powered fishing boat about the weather and the best route to the lighthouse, they pointed to a feature in the distance that I took to be the lighthouse and said, "Go that way, but be careful, a storm is expected at one-thirty this afternoon." Unless I changed my course or speed I would paddle right into to the coming storm. I headed closer to shore.

The fishers were wrong about the time, but not by much; the wind, rain, and lightning began at 1:25 p.m. As with the windstorm on the Snake River, I was amazed at the accuracy of the prediction. The storm's arrival found me close to shore where a few low trees provided some limited cover from lightning strikes, assuming that my composite paddle didn't serve as a lightning rod. For over an hour, a strong tailwind alternating with a crosswind made it impossible to steer a straight line. Only occasionally was there any relief to be had from the headlands and low marshy islands.

Looking for a campsite in early afternoon. I paddled up Deep Creek, which might better be named "Shallow Slough," toward the coordinates entered in my GPS for Ring Dike campsite. After paddling up the creek for three quarters of an hour, my GPS announced my arrival at my destination. The campsite was supposed to be distinguishable from the open marsh by a ring of large live oak trees, but I found no campsite, the only ground slightly higher than the marsh being small mounds with a few small trees and no water access. The creek was about the same width as Whisper II is long, and so shallow that I ran aground numerous times. Becoming concerned that even if I were to find a campsite, a low tide might trap me and make it impossible to retrace my route back to the bay, I found a place barely wide enough to turn around. Despite only one wrong turn on the way back, I had spent a big chunk of the afternoon in my fruitless search for a campsite I never found. I had to press on.

I had failed to learn the tidal pattern along the Gulf Coast, so I was not as aware as I should have been when the tide would be high or low. I am used to the tidal cycle along the mid-northeast coast where there are two almost equal tides each day, and the Pacific Northwest where there are two dissimilar tides each day, the higher of the two lows sometimes being almost equal to the lower of the two highs. I had been surprised to learn that Mobile Bay claimed only one tide per day. I thought I was then experiencing two not-quite-equal tides each day.

There was supposed to be another campsite two miles up the Pinhook River, but even with my GPS it was impossible to determine with much confidence which slough led to the site. Every indentation in the shoreline seemed as if it could lead to my destination but my GPS wasn't precise enough to differentiate one from another. Having already paddled nine hours, I was hot and tired. A sharp pain in my right wrist was sending me a strong warning signal to stop before I triggered tendonitis.

The next possible campsite was at a boat ramp on the Aucilla River, the entrance to which was, for once, right where my GPS said it should be. With the welcome aid of an incoming tide, I paddled two and a half miles up a sleepy river with moss covered cypress, willow and oak on its banks blocking the sun, to an almost new boat ramp and dock. The park was alive with fishers and picnickers. While setting up my tent, I met Katy and her partner Daniel, the owners of an airboat business near Panama City. They were well equipped to provide helpful advice about the waterways I had recently paddled, but they knew little about what lay ahead. I would have accepted their kind offer to take me shopping, but I hoped to resupply at the Econfina Lodge and convenience store the next day. As the sun set, a group of young men pointed to a ten-to-twelve-foot-long alligator near the river's end of the boat ramp. I glanced at my tent, set about three alligator lengths from the river. I didn't exit until the sun rose sufficiently for me to avoid stepping on alligators and snakes.

The next morning's ten-mile paddle from Aucilla to Econfina was easy. Although I began to sweat miserably while the morning progressed, there was little wind, and the sea was calm. The farther I paddled, the farther I was forced from shore by the shallow mud flats, but I did cross paths with two large green sea turtles swimming in tandem. For the final couple of miles, I worked my way around two log jams on a dreary narrow tidal estuary lined with pine flatwoods and oak-palm hammocks known as the Econfina River, where moss-covered trees blocked the sun. I was on guard for water moccasins and pygmy rattlesnakes that might drop from the overhanging branches. Seemingly out of nowhere, I came upon a well-maintained wooden dock and boat ramp with a sign telling me that I had reached my destination.

Arriving at the Econfina Lodge late in the morning, I spoke with the owners Joanne and Gary, while consuming a surprisingly tasty microwave beef brisket sandwich and electrolyte drinks in their convenience store.

Gary is a former firefighter who operates a fishing guide service and is an on-call captain for a towboat company. He offered to take me to the town of Perry the next day for supplies. I spent the remainder of that day cleaning my gear, eating, and napping in a delightfully soft and dry bed. Dianne, the person who maintains the lodge, was very kind and offered their laundry room to wash and dry my clothes.

Portage to the Suwannee River

It was now time to fish, cut bait, bail the boat or whatever the appropriate metaphor is with respect to the rest of the route to the Atlantic. I had intended to paddle the Big Bend to the mouth of the Suwannee River, and then head upstream on that river. However, both people and publications warned me that August is not the time to paddle the Big Bend. The medley of reasons included heat, bugs, closure of most campsites during the scallop season, frequent thunder and lightning storms, and the fact that the water is so shallow you must paddle two-to-four miles offshore from the marshy coast. I can handle lightning when I have a place of refuge, but if the water is too shallow to reach land, and if the land offers no cover a person in a kayak serves as nothing more than a lightning rod and human sacrifice. After consulting Joanne and Gary, I concluded that a fifty-mile portage to the Suwannee River via the town of Perry would be very difficult but preferable to paddling the Big Bend, even if it involved pulling Whisper II by hand along public roads.

The next morning at ten, I heard a horn honk and found Gary waiting in his big white pickup. On the way to Perry, where we would meet Joanne and her friend Bonnie, Gary briefed me on the fifty-mile portage. It was a short briefing because there was little of note along the route except for Rocky's Convenience Store and Campground about four miles west of Perry. There were a few houses along the way, but Gary warned me, "Don't stop at any homes unless you see someone outside. Most won't take kindly to someone knocking on their door asking for water or to camp on their property, and at least one will be openly hostile."

I asked Gary what he thought about my paddling up the Econfina to where it intersected with U.S. 98 to cut down on the portage length. He strongly advised against my doing so, because downed trees and branches blocked the river at numerous points and because I would encounter a favorable current only after dark. As a further inducement for me to travel by road, he noted that alligators and pygmy rattlesnakes were common along the river.

Gary took me to the post office in Perry where I mailed home some gear including a nighttime hatch cover, a lock and chain, and some clothes. While I was mailing the package, I thought back to the time I pulled into Glacier Park on my bicycle while riding across the US in 1999. It was a very warm afternoon, so I mailed home all my cold weather gear. The next morning it snowed.

After the post office, Gary and I met Joanne and Bonnie at Walmart. I bought food and medical supplies before looking at bicycles. The first leg of the portage was to be twenty-seven miles, a long distance for me to pull a kayak on foot in one day, in the heat and with limited services available. I didn't know how fast I could pull a loaded Whisper II with a bicycle, but I was about to learn. For $150, I bought what looked like a relatively sturdy bike with a rear rack. We loaded it into the back of Gary's pickup and went to lunch at the all-you-can-eat Fusion Buffet, a Chinese smorgasbord. After eating just about everything and enjoying the company of my new friends, the server brought fortune cookies. My friends agreed that the following three fortunes applied to me:

Not having a goal is more to be feared than not reaching one.

Some people dream of worthy accomplishments while others stay awake and do them.

And my favorite: *Smiling often can make you look and feel younger.*

Back at the Econfina Lodge, I improvised a tow connection between my new bike and my wheel-mounted kayak. The next morning, I set off while the sun was beginning to rise and pedaled the six miles to US

98 in less than two hours. Pulling the loaded kayak with the bike was a struggle. The bike was not geared to pull a heavy load, and although it was advertised as sized for someone over six-feet tall, I began to think that the engineers' human model must have had very short legs. Adding to my discomfort, the surgeon who performed the replacement on my right hip did it in a way that had my right knee consistently hitting or rubbing against the bicycle's top tube. Perhaps I made a mistake in buying the bike, but I was moving about 50 percent faster than walking.

After the sun took its place in the sky, the heat became suffocating. I struggled on, but worried about sunstroke, heat exhaustion, and the return of my heart arrhythmia. Within a few miles of Rocky's, I developed intense leg cramps. I couldn't raise my legs to get off the bike, so I stood on the road shoulder with the bike between my legs while I drank water with electrolytes. Most of the traffic was big trucks, and none stopped to help, although I hadn't really expected them to. When finally able to climb off the bike, I pushed it and Whisper II the rest of the way to Rocky's where I drank more electrolyte drinks, snacked, and recuperated from the long trek.

After a much-needed hour-and-a-half break, I was on my way to Perry, sometimes walking while pushing the bike with kayak in tow, and other times riding the bike while towing Whisper II. After arriving in Perry, I checked into a clean and comfortable Econo Lodge motel. My next stop was at a drug store to buy salve for my very sore butt. I then celebrated my arrival in Perry with a stop at Burger King for a Whopper, a crisp chicken salad, and a strawberry milkshake. My dinner tasted as good as anything I could get in a five-star restaurant.

The next day I had to cover the twenty-three miles of portage that remained, and I was still drained from the day before. I pedaled eighteen miles along US 27 to a road leading to the Mayo Correctional Institute. Along the way, the terrain changed from marshland to low sandy hills, although people accustomed to real hills would probably call these bumps. I walked and pushed the bike and kayak the next two miles to a convenience store at the intersection of US 27 and FL

53. While stopped for lunch, I tried to find out the shortest and easiest way to get to Lafayette Blue Springs State Park on the Suwannee River. I asked seven people, including several in a group of prison guards, and got six different answers. I chose the answer given me by the postman and headed southeast on US 27. After a couple of miles, I decided to confirm my planned route with a man pulling out of his driveway.

"You can save almost two miles if you take Northwest Meridian Road, and then turn left at a stop sign," he told me as he pointed to a sand road running east-west across the highway.

I didn't have much faith in his directions since every road named Meridian I had ever encountered ran north south. The man was in too much of a rush to explain local road nomenclature to me, but I was so tired that I decided to take a chance on the shortcut.

Pushing the bike and loaded kayak along a sand road in the extreme heat meant stopping to drink, wipe my forehead and my eyes, and rest every few hundred feet. I was about to turn around when Kevin, a slim, young man with a bright smile, pulled to a stop in the only vehicle I was to see on that road.

"Hey man, I saw you near Perry yesterday," Kevin called out. "Where are you headed?"

"I'm looking for Blue Springs and then headed for the Atlantic Ocean," I answered. "Am I headed in the right direction?"

"Sure are. Just turn left at the stop sign"

Kevin added that he also planned to change direction, both along the road and in his life. He wanted to connect with the earth just like I was doing. I took an immediate liking to Kevin. Since Blue Springs was our mutual destination, I thought I would see him again, but I never did.

Suwannee River

After stumbling up to the entrance to Blue Springs Park with Whisper II in tow, Larry, a park ranger, announced that they were expecting me as a result of Joyce's call to reserve a campsite. When Larry told me they also had cabins, I decided the heck with the hundred-dollar cost. *I'm going to luxuriate this night in comfort, I've earned it. I'll negotiate with Joyce later, when she sees the bill. A nice dinner out should do the trick.*

Larry also suggested that I bathe in the blue spring. I asked about alligators. His response, "This is Florida." I took a shower instead of bathing in the spring. I'm glad I did. I later learned that on October 19, 2015, James Okkerse, a 61-year-old visitor, was attacked and killed in the park's swimming area by a 12.5-foot-long alligator. Amazingly, the day before Okkerse's death, a snorkeler saw the alligator lying on the bottom and dove in to film it with an underwater video camera. The snorkeler emerged unscathed.

Larry took me to the park office where I signed in. Jennifer, the park superintendent, told me I could store my bicycle at the park in the event I wanted to use it on the next portage. While Larry drove me to the same convenience store, I had stopped at earlier, he confirmed that my portage had taken me from the swamp to an area that was primarily agricultural. He let me know that the river was about a foot above its normal level for this time of year. That meant a faster current.

"It will be the devil to paddle upstream," Larry said. "I don't know of anyone who has tried, and I don't know why anyone would want to"

After sleeping in the next morning, I briefly debated cooking a real breakfast, but settled on choking down several breakfast bars in my rush to move on.

Elizabeth, Jennifer's assistant, helped me take my bicycle to a storage building. Next, I pulled Whisper II the short distance to the river, stored the wheels in the rear compartment, and set off, paddling upstream against the current Larry had warned me about. Just before leaving, Larry stopped by the ramp in his pickup. He wished me *bon voyage*, but added, "I expect to see you back here by the end of the day."

While testing myself and the river, I was struck by the stunning natural beauty of the Suwannee with its tree-lined limestone banks so close I could almost touch them. The cooling water and bubbling sound of the numerous springs, and the many shades of lush green cypress, gum, birch, and pine hammocks were all worthy of an artist's pallet or a poet's pen. Even though he had never visited the Suwannee River, Stephen Foster made an excellent choice in memorializing the Suwannee in his classic and mournful melody "Old Folks at Home."

The Suwannee River rises in the Okefenokee Swamp (National Wildlife Refuge and Wilderness Area) in Georgia and winds its way 240 miles to the Gulf of Mexico. Two dams that once blocked the flow have been removed. Because shoals between Ellaville, Florida, near Interstate 10, and White Springs, Florida, make powerboat travel impossible without portage, the Suwannee is the only major waterway in the Southeast that is still unspoiled, a claim made in the pages of *Exploring Florida,* a website guide produced by the Florida Center for Instructional Technology. Despite fighting the current, I looked forward to paddling the mythical Suwannee. My route would take me from Blue Springs, Florida (RM 103), to Fargo, Georgia (RM 221). There I would begin my final portage.

To my great relief, and despite the doubts Larry instilled in me, I was able to make slow but steady progress paddling upstream against the current. Finding a sandbar to camp on was another story. When the Suwannee River is at mid-to-high levels as it was then, there are few sandbars on which to camp. I stopped at Dowling Park, Florida, at about noon to rearrange my gear in the unwelcome event I would have to sleep in Whisper II. Midafternoon, I found an acceptable sandbar and decided to stop there rather than tax my luck any further. I had paddled nineteen river miles in six-and-a-half hours, short of the twenty upstream miles per day I was hoping for, but I was okay with that. I had spotted only two other boats on the river. I also met two turtles that slid off their log when I approached, and two others who preferred to continue having sex to getting out of my way. I did my best to avoid disturbing their coupling. It was summer, and for turtles the living was easy.

The day's heat continued well into the night. I reluctantly decided to add my rain fly when I heard thunder close by. When outside the tent adding the fly, I stepped on a mound of ants. Their bites were painful. Had I known this was a precursor of future miseries, I might have reconsidered my goals and quit then and there. As had happened on many nights, my sweat puddled on my air mattress, giving new meaning to the word "waterbed."

Late the next morning, I knew I was approaching the I-10 Bridge from the buzzing sound of traffic, annoying in that it represents an unattractive part of civilization, but welcome in that it signaled progress on the river. About a half hour after first detecting the Doppler changing pitch of the traffic, I saw two men fishing from a boat just downstream from the bridge. When meeting people on a river, I usually ask about any potentially dangerous conditions. This time I didn't. This time I should have. In response to my question about drinking water, the men only told me I would soon encounter many springs.

Less than a mile after meeting the men, I paddled through a very large spring that burst from Suwannee's depths with surprising fury, much like the whirlpools I had encountered on the Missouri and Mississippi Rivers. The swirling water churned around my kayak and spun me in many directions like a compass searching for north. I kept Whisper II from capsizing but couldn't help but wonder what was next.

Mere minutes after the spring, I encountered my first shoal, a reach of the river where less erosive limestone rock constricts the stream and results in shallows and fast-moving water. I picked a course between two large partly submerged rocks only to be driven back by the current when almost through. For my second attempt, I made it a few feet farther before the current again swept me backwards. On my third and fourth attempts I didn't make it as far as the first two attempts. I thought of the saying, *"If at first you don't succeed, try, try again,"* but I put more credence in words often attributed to Albert Einstein. *"Insanity is doing the same thing over and over while expecting different results."* For my fifth attempt I tried a different approach along the right bank.

I was almost beyond the rapids when fast-moving water at a constriction between a rock and the riverbank slammed Whisper II into the rocky bank with a deafening bang. I almost hit my head on the sharp rock when the kayak tipped on her side. I grabbed a tree root and held on while trying to decide what to do next. I made a rather clumsy exit, stepping into a deep hole and almost tipping over while holding onto both the root and Whisper II's bowline. The boat took on about thirty gallons of water and soaked the deck bag containing my cell phone. My immediate fear was that the crash ruptured Whisper II's hull causing the front compartment to flood. I tried to remember if I had included my kayak repair kit in the package I had mailed home.

With Whisper on the riverbank, I pumped the water out and carefully checked the front compartment. I was both surprised and greatly relieved to find it dry. I had made a wise choice in spending the extra money for a stronger Kevlar kayak.

Since I still had to get past the rapids, I lined Whisper II along the bank, alternating between pulling myself and my kayak upstream while in the river holding onto tree roots, and climbing up on the bank composed of sharp limestone layers when the water was too deep. Twice, I almost slipped back into the river, but was able to stop myself by grabbing roots.

It was still morning when I reached Suwannee River State Park, once the site of the town of Columbus and the largest sawmill in Florida until the yellow pine forests were depleted. Normally I wouldn't stop so early, especially when worried about slow progress, but I lost a water bottle when I flipped out of Whisper II and wanted to replenish my water. I walked unsteadily up the boat ramp and met Mary, who was sitting outside her RV.

Mary smiled and said, "You look like you could use a drink"

While I guzzled the water and soft drinks she gave me, I answered her questions about my journey and asked about her life. When I attempted to call Joyce on my drowned cell phone without success, Mary offered hers.

"You must be well known," Mary said when I ended the call.

"Not so," I replied, "Not many know about my trip."

"I'm going to correct that if you allow me to take your photo and put it on Facebook.

I am not a fan of social media, but I consented.

While departing, my new friend and benefactor Mary handed me a sack lunch. Back on the river, I reached into the bag and pulled out a giant individually wrapped dill pickle. I craved salt and it tasted great. Then I found about a half pound of cantaloupe melon cubes, also great. The third attraction was a bag of blueberries. Joyce later explained the reason my intestines almost exploded was because I had become unaccustomed to fruits and spices. After devouring these delicacies, I had to rush to shore, and only made it just in time.

I spent another night in my sauna-like tent. Even without my cell phone alarm, I was awake long before sunrise. I had some trouble packing because I was working in the dark, the batteries in my headlamp having run down the night before and my weather radio having given up. My battery-hungry GPS was still working, and for that I was grateful.

The Shoals

Late in the morning, I came upon a boat ramp leading to the Spirit of Suwannee Music Park, an 800-acre resort and campground that attracts people from all over the country to its famous music festivals. While proceeding upstream past the ramp, it dawned on me that I had seen many canoes and kayaks on a rack at the top of the ramp. I broke my never-turn-around rule and headed back.

At the top of the ramp, I found the Suwannee Canoe Outpost owned by Steve Baxter and run by Steve with the help of Debbie and David Pharr, the former owners. Even though it was Saturday, and they would normally be very busy, David told me they were between trips. He offered to take me to get supplies or help in other ways. I gratefully accepted his offer.

While on the way to Walmart in the town of Live Oak, Florida,

I asked David how often people kayak upstream. He said that in his twenty years on the river, I was the third he'd seen. He claimed one of the other two had canoed as far as Branford (RM 76), then called David to ask if he would drive him and his canoe to the St. Marys River. The person David described seemed like the same paddler who had published a blog in which he implied that he had paddled the entire 221 miles from the Gulf of Mexico to Fargo, Georgia. I had my doubts about the story since the timing didn't make sense. David also thought that this was the same person and said he hoped he hadn't spilled the beans. The implication that someone could do the entire distance in a canoe without any problems might create a false sense of security for other paddlers, as it most certainly had for me.

While at Walmart I bought a new cell phone, peanut butter, electrolyte drinks, and batteries. After returning to the Outpost, I attempted to transfer data from my old phone to my new phone without success. Lou, a military communications expert waiting to launch a canoe, was somehow able to accomplish what for me was impossible. I later crossed paths with Lou and a friend of his while they leisurely floated by me on their way downstream. Seeing them reminded me that I was looking forward to the St. Marys River where I mistakenly fantasized floating downstream in the sunshine with a cold drink in my hand.

David gave me a map he created entitled, *The Suwannee River Boating, Canoeing and Recreation Guide,* which showed Little Shoals about twenty-three miles ahead, and Big Shoals about four miles upriver from Little Shoals. He cautioned me that I would have to portage Big Shoals, and depending on water levels, there could be more little shoals than those shown on his map. The good news was that any shoals I encountered above Big Shoals should not be that challenging because the river spread out more. However, David warned that the less steep banks upstream of Big Shoals meant the presence of more alligators. I don't remember David cautioning me about conditions at Little Shoals, but I wished he had.

Late the following morning, I arrived at Stephen Foster Folk Culture Center State Park, named after the composer of "Old Folks at Home" sometimes referred to as "Way down upon the Suwannee River." The manager of the gift shop allowed me to charge my new phone while I ate a pint of chocolate ice cream and spoke with a park ranger about the route ahead. The ranger cautioned me about Big Shoals but said I should be able to negotiate Little Shoals. I thought he said that the current was no more than 2 mph. He also told me that I would find few campsites in the vicinity of the shoals but invited me to call him if I needed help or a place to spend the night.

A river gauge at the Culture Center showed the river to be at fifty-six and a half feet (based on North American Vertical Datum of 1988). Several publications suggest it is best to kayak the Suwannee when the river level is between fifty-one and fifty-nine feet at the nearby White Springs Gauging Station. According to David Pharr's map, a water level lower than fifty feet results in many areas too shallow to paddle while at a level above sixty feet there are few sandbars on which to camp, and the river becomes appreciably more dangerous. Given the erratic rainfall this year I felt fortunate to be paddling at a good water level.

About three miles above Stephen Foster Culture Center State Park, I observed some small shoals. What I first saw were swirling currents of foam-filled water, which formed surprisingly beautiful patterns. If I had any artistic talents, I might have stopped to sketch them, as many artists have done. I negotiated the first shoal without any problem. I soon came upon another shoal preceded by more foam. Because of my success at shoal number one, I approached this one with unjustified composure. What I found was a series of rapids where the current near the center of the river was several multiples of the 2 mph the ranger described.

My heart began pounding. This was not going to be easy. To avoid the worst of the current, I made my way up the left bank by pulling on tree roots between paddle strokes. About halfway up the rapids, I had to detour around the elephant foot roots of a tupelo tree. The faster current on the river side of the tree suddenly swung Whisper II's bow around broadside to the current. Before I could take any corrective action, I went over.

Spilling out, I was somehow able to grab both Whisper II and my paddle. I stayed eerily calm while being swept downstream for several hundred yards, watching some of my gear float away. *You dummy,* I said to myself, *why didn't you secure your gear?* I also berated myself for having put Whisper II in danger of ramming into a rock. Several times my feet hit bottom and I was able to push Whisper II away from rocks and closer to the left bank. I was finally able to stop my downstream plunge by grabbing onto some twisted tree roots.

After reaching shore and bailing Whisper II, I took stock of the damages. I'd lost another water bottle, David Pharr's map, my favorite floppy hat and, most importantly, my second and last pair of glasses. I can read without glasses, but my distance vision is seriously impaired. As I worked my way back upstream, sometimes in the water and sometimes crawling on my hands and knees along the six-foot-high bank, I had to hold on tightly to roots so as not to slip back downstream to the Gulf of Mexico. The thought that any of those roots might have concealed a cottonmouth moccasin has kept me awake many a night.

Not far above this big Little Shoal, I encountered another little shoal that warranted the little description even though it also required pulling Whisper along the bank. Again, I encountered the foam. My extreme thirst convinced me to drink the river water, after first adding iodine tablets. My guess, still unconfirmed, is that phosphates, found in fertilizers, probably caused the foam. I wondered if these were the same phosphates, that when flavored, were sold as soft drinks in old time soda fountains.

Late afternoon I'd had enough of this fumbling and decided it was time to look for a campsite. When by 6 p.m. I still hadn't found a suitable spot, I settled on a marginal brush covered plot of sloping ground only about eighteen inches above the river. Remembering Rule One, I secured Whisper II to a large tupelo tree. The rain started pelting soon after I pitched my tent. I pulled Whisper II even farther above the river. It was raining too hard to use my stove outdoors, and since I don't like to risk a fire in the tent, I ate a cold meal of beef jerky and peanut butter while the sound of rain beating on my tent helped soothe my gloom.

I called Joyce to see if she could order another pair of glasses for me. She didn't seem very optimistic that they would get to me before I finished, whenever that would be. Joyce conveyed the distinct impression that I was placing her under a lot of stress when she said, "You are placing me under a lot of stress. You owe me big time." While I tried to sleep in my underwear on a sweat-soaked mattress I wondered what "big time" meant.

The next morning marked the beginning of week four. The days were getting shorter as the end of summer approached, and because I was in the western part of the Eastern Time Zone, the sun didn't rise until about seven.

Everything was wet from the rain, humidity, and my sweat. Less than an hour after starting, I came upon more swirling foam, indicative of another rapid. I looked for a marked portage route, which would mean I was at Big Shoals. Not finding a portage, I climbed in and out of the river as I pulled Whisper II along the left bank. I was using different muscles than I used while paddling, rapidly becoming tired, my sweat contributing ever so slightly to the river flow. The challenge of getting past the rapids and avoiding snakes kept me on full alert and kept me from focusing on my other problems.

The rapids consisted of several drops of two or more feet and one smaller drop. The rock looked surprisingly sharp for limestone. The fact that the shoals were there indicates that this rock was harder and less erosive, and thus less rounded than other nearby rock. The sharp rocks made this a dangerous rapid, but it was easier for me to negotiate than the one that had capsized Whisper II. I erroneously concluded that this was just another little shoal.

Lost Again

After my problems at the real Little Shoals, I desperately wanted Big Shoals behind me. I kept looking for the telltale swirling foam and rumbling noise that would tell me that the shoals were getting close. When I didn't see any foam or hear any rumble by 11:30 a.m., I began to wonder if I had somehow passed Big Shoals, or worse, had paddled up some unmapped tributary. When, at noon, I reached a boat ramp with a sign that read *Cone Ramp*, I realized that the last shoals I'd passed through, the ones with several two-foot drops, were in fact Big Shoals and that my worry was behind me. Markings of portages and other features are rare for the almost non-existent upstream travelers. Hence, my confusion.

While at the Suwannee Canoe Outpost I bought the book *Canoeing and Camping on the Historic Suwannee River: A Paddler's Guide* by Rose Knox and Graham Schorb. The authors do a commendable job of re-creating the era when steamboats plied the river and luxury hotels lined the banks in several communities, including White Springs, the town I had just unknowingly passed. According to the authors, White Springs' mineral waters were also a gathering place for Native Americans.

As I had done near Salt Creek, Missouri, in 2015, I was now crossing paths with Hernando de Soto. When de Soto arrived in Florida in 1539, thirteen tribes (the Timucua being the largest) thrived in this area. By the mid-eighteenth century there were few Timucua living, most having died from disease, war, the exploitation of their resources, and the ravages of slavery. *The Atlas of Indian Nations,* by Anton Treuer, traces the history of the Seminole, the tribe many people think are native to Florida. According to the author, the Seminole moved south from Georgia and Alabama to occupy the land previously held by the Timucua. The Seminole, along with freed slaves, the few surviving Timucua, and displaced members of the Creek Tribe, lived in this part of Florida in the 1800s. They held European settlers largely at bay during three wars lasting from 1817 to 1858 but were eventually forced to flee.

Those tribal members who escaped removal and rejected agreements made with the government withdrew to remote reaches of the Everglades. Today, descendants of these so-called renegade people number about 2,000. The Seminole opened a high stakes bingo operation on their reservation in 1979 defying Florida law. In 1981 the tribe won the landmark case of Seminole Tribe of Florida v. Robert Butterworth, legitimizing its rights to operate a gambling casino and transforming the economic landscape of Indian lands throughout the US.

Joyce and I once visited the Seminole's casino in the Everglades and occasionally stop at the Tulalip casino near Marysville, WA for lunch or dinner. My family and I sometimes discuss the improvements to the lives of Native Americans brought about by the tribal casinos near where we live. Now, the tribes are sharing their largess with surrounding communities. Unfortunately, except for Florida's extreme south where the Seminole and several other tribes still have small reservations, the once populous Native American tribes of Florida are no more.

The riverbanks were now lower and the river wider than it had been downstream of the shoals, just as David Pharr said it would be. While Whisper II continued upstream, much of the country experienced a total solar eclipse. Being in an area where approximately 89 percent of the sun was obscured, I sensed only a slight change in the amount of sunlight, but at the peak hour for the eclipse, the wind became blustery, and the temperature fell about ten degrees. I was a little disappointed that I didn't experience more of the eclipse and didn't have more to write about in my journal.

Late in the afternoon, after being on the river for more than ten hours, I pulled ashore to camp on a pleasant bar of white sugar sand a couple of miles below the FL 6 Bridge. Several people had warned me that this was the land of big alligators, apparently because hunters often leave deer carcasses along the river. I wanted to remain diligent, but without my glasses it was impossible to do so. Logs looked like alligators and alligators looked like logs.

The blustery wind made it difficult for me to pitch my tent. Thunder and lightning in the distance convinced me to add the rain fly.

Normally, the absence of air circulation in the tent would have made it unbearably hot, but the drop in temperature, caused by the eclipse, allowed me to write in my journal without sweating over the pages.

The next morning, I still had twenty-eight miles to reach Fargo. I wanted to make it in one day, but soon encountered several obstacles. About an hour after shoving off, Whisper and I hit another shoal. This one was easy to negotiate because the water depth was under three feet and there were no big trees along the shore to block my path. I began to worry that I may have to stop because my arrhythmia seemed to have returned, but what really bothered me were the legions of fire ants that had found their way into Whisper II's cockpit.

I have no idea how the ants booked passage, but they were most unwelcome. They must have been trained in military techniques. The first group mounted a mass attack and then withdrew to a defensive position on my feet where the tight cockpit made it impossible for me to reach them. Next, they sent out advance scouts before attacking both of my legs in a pincer movement. When they climbed to the fleshier parts of my thighs, I began to think that one bite from an alligator might be preferable to the bites from countless ants. I was saved from worse injury by the tight bike shorts I wore under my paddling shorts. They prevented the ants from invading my private parts. Later that day when examining the damage to my legs I discovered over eighty welts from ant bites. Those welts persisted on my thighs for five months.

I stopped at Roline Launch (RM 202), around noon for a half hour to make phone calls and kill ants. I am reluctant to kill any animal, even an ant, but the fire ants on Whisper II and me were summarily tried and executed for their crimes.

Roline was the last human-made landmark I would see on the Suwannee. By midafternoon, I began to doubt I would make Fargo before dark, but it was impossible to know because of the difficulty of fixing my position. There was supposed to be a marker welcoming southbound river travelers to Florida, but I never saw it, either because it wasn't there or because it was positioned for only downstream travelers to see.

Beyond Roline, I estimated my location on the river by multiplying the hours kayaked by about 2.5 mph, my estimated speed over the ground. I was still executing fire ants while looking for a sandbar at about 4 p.m., but good sandbars were few and very far between. Shortly before 5 p.m. I was delighted to find a sandbar with fine white sand and a flat surface near the top. Upon further examination, I noticed that the shoreline was marked with what looked like the tracks of large alligators. I moved on. The next possible campsite was near a backwater pond and appeared to be excellent habitat for alligators, but there were no alligator tracks. I warily made camp. After pitching my tent, I went back to killing ants.

When setting off the next morning, my GPS showed that there were three-and-a-half straight-line miles to Fargo. This put me at about RM 216, a mile and a half or so below below Suwannoochee Creek, which joins the Suwannee River from the west and two miles below Cypress Creek, which joins the Suwannee River from the east. With my diminished vision and having misjudged my location, I never did see Suwannoochee Creek. When I came upon a fork in the river, I thought that the fork from the east would keep me on the Suwannee River. However, that fork was perceptively narrower and shallower and was flowing much faster than the river I had been paddling. Like Lewis and Clark upon reaching the Marias River, I hesitated. Unlike them, I didn't camp at the confluence for ten days while sending out scouting parties before deciding which fork to take.

I too hastily concluded that the apparently higher volume of flow meant that the branch joining the Suwannee from the east was the Suwannee River. Big mistake. Slowly fighting my way upstream through tangled barriers of downed trees, I had to climb out of Whisper II and pull my kayak past the tangles several times. I was lucky not to capsize or have a cottonmouth fall from a branch. The current was moving rapidly. After about two miles of this struggle, I came to a bridge. Thinking I was at the Fargo boat ramp at state highway 94, I unloaded Whisper II and pulled her out of the river bottom and up the road embankment, stopping along the way to swat mosquitoes and spray myself with mosquito repellent. A sign near the bridge said Cypress Creek.

After placing Whisper II on its wheels and reloading, I flagged down a motorist who confirmed that I had lost my way, that this was not the Suwannee River, but added that I was now headed in the correct direction to Fargo. Rather than retrace my steps back downstream on Cypress Creek to the Suwannee River, I pulled Whisper II one mile along US 441 to its junction with GA 94 and another mile to Fargo. I crossed the Suwannee River a few hundred yards from downtown. An ignominious end, but I figured I'd struggled enough for one day.

Portage to the Saint Marys River

After pulling Whisper into the parking area for the Suwannee River Outfitters and Lodge, I met John, partner to Bonnie, the other owner. Bonnie manages the inn and restaurant while John is the outfitter and guide. John is also an accomplished beekeeper and the mayor of Fargo, a town of about four hundred residents. As I had been continuously reminded, August is most definitely not the preferred time to be on a Florida adventure, so I was not surprised to find I was the only guest at the lodge.

Over the past week, I had been rethinking my next portage from Fargo to the St. Marys River. The portage distance was forty-one miles, shorter than this year's first portage but there was no place to camp or spend the night and the route was essentially devoid of houses and businesses. The lone exception was a convenience store on a sand mound in Moniac, Georgia, twenty-three miles east of Fargo.

David and Bonnie Pharr would soon arrive in Fargo with the bicycle I left at Blue Springs, but towing Whisper with the bike could put me close to heat exhaustion or sunstroke. I decided to ride the bicycle from Fargo to the St Marys River without pulling Whisper II. I would then return to Fargo by motor vehicle, getting a lift with John's son Lanier. The next day John would transport Whisper and me back to the river with his truck.

My plan was complicated. More importantly, this was not an easy decision for me to make. I was committed to completing this journey under my own power, which I would still do, but I couldn't escape the feeling that I was cheating by having John haul Whisper II along the portage route. I had justified traversing the Rocky Mountains by bicycle without towing Whisper because Lewis and Clark had not hauled their canoes across the mountains. Somehow this seemed different.

After completing arrangements for the next day with Bonnie and John, and paying them a small fee, I took a long cool shower and napped in a dry, comfortable bed for the first time in a week. Despite my itching legs, I was so tired that sleep came quickly. Awakening at lunchtime, I went across the street to the Suwannee River Cafe and enjoyed a hamburger, sweet potato fries, and a salad. The restaurant didn't serve ice cream, so I went to the nearby convenience store, bought some ointment for the fire ant bites, and devoured a pint of fudge swirl ice cream.

While spending the afternoon mending and cleaning my gear, I removed what seemed like several pounds of accumulated sand. Since the lodge restaurant was closed, the cafe across the street was the only restaurant in town. For dinner, I ordered fried chicken and coleslaw, and washed it all down with several large glasses of refreshing lemonade. I should have remembered Joyce's advice about drinking too much juice. I didn't get much sleep that night.

Feeling better the next morning, I left Fargo by bicycle for St. George and the St. Marys River. I stopped in Moniac to see if I could learn anything about the river route ahead. A police officer burst my bubble when he said I might be able to paddle down the St. Marys to the Atlantic in one month, but I should plan on two. This could be a major problem. Joyce had told me that Hurricane Harvey was supposed to arrive in north Florida in three to four days.

With a modest headwind, temperature in the mid-90s, and a bicycle that was a poor fit for me, it took four and a half hours to reach St. George and another fifteen minutes for the downhill run to the St.

Marys River. The river looked high and while the current was moving fast, it appeared navigable. Returning to St. George, I bought supplies at the supermarket and the Dollar General store. While waiting to be picked up by John's son and his friend, I made more inquiries about the St. Marys River. All estimates regarding how long it would take to reach the Atlantic from St. George put me there in less than a month, but none suggested I could do it in less than a week. I was told that several people had recently drowned in the high water and that I should carefully examine every branch I passed under to make sure a poisonous cottonmouth, having fled the low ground, wasn't poised to drop from above. Having lost both pairs of glasses, a careful examination would not be possible. Other than quitting, there wasn't much I could do to improve my situation. I decided to move on.

A young man, a shopper, asked if the Intracoastal Waterway connected the Gulf Coast with the Pacific Ocean. A young woman asked if all the rivers between the West Coast and the Atlantic Ocean flowed downstream. Was this lack of knowledge the result of too much time spent on their smart phones? Was it because of the small images on digital screens in place of large area *paper* maps? I'll never know.

On the way back to Fargo, we stopped at the Moniac convenience store. Lanier asked a friend if we could borrow the *Georgia Gazetteer* map book so that I could better understand the St. Marys River. We then stopped at a state agricultural inspection station where the officer on duty made copies of the three map pages I needed. That night, map pages in hand, I called my son Greg to help me address some of the unknowns that still haunted me. In less than fifteen minutes on his smart phone (yes, they can be helpful) Greg learned the number of miles to the Atlantic Ocean, located the very few places to camp along the way, and told me that the water level in the river was still in flood stage but was beginning to drop, albeit slowly.

The next morning Mayor John took Whisper II and me to the boat ramp east of St. George. On the way he told me that after losing their timber mill, Fargo's population declined from over 1,000 to fewer than four hundred. Even the almost new Suwannee River Visitors Center was forced to close. With little crime and no police force, a volunteer fire department and no property taxes, Fargo gives John reason to hope that his hometown might still attract an industry and reverse its decline.

St. Marys River

John waited until I was ready to shove off and then bid me goodbye. Unlike the park ranger at Blue Springs, he didn't add that he expected to see me return that night, but maybe he should have. I hadn't paddled more than a mile on the tea-colored river lined with stately bald cypress and tupelo trees before my rudder mechanism caught in a downed tree. I started to capsize in the strong current, and although Whisper II took on water, I was able to right her by grabbing a branch. After getting to shallow water and bailing, I moved into an area where the river had overflowed its banks. I followed the current until it finally disappeared. I was lost in the swamp.

Paddling around the dark waters, probably in circles, for over an hour looking for the channel, I felt close to panicking. The rudder mechanism kept catching in tree branches. I could see no riverbank and didn't know how to escape the backwater. The musty odor of decaying vegetation that I had previously found pleasant now gave me the creeps. My GPS was not precise enough to help and the water was too deep to step out of Whisper II to get access to my cell phone and emergency beacon, which were in a watertight stern compartment. Even if my cell phone were available, I had gotten this far without relying on others for rescue and I didn't want to start now. If I were in the habit of cursing, I may have filled the air with expletives. I thought that at least I could use my GPS to record my tracks, and in this way avoid paddling in circles. I finally observed a slight current. It wasn't much more than a trickle, but I followed it like a bloodhound pursuing a scent. The current gradually became stronger and eventually led me back to the flowing river.

No sooner did I have Whisper II back on the river when the fire ants returned in force. Likely, I had accidentally dislodged a colony of ants on a branch in my desperate search to find the current and free the boat. How they got in Whisper II really didn't matter. I had to endure frequent bites for the eight more hours it took me to paddle to Traders Hill boat ramp and Park, all the way trying to avoid taking a wrong turn into the backwater. When I pulled up to the park shortly before 5 p.m. my legs were a lunar landscape of welts.

The park, with its expansive well cared for lawns and wading area, was only two hundred yards downstream from an alligator wallow. Wondering if camping was allowed, I paddled by the fishing pier to ask the lone fisher, a very large man sitting on a very small bucket.

"Hello," I called out. "Can I camp here?"

"Of course, you can. You're famous. I saw you on TV."

"What about alligators?"

"Don't go swimming and you'll be okay."

I couldn't understand how he knew about me until I remembered my benefactor, Mary, who packed my lunch several days ago, taking my picture and posting it on Facebook. I took the fisherman's advice about not bathing in the river, but I did quickly rinse off, all the time looking for two beady eyes.

I woke the next morning before sunrise still uncertain about the path that Hurricane Harvey would take and whether I should be worried. Joyce's weather reports made it clear that, hurricane or not, an adverse northeast wind approaching 20 knots would build up over the next few days. Not relishing the idea of struggling against such a powerful adversary on the lower and much wider end of the St. Marys River (the lower end flowing through a marsh with few trees or bluffs to buffer the wind) I picked up my pace.

The first half of the day saw me in the general vicinity of Folkston, Georgia, a large enough community to support two boat ramps and a few homes on the river. Trees clogging the river bottom had become less prevalent as the river moved away from the bog swamp into semi-developed areas. About noon, I passed the river communities of Flea

Hill, Georgia, and its cross-river companion, Kings Ferry, Florida. I wondered if Florida always selected more grandiose community names than Georgia until I looked at my map and noticed Kingsland, Georgia, not far from the river. After passing the two small river towns, I saw nothing but low-lying marsh, with no places to camp for several hours.

Just before reaching the confluence with the Little St. Marys River, I passed a community of stately homes along the right bank, all with the most up to date security systems and warning signs. I thought about approaching the back gate of a home, but Florida's self-defense law allowing armed vigilantes to shoot people that scared them dissuaded me from doing so. Finding no one outside who might invite me to camp in their backyard, I proceeded past the Little St. Marys River and into more marsh. As the sun threatened to sink below the horizon, I still had not found a place to camp. This was not the leisurely float trip with cold drink in hand that I had daydreamed about.

Approaching ten hours of hard paddling, with the only occasional fire ant bites, I prayed that Greg's prediction of a boat ramp at the US 17 Bridge would prove correct. If wrong, I would probably spend another night attempting to sleep in Whisper II.

I came abreast of a gravel ramp just beyond the bridge that at first looked promising, but it was so close to the level of the river that the high tide expected during the night might pick me up and float me. A fisherman familiar with the area pulled up in a pickup while I contemplated my dilemma. He assured me that the location where I'd hoped to pitch my tent was a good six inches above the high tide level and large boat wakes were not likely during the night. He also checked the tides on his smart phone and told me that I would encounter a strong adverse tide the next morning unless I got a very early start.

Hoping this would be my last night on the river, I decided to celebrate with beef stroganoff, my favorite freeze-dried meal, accompanied by peanut butter and my last cup of peaches in syrup for dessert. Not exactly gourmet fare, but good enough for comfort food.

The next morning, I broke another one of my cardinal rules. Hoping to beat the adverse current and wind, I was on the river more than an hour and a half before sunrise. Cloud cover obscured the moon. It was nearly as dark as the inside of a cave. My feeble headlamp wasn't much help, but it did show my position and likely saved me from a head-on collision with a fishing boat that sped by. Except for the short time when I could see lights along Interstate 10, I had to rely on GPS to navigate. Because my GPS eats batteries with a voracious appetite, I used it sparingly. When the sun finally did rise, the wind remained light and the tide favorable, my spirits lifted. The water had transitioned from the tea color found upstream to the blue green of the ocean. That, along with the many gulls, were signs the finish was near. Added to the countless gulls were the many herons and egret wading in the shallows in the surrounding tidelands, now more than a mile wide. Too much exposure to adverse weather, for sure, but the promised winds hadn't yet picked up and the prospect of finishing that day still looked good.

The Finish

Late morning the wind hit. I was floating past downtown St. Marys, with only six miles to go to reach my final destination, the St. Marys Boat Service on North River. I paddled by an anchored thirty-five-foot sailboat and saw a man with the gloomy demeanor of someone who had just awakened. He found a chart and showed me that I had to paddle around a nearby point to get to North River. He added that I should expect to encounter a strong adverse tide and wind along the way and to not imagine it would be easy. He was correct.

While trying to round the point, I paddled until my arms felt they were on fire but made almost no progress. I considered pulling ashore or heading back to St. Marys, but I so wanted to finish that I put every bit of strength left in me into paddling forward. I finally rounded the point an hour or so before noon. I took a break and called Joyce to report that I was near the finish. She could tell I was ready to be done with this. She said she'd call friends and family to let them know I'd made it and I was safe and sound.

Not ten minutes later, I was hit by one of the most intense squalls of the entire trip. Before the rain hit, I saw that the water in the exposed bay was being whipped into a gray froth. I later learned from a radio report that wind gusts exceeded 30 knots. When the rain hit, it slammed me and Whisper II at a near horizontal angle for at least a half hour, limiting my sight line to the shore. I thought of the words written by William Clark in his field notes upon seeing what he believed to be the Pacific Ocean. "Ocean in view! O! the joy." I wanted to have that feeling but began to doubt I would any time soon.

I did eventually fight my way to St. Marys Boat Service and arrived just as the rain stopped. Some men were on the dock hoisting an inter-island ferry with a travel lift. Among them, Rocky Smith, owner of the boatyard, announced himself as my host. The greeting I particularly remember though, came from one of his dock workers. "Welcome to Saint Marys. Wow, you sure look scrawny."

Postscript VIII

Rocky and his staff went beyond the call of duty helping me prepare Whisper II for storage in one of their sheds. At the yard I met Andy, another adventurer. Andy had not been as fortunate as me. He wrecked his forty-two-foot catamaran when wind and waves forced his sailboat over the rock jetty where the St. Marys River enters the Atlantic Ocean. During that day and the next, I explored St. Marys' historic downtown and waterfront. I enjoyed gourmet food at the local restaurants on my quest to regain the fifteen pounds or so that I had lost. On my day of departure, Jerry, co-owner of the old Riverside Hotel, drove me to the Amtrak station in Jacksonville. That began my train trip home.

This was the end of a long and arduous voyage. While retracing the route of Lewis and Clark, I observed the fabled purple mountain majesties in Idaho and endless waves of grain in Montana and the Dakotas. While on the Missouri River, I came within fifty miles of Canada, and this year I floated in the warm waters of the Gulf of Mexico. I paddled and portaged from sea to shining sea. Over the course of 4,700 miles, I traversed thirty-one dams on nineteen waterways and rivers. I touched land and water in seventeen states. I was touched by the history and beauty of this country, and, it must be said, by the graciousness and hospitality of so many people, in so many places. I paddled and portaged through the heart of the country. *America the Beautiful*, as expressed in the anthem, was even better than I'd hoped it would be. It was amazing. And in my memories of this quest, so it shall remain.

My arrythmia returned during, or soon after, the voyage. My frequent dehydration or the fire ant bites may have been the cause. When the doctors told me I would not need a new heart valve for another couple of years, I started to hatch a plan to paddle from St. Marys up the east coast to New York. I was within two weeks of beginning my trip when I learned that Whisper II had been stolen from St. Marys Boat Service. I am now recovering from an operation to install a new heart valve and am in a holding pattern for a new kayak.

Author in kayak at big Lagoon

The Ditch

Bike Trailing Whisper

Blue Springs Pool

Suwannee River

A Note of Appreciation

I t is an honor for me to acknowledge those who helped in the preparations and writing of this book and those who were with me on the rivers. To my parents, who allowed me the freedom to travel well beyond their comfort zone, I owe my love and appreciation. My two sons, Greg and Mike, and my friend Bob Schaal were with me when the going was tough on the river and portages. Always present to answer the call for help were my daughter, Amy Coyle, and her husband, Sean. My five grandchildren, Kyla, Owen, Landon, Katy and Jack, were there when I needed kayak equipment for my birthdays, artwork to boost my spirits, and hard-to-find metaphors for my text.

But most of all I owe appreciation to my wife, Joyce, who never let me down and whose support was essential for both the trip and the book. Even I am not so dense as to not notice I was putting Joyce under a lot of stress when she told me, "You are putting me under a lot of stress, you owe me big time." One of the reviewers for this book, Dr. Barbara Gitenstein, echoed my sentiments: "The story is Hank Landau's, but perhaps his wife, Joyce, is the heroine."

My most sincere thanks to "River Angels," many friendly people and three grumpy souls who helped guide me along the way. Most of them are listed in the text or in the "Daily Logs" on my website. I apologize to those who are not listed and those whose names may not be listed correctly. I was diligent in keeping notes, but some of my notes were obliterated by spray, rain, mud, and condensation, and there were a few times when stress or forgetfulness caused me to miss something.

Chris Cunningham, editor of the too-soon-departed *Sea Kayaker Magazine*, was the first to inform me that writing an adventure story required skills that were then unknown to me. Others who assisted the voyage, the research, and the writing and who may not be acknowledged in the text or "Trip Logs" include the following: Jan Ahlquist-Niemi, Pat Albaugh, Doug Alderson, Jerry Alexander, Allen Family, Tim Arntzen, Connie Bad-Horse, Bailey and Bank families, John Baker, David Bandy, Steve Baxter, Phil Benge (USACE), Sharon and John Bitter, Peter Block, Mike Boehnke, Charles Brady, Kelly and Gina Bramble, Jerry and Gaila Brandon, Kenneth Breiten (USACE), Rev. Sandy Brown, Jacki Bultsma (USACE), Ginny and Steve Burger, Heather Burke (USACE), Jim Butkiewicz, T. Caldwell, Ralph Camp, Jim Card (Adm. USCG Ret.), Ken Cardwell, Tote Carpenter, Mike Clark, Mike Cooper, Steve Cournoyer, Ed Crouch, Dale Davies, the Dawl family, Bob and Gretchen Dixon, Dog River Marina (Bob Schwarz, Sonny Middleton, Linda, Ricky, Paul, and Joe), Cindy Easterson, Bill Ellis, Epic Writers Group, Lauren Evans, Gale Fiege, Lee Fitch, Mary Fitch, Chris Flow, Jimmy Fogle, James Gale (USACE), Roger Galladay (USACE), Richard Galloway (USACE), Harley Gebhardt, Ann Glassley (USACE), Joe Goddard, Jack Gould, Bonnie Griffis, Karen and Ed Hargrove, Steve and Marla Harris, Jeffrey Hawk (USACE), Bill Heimann, Peg Hellandsaas, Kris Hendrickson, Dwane Hendrix, Richard Hilt (USACE) Pat and Gil Holzmeyer, Dawn Hooper, Todd Hornback (USACE), Steve Hromoda, Jolene Hulsing, Daryl Jackson, Mimi Jackson, Curtis Johnson, Duane Johnson, Kristiana Johnson, Dr. Lloyd Johnson, Jeff Keller (USACE) John Kennedy, Fritz Ingraham, Harriet King Ingraham, Kyla Landau,

Tracy and David Lannie, John Larpenteur, John La Randeau (USACE), Joe Little, Chet Lowry, Carla Majernik of Adventure Cycling, Bill Marisk, David and Michelle Matters, Daniel and Katy McCurdy, Craig McDonnell, Lora Jane McIlwain and Randolf, Jerry McPherson, Gary Mears, Gary and Terressia Miles, David Miller, Norman Miller of Missouri River Paddlers, Sonny Middleton, Scott Mitchuson and Donna, Kristina Moen, Bill Nedderman, Terri, Tami and Cody Nelson and Jessica, Rev. Steve Nelson, Mike and Jean Norder, Oahe Marina (Steve Rounds, Darwin, Dalton, Ciara, and Chance), Jan Ostlund, John and Yung Park, David and Debbie Pharr, Ken Pickle, Curt Porter, Aaron Post, Joe Pratt, Steve Reichart, Joe Carl Rice and Tuesday Writers Group, Glenda Richard, John Roberts, Steven Roberts, Timothy Roberts (USACE), Chris Robertson, Steve Rounds, Buddy Rush, Johna Rush, Bob Schaal, Harold Schaal, Chuck Schaub, Dan Schepis, Mr. Scipio, Arnell Scott, Pat Shields, R. C. Silvestri, Martin and Trey Slaughter, Bill Smith, Mark Smith, Myron Smith, Mary Kay Sneeringer, Pete Solomon, Charles Sorrenson (USACE), Ken Stanhope, St. Marys Boat Service (Rocky, Missy, and Clayton Smith and crew), Larry Steffan, Dave Teitzel, Paul Thomas (USCG), Dan Thompson, Steve Thorp, Denny Tillman, Terri Todd, Dan Tonsmeire, Wayne Tracksel, Valley Cats Off Road Club, Mary Van Horn, Larry Vogel, Denise and David Ward, Tara Waterson, Gregory Watson (USACE), Eric Weber, Ann Wermus, Perry Whitaker, Dale White, Patti Williams (USACE), Eileen Williamson (USACE), Marsha Wilds, Teresa Wippel, Scott Woerman, and Bob Wright.

The first time Karin Redmond, my editor and new friend, told me, "Show, don't tell" in uppercase print, I had little idea what she meant. Karin showed remarkable patience in guiding me along the writer's path. Dr. Scott Driscoll, language professor at the University of Washington, built on Karin's guidance for the last few chapters. Many thanks to the patience afforded to this first-time author by Danielle Koehler of Dalitopia and John Koehler, Joe Coccaro, and Lauren Sheldon of Koehler Books.

Bibliography

Part One: The Pacific Ocean to St. Louis

Ambrose, Stephen E. *Undaunted Courage: Meriwether Lewis, Thomas Jefferson and Opening of the American West.* New York, NY: Simon and Schuster, 2005.

Adams, Karl. *Wake of the Wind Dancer: From Sea to Shining Sea by Paddle and Sea.* Bloomington, IN: iUniverse Inc., 2009.

Adventure Cycling Association. *Bicycling the Lewis and Clark Trail.* Michael McCoy, Field Editor. Helena, MT: Falcon, 2003.
———. "Lewis and Clark Bicycle Trail." Detailed maps, frequently revised.

Burkhardt, D. C. Jesse. *Railroads of the Columbia River Gorge.* Charleston, SC: Arcadia, 2004.

Dakota Ads. *Welcome to Upper Lake Oahe, Whitlock to Pollock.* Gagner & Assoc. Undated

Delorme. *Road Atlases & Gazetteers* for Washington, Oregon, Idaho, Montana, North Dakota, South Dakota, Nebraska, Iowa, Kansas and Missouri.

DeVoto, Bernard. *The Journals of Lewis and Clark.* New York, NY: Houghton Mifflin, 1953.

Evergreen Pacific Publishing. *River Cruising Atlas: Columbia, Willamette and Snake Rivers.* Everett, WA: Evergreen Pacific, 2001.

Fanselow, Julie. *Traveling the Lewis and Clark Trail.* Helena, MT:

FalconGuides, 2007.

Hay, Keith G. *The Lewis and Clark Columbia River Water Trail: A Guide for Paddlers, Hikers and Other Explorers*. Portland, OR: Timber Press, 2004.

Larpenteur, Charles. *Forty Years a Fur Trader on the Upper Missouri: The Personal Narrative of Charles Larpenteur, 1833-1872*. Lincoln, NE: A Bison Book, University of Nebraska Press,1989.

Least Heat Moon, William. *River Horse: Across America by Boat*. New York, NY: Penguin Books, 1999.

Leopold, Luna B. *A View of the River*. Cambridge, MA: Harvard Univ. Press, 1994.

Miller, David L. *The Complete Paddler: A Guidebook for Paddling the Missouri River from the Headwaters to St. Louis, Missouri*. Helena, MT: Farcountry Press, 2005.

Miller, George R. *Weather Disagreeable: Lewis and Clark's Northwest Journey*. Portland, OR: Frank Amato Publications, 2004.

National Parks Service. *Knife River Indian Villages*. A pamphlet, 2004.
———. *Lewis and Clark Trail*. A pamphlet, 2002.
———. *Little Bighorn Battlefield*. A pamphlet, 2004.
———. *The Washington Experience*. A pamphlet, 2005.

NOAA. *National Climatic Data Center*, Nov. 1998.

Oregon State Marine Board. *Boating Guide to the Middle Columbia River*. Support from the USACE and others, Undated.

Schultz, James Willard (aka Apikuni). *Floating on the Missouri*. Edited by Eugene Lee Silliman. Norman, OK: Univ. of Oklahoma Press, 1979.

Silvestri, R.C. *A Paddle Across America*. USA, Xlibris Corporation,

2008.

USACE. *Aerial Photography and Maps of the Missouri River: Ponca State Park, Nebraska to St. Louis, Missouri.* 2009.

———. *Aerial Photography Maps of the Missouri National Recreation River: Gavins Point Dam, South Dakota to Ponca State Park, Nebraska.* 2004.

———. *Aerial Photography: Maps of the Missouri National Recreation River: Fort Randall Dam, South Dakota to Santee, Nebraska.* 2004.

———. *Bonneville Lock and Dam.* A pamphlet, 2006.

———. *Fort Cascades Trail Guide.* A pamphlet, 2006.

———. *Fort Peck-A Half-Century and Holding,* Vol. 11, No 2, Summer 1987.

———. *Fort Peck Dam & Lake, Montana.* A low-resolution map, 2006.

———. *Lake Oahe: Oahe Dam: Boating and Recreation Guide.* Detailed maps.

———. *Lake Francis Case: Fort Randall Dam: Boating and Recreation Guide.* Detailed maps, 1997.

———. *Lake Francis Case: Fort Randall Dam: South Dakota.* A pamphlet, 2012.

———. *Lake Sakakawea: Garrison Dam: Boating and Recreation Guide.* Detailed maps.

———. *Lake Sakakawea: Garrison Dam: North Dakota.* Low-resolution map, 2010.

———. *Lake Sharpe: Big Bend Dam: Boating and Recreation Guide.* Detailed maps, 2004.

———. *Lake Sharpe: Big Bend Dam: South Dakota.* A pamphlet, 2009.

———. *Lewis and Clark Lake: Gavins Point Dam: Boating and Recreation Guide.* Detailed maps, 2003.

———. *Lewis and Clark Lake: Gavins Point Dam: Nebraska / South Dakota.* A pamphlet, 2003.

———. *Lower Snake River Recreation Guide.* A pamphlet. Undated.

————. *Portaging the Mid-Columbia River Dams.* A pamphlet.

————. *Oahe Dam and Lake: South Dakota / North Dakota.* Low resolution map, August 2008.

————. *Snake River Recreation Area.* A pamphlet. Undated.

US Dept. of Interior, BLM. *Floating the Upper Missouri.* A pamphlet, undated.

————. *Upper Missouri River Breaks National Monument Boaters' Guide: Fort Benton to Judith Landing.* 2011.

US Fish and Wildlife Service, *Charles M. Russell National Wildlife Refuge, Guide Map and Information.* May 2009.

————. *Upper Missouri River Breaks National Monument Boaters' Guide: Judith Landing to Kipp Recreation Area.* 2008.

Wikipedia.org. "Lexington, Missouri." Last modified June 11, 2022. https://en.wikipedia.org/wiki/Lexington,_Missouri.

Part Two: Beyond St. Louis

Adams, Karl. *Wake of the Wind Dancer: From Sea to Shining Sea by Paddle and Sea.* iUniverse Inc. 2009.

Apalachicola National Estuarine Research. "Lower Apalachicola River Corridor, Road Map to Recreation." 2016.

Delorme, *Florida Atlas & Gazetteer.* Yarmouth, Maine: Delorme Atlas & Gazetteer, 2006.

Delorme. *Georgia Atlas & Gazetteer.* Yarmouth, Maine: Delorme Atlas & Gazetteer 2010.

Delorme. *Road Atlases and Gazetteers* for Illinois, Kentucky, Tennessee, Mississippi, Alabama, Georgia and Florida.

Florida Center for Instructional Technology, *Exploring Florida, The Suwannee River*. 2002.

Florida Department of Environmental Protection Office of Greenways and Trails, *Florida Circumnavigational Saltwater Paddling Trail*. Undated

Florida Paddle Trails Association. Paddling Trails. Visit Florida: Google Earth Pro Route Guide. Accessed May 2017. www. floridapaddlingtrails.com

Genealogybank.com. "Appalachia Indian Tribe: History of Poarch Band of Creek Indians."

Geo Plot System by Atlantic Mapping Inc, "Kentucky Lake Recreation and Fishing Guide." Accessed, August 2015. Undated paper copy copyright 2015. www.atlanticmapping.com
————. "Lake Pickwick Recreation and Fishing Guide." Accessed August 2015. Undated paper copy copyright 2011.

Hay, Jerry M. *Ohio River Guidebook, Inland Waterways*. 2014.

Knox, Rose and Schorb, Graham, *Canoeing and Camping on the Historic Suwannee River: A Paddlers Guide*. Cocoa, FL: The Florida Historical Society Press, 2012.

Myers, Fred, *Tenn-Tom Cruise Guide*. Fred Myers Publisher, 2005.

Pharr, David, *Suwannee River Boating: Canoeing and Recreation Guide*. Maggie Valley, NC: River Graphics, 2016.

River Gator; "The Lower Mississippi River Trail." Accessed July 2015. www.rivergator.org.

Tennessee-Tombigbee Waterway Authority. "Tennessee-Tombigbee Waterway, Facts at a Glance." www.sam.usace.army.mil/Missions/ CivilWorks/Recreation/Tennessee.

The Historical News, Southern Historical News, Inc, August 2017.

Tomalin, Terry, "A Look at Florida's Native American History," Visit Florida, https://www.visitflorida.com/things-to-do/cultural/native-american-heritage/.

Treuer, Anton. *Atlas of Indian Nations*. Washington, DC: National Geographic Society, 2013.

USACE, *Touring the Tennessee-Tombigbee Waterway*.

US Fish and Wildlife Service, *Okefenokee National Wildlife Refuge*, undated.
———. *Okefenokee National Wildlife Refuge*, undated.

Wikipedia.org. "1993 Big Bayou Canot rail incident." Last modified June 30, 2022. https://en.wikipedia.org/wiki/Big_Bayou_Canot_rail_accident
———. "Apalachicola People." Last modified March 2, 2022. https://en.wikipedia.org/wiki/Apalachicola_people
———. "Fort Walton Mound." Last modified June 28, 2022. https://en.wikipedia.org/wiki/Fort_Walton_Mound
———. "Hernando de Soto." Last modified June 21, 2022. https://en.wikipedia.org/wiki/Hernando_de_Soto
———. "Indian Removal Act," Wikipedia, last modified July 15, 2022. https://en.wikipedia.org/wiki/Indian_Removal_Act
———. "Intracoastal Waterway." Last modified July 17, 2022. https://en.wikipedia.org/wiki/Intracoastal_Waterway
———. "Tennessee–Tombigbee Waterway." Last modified July 25, 2022. https://en.wikipedia.org/wiki/Tennessee/Tombigbee_Waterway.

CPSIA information can be obtained
at www.ICGtesting.com
Printed in the USA
BVHW042252161022
649596BV00001B/8

9 781646 637805